Poetics of the Local

Poetics of the Local

Globalization, Place, and Contemporary Irish Poetry

SHIRLEY LAU WONG

Cover: *Warm Day 12.06* (2022) by Bernadette Madden. Photographed by Gillian Buckley.

Published by State University of New York Press

© 2023 State University of New York

All rights reserved

Printed in the United States of America

No part of this book may be used or reproduced in any manner whatsoever without written permission. No part of this book may be stored in a retrieval system or transmitted in any form or by any means including electronic, electrostatic, magnetic tape, mechanical, photocopying, recording, or otherwise without the prior permission in writing of the publisher.

For information, contact State University of New York Press, Albany, NY
www.sunypress.edu

Library of Congress Cataloging-in-Publication Data

Name: Wong, Shirley Lau, author.
Title: Poetics of the local : globalization, place, and contemporary Irish poetry / Shirley Lau Wong.
Description: Albany : State University of New York Press, [2023] | Includes bibliographical references and index.
Identifiers: ISBN 9781438493824 (hardcover : alk. paper) | ISBN 9781438493831 (ebook) | ISBN 9781438493817 (pbk. : alk. paper)
Further information is available at the Library of Congress.

10 9 8 7 6 5 4 3 2 1

For my father, 王子浩, *and my mother,* 劉志超.

Contents

Acknowledgments	vii
Introduction: Poetics of the Local	1
Chapter 1. Occasional Poetry and the Creative Economy	25
Chapter 2. Some Versions of Irish Pastoral	57
Chapter 3. The Loco-descriptive Details of Belfast	87
Chapter 4. Paul Muldoon and the Difficulty of Comparison	115
Coda: Race, Place, and the Grounds of Irish Geopolitics	147
Notes	167
Bibliography	207
Index	227

Acknowledgments

This book is about the links forged between places near and far, which is also an apt description of the communities of friends, colleagues, editors, mentors, and other interlocutors who have buoyed and made altogether possible this project. I would first like to thank the two anonymous readers who offered incisive and generous reviews on the initial draft of this book. Like much labor in academia, their work was both invaluable and yet easily rendered invisible; while I cannot name them, I want to underscore how this book has been enriched by their insightful feedback. My profound thanks go also to my editor at SUNY Press, Rebecca Colesworthy, who enthusiastically supported this project, even as it incurred the delays and bumps of an interstate move, a change of workplace, and a global pandemic. Thank you also to Julia Cosacchi, Jenn Bennett-Genthner, and the rest of the production team at SUNY Press for their adroit assistance.

Like its author, this book has had many homes over the past decade, beginning first at New York University. I had the great fortune of a supportive dissertation committee in Maureen McLane, Peter Nicholls, and Robert Young, who not only shepherded the writing of my dissertation but also steered me through all the other hurdles that come with graduate school. Maureen as well as Jini Kim Watson were wonderful mentors who had the uncanny ability to send an email or a text message at the moments when I most needed a guiding hand or kind word to navigate the profession. I also am grateful to count as mentors Patrick Deer, Elaine Freedgood, Lytle Shaw, and John Waters. My time in graduate school was spent with a cohort of whip-smart and kind humans. I am especially grateful that NYU gave me the lifelong friendship of Laura Fisher and Jennifer Spitzer, who have acted as readers of book chapters, emails, and every genre in between; conference hotel bar companions and roommates; writers of encouraging texts at the end of long work days; in short, my lifelines.

At Westfield State University, I found another wonderful community in the English department, whose members nurtured me when I was a fledging assistant professor. In particular, I thank Carol Bailey, Sophia Sarigianides, Catherine Savini, Beth Starr, and Emily Todd, for modeling how to be the kind of colleague and teacher who is more interested in lifting up others than one's own self. Westfield's Semester Time Award for Research and Scholarship afforded me much-needed research time at a crucial early stage of this project.

Since joining the US Naval Academy, I have been fortunate to be a part of another vibrant department of scholars and teachers. I am grateful to the members of my writing group in the USNA English department—Gabriel Bloomfield, Audrey Wu Clark, Mike Flynn, Alyssa Quintanilla, Michael Wagoner, Jane Wessel—for workshopping parts of this project. Publication of this book was made possible in part by assistance from the Ernst Volgenau Fellowship at USNA.

Some of my greatest forms of support have been at other institutions. I am grateful to Omaar Hena, Walt Hunter, Laurie Lambert, Mary Mullen, Sarah Townsend, and Amelia Worsley for their intellectual comradeship and their perpetual good cheer. Joe Cleary's scholarship and generosity as a mentor have been essential to this work.

There are many people in my life who have not read a word of this book, and yet their love and bigheartedness have shaped it in the most meaningful ways: the Johns clan (Jenny, Lauren, Sarah, Kate, and Rob) provided me a family when my own was far away; Jared Kushner, Megan Melnyk, Henna Messina, and Laura Rosner helped make New York a home for me.

My deepest gratitude goes to my family: my brother, Michael, and my parents, Patrick and Cecilia, to whom I dedicate this book. It seems a cliché, but it is nevertheless true in my case: my parents weathered the challenges common to many immigrants, always making the difficult and practical choices, all so that I could chase a more impractical path in life. Colin Blair has unfailingly championed this book and my career at times when I felt like giving them up, holding my hand literally and figuratively, from New York to Western Massachusetts to Baltimore. Every day I am inspired by his brilliance and curiosity, his selflessness and natural instinct to put others before himself. Thank you for your love, for always being by my side through all the places this life has taken us.

∽

An earlier version of the introduction was originally published in "Globalizing the Province: Rethinking Place and Scale," *The Global South* 10, no. 1 (2016), and an earlier version of chapter 2 was published in "Country Bumpkin and Cosmopolitan: Some Versions of Postcolonial Pastoral," *The Global South* 7, no. 2 (2013). All rights reserved, republished by permission of the copyright holder, and the present publisher, Indiana University Press (www.iupress.org).

"Developers" from *The Breadbasket of Europe* by Alice Lyons is reprinted by kind permission of the author.

"Six Sycamores" from *Painting Rain* by Paula Meehan is reprinted by kind permission of Wake Forest University Press, Winston-Salem, NC, and Carcanet Press, Manchester, UK.

Excerpts of *The Rough Field*, sixth American edition, by John Montague are reprinted by kind permission of Wake Forest University Press, Winston-Salem, NC, and the estate of John Montague.

"Tourism" from *Between Here and There* by Sinéad Morrissey is reprinted by kind permission of Carcanet Press, Manchester, UK.

Introduction

Poetics of the Local

> The poet's eye, in fine frenzy rolling,
> Doth glance from heaven to earth, from earth to heaven;
> And as imagination bodies forth
> The forms of things unknown, the poet's pen
> Turns them to shapes and gives to airy nothing
> A local habitation and a name.
>
> —William Shakespeare, A *Midsummer Night's Dream*

> No space disappears in the course of growth and development: the *worldwide does not abolish the local.*
>
> —Henri Lefebvre, *The Production of Space*

I.

In his 1978 essay, "The Sense of Place," Seamus Heaney laments what he sees as the diminishing presence of Ireland in the work of contemporary Irish poetry as new generations of poets slowly unmoor their identity from the country's landscape. Replacing the "sense of place" is a deterritorialized perception of Irish identity and place. "We are no longer innocent, we are no longer parishioners of the local. We go to Paris at Easter instead of rolling eggs on the hill at the gable," the poet bemoans, " 'It's a far cry from the Moy.' "[1] While Heaney expresses his concern with some degree of irony, there is nonetheless a zero-sum game at work in his nostalgia in which globality and a globalized identity always come at the expense of locality and a local identity. Conceived as opposite ends of a binary, the local and global are mutually exclusive and even hostile categories of cultural identity. It seems that the Irish poet cannot have Paris and the Moy too.

Heaney's sentiments reverberate well beyond the bounds of Irish literature and cultural criticism. Doreen Massey identifies how similar anxieties over the so-called "loss" of the local have emerged in an era of globalization. Such concerns circulate around the dissolution of "any sense of a local place and its particularity" and look longingly to a time "when places were (supposedly) inhabited by coherent and homogeneous communities."[2] The reactionary undertone of such anxieties is not lost on Massey, who argues that the "seeking after a sense of place" can slide dangerously into "certain forms of nationalism, sentimentalized recovering of sanitized 'heritages,' and outright antagonism to newcomers and 'outsiders.'" While Massey writes nearly three decades ago, the nostalgia for the local rings all too familiar in the contemporary moment as waves of resurgent ethnonationalism—with white supremacists resuscitating the Nazi slogan "Blood and soil"—sweep across Europe and the US.

A book on the poetics of the local may then seem outdated and ill-timed. But rather than looking to the local as a relic of a bygone era, I trace the ways that Irish poets have approached the local as a critical interlocutor with the forms of globalization they have found alienating and destructive. The poets in this book have strayed from the more laudatory accounts of globalization, which view it as a blissful period of geopolitical and cultural interconnections facilitated by innovations in travel and telecommunications. Instead, they call attention to the uneven experiences of economic development and cultural interchange under global capitalism, which has indeed connected places near and far but only within deeply asymmetrical relations of power.[3] Following the lead of these writers, this book approaches the local and the global as not antagonistic but rather intersecting modes of engaging with the world. The local is often seen as a source of authenticity, a fragile site under duress as the monolithic machinations of globalization threaten to subsume everything within their grasp. Worse yet, the yearning for place reads like a coded kind of nativism, a backlash against migration and other forms of global movement. In the context of contemporary Irish poetry, the enduring centrality of place can be seen (sometimes deservedly so) as an embarrassing symptom of its formal and political conservatism. But in *Poetics of the Local*, I argue that the continued presence of place in Irish poetry should not be dismissed as just the vestiges of a nostalgic nationalism but instead understood as a meditation on the material and emplaced effects of globalization—a way of discerning and therefore interrogating what are seemingly invisible and faraway processes.

Such an approach helps us view the history of Ireland in the twentieth century as more than the exclusive narrative of the creation of the Republic and the Troubles, and therefore also helps us situate Irish poetry in a more variegated political and economic frame.[4] Though the processes of decolonization were integral to the nation's history, they reverberate elsewhere than in Ireland's relationship with the United Kingdom. I reroute attention to events such as the country's accession to the European Economic Community (EEC) in 1972; the installation of corporate tariff breaks in the 1980s and the subsequent influx of multinational corporation investments; the 1990s boom period of the Celtic Tiger and its spectacular crash in the first decade of the new millennium; the 2004 referendum, which changed the basis of Irish citizenship from *jus soli* (automatic citizenship to those born in Ireland) to *jus sanguinis* (citizenship determined by the nationality of one's parents). Such events are watershed moments that have equally marked Ireland's postcolonial condition. As the ongoing fallout from Brexit and the Irish financial crisis makes evident, Ireland's role in global politics cannot be contained within a schematic metropole-and-colony dyad. Critically engaging with discourses of globalization, the poets in this book point to broader literary and economic systems—an emergent, transforming global situation that confounds any simplistic nationalist identity. At the heart of *Poetics of the Local*, then, is a centralizing question: at a time when the languages of open-market economics, urban development, and world literature were promoted as "transcending" the local, how did Irish poets understand the place of Ireland in the world?

This book pursues this line of inquiry by examining a series of spaces implicated in the growing pains of a rapidly globalizing Irish economy: Alice Lyons's "ghost estates," the empty housing projects built during the Celtic Tiger and then abandoned after its crash; St. Stephen's Green, the historic Dublin square whose grand Georgian architecture was subsidized by financial capital, as Paula Meehan explores in her poetry; the disappearing agricultural order in Seamus Heaney and John Montague's pastoral poetry; the urban "regeneration" of Belfast during and after the Troubles, as depicted by Ciaran Carson, Sinéad Morrissey, Alan Gillis, and Leontia Flynn; the cross-cultural communities imagined by Paul Muldoon.

In exploring both the material and imaginative configurations of these spaces, I wed together critical lenses from globalization studies, critical geography, and ecocriticism. At the same time, through close textual analysis, I show how these writers renovated poetic genres, modes, and forms—including the occasional, pastoral, and loco-descriptive poems, and the figures of apostrophe and conceit—to articulate new forms of place and belonging in contemporary Ireland. By many accounts, Ireland is one of the most, if not the most, globalized country in the world.[5] Yet, as demonstrated by the work of these aforementioned writers, place has continued to loom large in contemporary Irish poetry. This book reads poetry in light of the transnational forces of neoliberalism and uneven development, showing how these global forces and conditions have shaped poetic innovation in Ireland. In doing so, my project moves in two directions: on the one hand, it asks how the local inheres in Irish poetry at a moment when discourses of globalization are dominating politico-economic policy. On the other, it argues that Irish history and cultural production, particularly poetry, have not only participated in but can also give new insights into emerging scholarship on global poetics and other literatures produced under conditions of globalization.

While "local" and "place" are obvious conceptual bedfellows, at first glance "local" and "globalization" may seem fundamentally at odds with one another. "Local" derives from the Latin *locus*, but its earliest usages in the English language did not refer to a geographic place but rather emerged first in the fields of medicine and theology. In medicine, "local" referred to a contained area of the body on which topical medicine was applied (such as a local anesthetic), while in theology it signified the space of the immanent and human as opposed to that of the celestial and spiritual. (In his 1777 work *Disquisitions*, for instance, Joseph Priestley writes that the "Cartesians have . . . maintain[ed] that spirits have no extension, nor local presence.") Material and spiritual, encircled and unbounded: the local, since its earliest origins, has captured a wide sense of scale from the most delimited zones of the body to the heavens above.

Similarly, globalization has been defined by a preoccupation with scale. While the term "globalization" carries a much less storied past, having only begun to appear in the 1970s, it has since generated a wide range of meanings. David Harvey defines the experience of globalization as that of "time-space compression," the concept he coined to describe the breakdown of spatial barriers and distances caused by the acceleration of capitalist production and exchange. Writing more recently, Harvey views globalization as a fundamental "shift in the geographical scale at which capitalism is organized" with a reorganization of geopolitical power away from the nation-state and toward supranational institutions like the World Bank, World Trade Organization, and International Monetary Fund.[6] Anthony Giddens has frequently challenged Harvey's focus on globalization as an exclusively economic phenomenon, but he likewise understands globalization as a change in scale caused by the "intensification of worldwide social relations which link distant localities in such a way that local happenings are shaped by events occurring many miles away and vice versa."[7]

My book leans on the local as one of its central terms because it is an inherently relational concept—conjuring at once the materially grounded spaces of the natural and built environments and also the territorially unbounded movements of global capitalism. Of course, it is now old hat to recognize that the local is shaped by far-flung global forces. But what has been less clear is how such shifts in scale can be attended to in our modes of literary and cultural analysis. Clichés like "think global, act local" and "glocalize" paper over the complex shifts of conceptual register that are required of such thinking. Ursula Heise critiques a similar line of rhetoric in US environmentalism, pointing out that the "local is not just a seamless extension of the global."[8] This book, then, forefronts the question of how to think across and think together the seemingly incommensurate scales of the local and global. How can literary scholars negotiate between the macro-level analyses of globalization studies with the micro-level sensitivities of close reading? How can poetry help us negotiate these different conceptual registers? At a time when the nation-state and the world are no longer the obvious frameworks of analysis, what is the scale of literary study?

To answer such questions, we can look to modernist studies, where scholars have turned to the concept of scale itself as a way of widening the field's geographic reach and expanding its archives and languages.[9] Central to such conversations is modernism's scalability, or the broadening of the field's modes of analysis and the very definition of modernism itself to include periods and cultures outside the traditional purview of late-nineteenth- and early-twentieth-century European and American literature and art. The anthropologist Anna Tsing defines scalability as the "ability to make one's research framework apply to greater scales, without changing the research questions," and her definition reveals how scale is often implicitly synonymous with scaling up.[10] (For instance, a business plan is scalable and only has value to a company if it can be "scaled up" and implemented in larger markets.) This sense of scalability is recapitulated in recent treatises on scale that privilege the macro, global, and maximal. In a special issue on "Scale and Form; or, What Was Global Modernism?," editors Thomas S. Davis and Nathan Hensley pioneer a model of modernist studies that "coordinate[s] macro-level analyses of the world-as-system—the maximalist model—with particularized attention to individual cultural objects or moments within them."[11] But their emphasis ultimately tilts toward the former; as they later write, modernism is always "best understood as a maximal rather than restricted phenomenon." In her call for a "planetary modernism" that would open up the "capacious archive of global modernities," Susan Stanford Friedman argues for abandoning definitions of modernism as a distinct historical period and designating it instead as a "loosely configured set of conditions that share a core meaning of accelerated change."[12] While she argues that it is crucial to attend to the "small scale of localized, even textualized particularities," her study seems to belie such an attention to the local and particular. Friedman's model of planetary modernity rests on scaling up the definition of modernity to include "stories" that envelop everything from the Mongol Empire to the Song and Tang dynasties to contemporary Shanghai in a single chapter. Rather than being subsumed under the umbrella of "Western modernity," the whole world is now incorporated under the new moniker of "planetary modernity."

Gendered spatial tropes underpin the privileging of the "planetary," which pits the "maximal" against the "localized." In conventional oppositions of the local and global, the local is associated with the feminized spaces of the private, insular, and domestic. Feminist scholars have long critiqued the discourses of nationalism that have embodied the nation as passive, feminized victims of male imperial power. Elizabeth Butler Cullingford argues that male Irish poets often personified the nation as idealized visions of Irish womanhood, reducing both land and women to the status of material objects to be reclaimed from colonial aggressors: "Politically, the land is seen as an object to be possessed, or repossessed: to gender it as female, therefore, is to confirm and reproduce the social arrangements which construct women as material possessions, not speaking subjects."[13] In a similar vein, Geraldine Pratt and Victoria Rosner point out that even the seemingly innocuous call to "think global, act local" reinforces the gendering of space "by associating the global with theory, objectivity, and causation, while depicting the local as embodied, unthinking, and determined by outside forces."[14] To scale up, then, is to circulate within the abstract and sophisticated machinations of the global; to scale down, by contrast, is to fall into crude and "unthinking" materialism.

We can see a similar assumption at work in Jahan Ramazani's critique of what he calls "loco-materialist approaches" in poetry criticism, which offer a corrective to the "placeless" formalism of New Criticism and deconstruction by "explor[ing] poems in relationship to the historical sites from which they emerge."[15] While Ramazani acknowledges some of the critical insights of loco-materialist scholars, he finds them guilty of what he calls "locational fallacy," of conflating the setting of a poem with its real-life referent. He reminds loco-materialists that, "Poems may not be 'about' places in the same way that a pin can be pushed into a real or digital spot or that GPS can calculate a position."[16] According to Ramazani, an overemphasis on a poem's locality both misses the formal workings of poetry and misunderstands how the local itself is far from a stable and homogenous referent, particularly in a globalized era: "Such loco-materialist arguments . . . advance a model of the poetry of place . . . that is ultimately insufficient to the complexities of poetic mimesis and formal mediation, perhaps especially under global modernity."[17] However, one might query the claim that an attention to place is necessarily at odds with an appreciation of poetic form. But more concerning is how Ramazani divulges an underlying assumption that folds together the local with the indexical in his critiques of loco-materialists. For instance, he describes their "implicit representational ideal" as the "empirical documentation of a limited historical space." But few scholars would argue—or, indeed, have argued—for reading poetry in order to supply "empirical documentation" of a place; even fewer would judge a poem's value on the fidelity of its description or its ability to produce an "authentic reproduction of the singularities of singular places." If the locational fallacy rests on the overvaluing of a poem's place, Ramazani's account of loco-materialism rests on the conflation of the local with verisimilitude and indexicality.

The poetry of Sinéad Morrissey elucidates the complex relationships between locality, materiality, and poetic form, and demonstrates how an attention to place need not assume an ideal of indexicality. At first glance, Morrissey's poem "In Belfast" seems to lure the reader into the trap of locational fallacy, as the title and recitation of place-names (including references to the Lough, Royal Avenue, Albert Bridge, and the Transport Workers' Union) firmly anchor the poem in the writer's home city. Morrissey emphasizes the architectural and even meteorological solidity of Belfast, which comprises grandiose Victorian buildings ("ballast of cooper and gravitas") weighed down by an "iron sky" leaden with rain and fog. But all that is situated melts into air in the second half of the poem as the city dissolves into a haze of rain and mist: "The city weaves itself so intimately / it is hard to see, despite the tenacity of the river / and the iron sky; and in its downpour and its vapour I am / as much at home *here* as I will ever be."[18] The city's intimacy does not so much assure a sense of place as make it difficult to discern altogether. In the poem's opening line, the deictic "here" grounds the poem in a specific, rooted site: "Here the seagulls stay in off the Lough all day." But by the poem's conclusion, Belfast's architectural and environmental materiality is supplanted by the speaker's uncertain feelings of being "at home here." As words that gesture toward people and places, deictics are usually assumed to point to worlds outside the pages of the poem. But Andrew Weaver notes that deictics "'shimmer' between a possible, provisional specific interpretation and a possible, provisional general interpretation . . . '[H]ere' can be both a particular—though unspecified—place . . . as well as a self-reflexive gesture to the poem itself."[19] In Morrissey's poem, we are similarly unsure of where exactly "here" is; the poem's deictic ambiguity resists any attempts to fix it definitively in either the space of the city or the poem itself. Rather than acting as a pushpin on a map, the poem shimmers between material and poetic place. Despite the poem's emphatic location "In Belfast," Morrissey's work is far from a simple documentation of Belfast's topographical textures. Morrissey instead emphasizes how the local (after all, what is more local than "here"?) is an unsettled site, the product of a set of highly mediated cultural and historical practices.

But Morrissey's unsettling of the local bespeaks more than just the restlessness she feels in her home city; her poetry also registers Belfast's uneasy transition from the locus of sectarian violence during the Troubles to a now "post-conflict," global city. Morrissey is part of a generation of "Peace Poets," or Northern Irish writers who established their careers after the IRA cease-fire in 1994 and Belfast Agreement in 1998.[20] (In this book's third chapter, I further analyze the work of this cadre of poets.) Morrissey shares with her cohort a deep skepticism over what they see as the false promises of the Peace Process, which has couched peace and reconciliation in primarily economic terms. The architects of the Peace Process attracted support by promising participants a "peace dividend," or economic growth in the form of foreign investments and Northern Ireland's integration into global markets.[21] Morrissey experiments with deixis again in "Tourism" to ridicule the commodification of the city's sectarian geography, now repackaged and peddled as heritage tours to lure curious European visitors: "We take them first to those streets / they want to see most, at first, / as though it's all over and safe behind bus glass." But in the final stanzas of the poem, Morrissey's scorn dissipates into a surprisingly open, albeit also wary, welcome for future visitors:

> Unabashedly, *this* is our splintered city,
> and *this*, the corrugated line between doorstep and headstone.
> *Next*, fearing summary,
> We buy them a pint with a Bushmills chase
> And *then* on to the festering gap in the shipyard
> The Titanic made when it sank . . .
> So come, keep coming *here*.
> We'll recklessly set chairs in the streets and pray for the sun.
> Diffuse the gene pool, confuse the local kings,
> infect us with your radical ideas; be carried *here*
> on a sea breeze from the European superstate
> we long to join; bring us new symbols,
> a new national flag, a xylophone. Stay.[22]

At first, the deictic "this" acts as a possessive that cements the speaker's custody of "our splintered city." Operating as both tour guide and native informant, the speaker seems to physically point to the remnants of the city's sectarian and deindustrialized past: "this, the corrugated line" of old Republican-Unionist barriers, "Next . . . the festering gap" where Belfast's once thriving shipbuilding industry stood. (This makes all the more sense if we remember that "deixis" originates from the Greek *deiknunai*, meaning to point or show.) But by the poem's close, the deictic markers have loosened their firm grip on the city. As Belfast is rebranded in a post-conflict era of global capital, its history of "local kings" and very "gene pool" about to be "infected" by the influx of tourists (and more significantly EU investments), the deictic "here" points to a city whose identity is on the cusp of being entirely remade by "new symbols / a new national flag." Yet the poem does not close with an ethnonationalist nostalgia for a now-lost Belfast, as the speaker directly addresses and invites the visitors to "keep coming here" and even to "Stay." (Moreover, Morrissey has spoken optimistically of the racial and cultural diversity that immigrants would bring to Northern Ireland.)[23] Instead, while the poem ends on a note of hospitality and openness, Morrissey also cautions against equating globalization (the "European superstate / we long to join") with more genuine forms of cosmopolitanism.[24]

Ramazani is right to stress that, "before equating the global with present-day 'capital and data,' let's remember that the poets were there before the economists . . . The globe is more than global capital."[25] But Morrissey offers the rejoinder that it is equally important not to privilege utopian imaginings of the world over a critical analysis of the material effects of globalization—nor are poetry and politico-economic critiques of global capitalism necessarily opposed modes of engaging with the world. In her poetry, Morrissey shows how the particularities of the local cannot be separated from the processes of globalization and uneven development that make them visible and experienceable in the first place. While the writers in this study come to varying and sometimes conflicting conclusions, they are united by a shared commitment to make legible what are insignificantly local places—too "local" to be addressed by the terms of globalization studies. The turn to the local—despite being laden with problematic senses of nostalgia (and sometimes precisely because it does shoulder associations with nativism and ethnonationalism)—allows these writers to see how global capital manifests within specific places, whether in the architecture of post-cease-fire Belfast or the ghost estates that dot the countryside of the post-recession Republic. By fixating on these local sites, these poets negotiate between the macro and micro levels of analysis, between the abstract language of globalization and the more concrete figurations of poetic language. In so doing, the writers discussed in *Poetics of the Local* not only demonstrate how the supposedly deterritorialized and dematerialized processes of global capital make themselves known in place and space; they also show how their poetries of place can become an effective means of reflecting on and interrogating globalization.

II.

While I seek to make porous and flexible the geographic boundaries of my book, I also want to make the case that contemporary Irish poetry is a key site from which to contemplate the complex relationships between globalization, locality, and place. The archive of contemporary Irish poetry that I explore—written from the late 1960s to the present—coincides with some of the country's most seismic geopolitical upheavals and falls under what has been designated the post-1973 era of late capitalism by Marxist scholars like Fredric Jameson and Giovanni Arrighi. As these scholars have argued, the cultural dominant in this era takes the name "postmodernism," and its political dominant is neoliberal globalization. This same period has also been witness to Ireland's most decisive economic shake-ups in the twentieth century: its accession to the EEC in 1973, the brief economic boom of the Celtic Tiger from the mid-1990s to 2008, and the subsequent financial crisis. Moreover, the violence of the Troubles reached its zenith in the 1970s and was pushed into the spotlight of international news media after the events of Bloody Sunday in 1972. But despite the fact that this tumultuous period of economic and political unrest coincides almost precisely with the Marxist periodization of late capitalism and globalization, relatively little scholarship has situated Irish poetry within these global flows.[26]

In *Poetics of the Local*, I bring global theory to bear on this archive of contemporary Irish poetry by turning to analyses of globalization that take into account the materiality of space and place. Earlier scholars of globalization often utilized the language of flow and scape to describe what they saw as the fluidity and movement of globalization. But in recent years, especially as ecocriticism has permeated global studies, theorists have instead emphasized more spatially informed and "grounded" theories of globalization. Saskia Sassen understands growing forms of inequity (such as rising poverty levels, land evictions, austerity measures forced upon peripheral economies) as a series of "expulsions," or instances when vulnerable peoples and places are displaced and "expelled from the core social and economic orders" by new technologies of financialization and resource extraction.[27] Similarly, Annie McClanahan revises older Marxist notions of finance capitalism as totally dematerialized, arguing instead that the material processes of "violent political force, scarce natural resources, and brutalized working (or not-working) bodies . . . underwrite [financialization's] apparent abstraction."[28] In his theory of world-ecology, Jason Moore dissolves the binary that separates social and environmental history, arguing instead that capitalism has always been a socio-ecological process comprised of "ecological regimes." Borrowing from Henri Lefebvre and other Marxist geographers, he explains that "all social relations are spatial relations; social relations develop through, and actively co-produce, space . . . Space is, then, not simply 'out there' but joins in specific complexes of social relations and 'built environments.'"[29]

These geographically informed lenses allow us to recalibrate the ways we have approached the histories of colonialism and dispossession in Ireland. For instance, the period of early modern Irish plantation included not just the displacement of native populations but also the mass deforestation of oak forests that made way for farmland and provided lumber for the English shipbuilding industry. The destruction of Ireland's ecological biodiversity reached apocalyptic proportions with the Great Famine in the 1840s, an environmental disaster spurred by a monocultural food system that was developed to feed a growing peasant labor force. Sharae Deckard argues that Irish history must be situated beyond its colonial relationship with the UK and as part of a wider global history of capitalist accumulation, in which the country's natural resources were extracted to provide new sources of cheap energy: "The reorganization of Ireland's biologically diverse bogs and forests into rationalized sites of capitalist monoculture was crucial to the erosion of Irish self-sufficiency and the integration of the island into the capitalist world-ecology."[30] Although there is no shortage of Irish scholarship that concentrates on land and landscape (Deckard concedes that the "significance of land and agriculture is almost overdetermined in Irish historiography"), there still remains important work to be done to read these histories of dispossession within broader politico-economic and ecological frameworks.

How then might we analyze the persistent importance of place in contemporary Irish poetry within these global frameworks? Scholars of Irish literature have long meditated on the relationships between place and identity, but often within the parameters of the nation-state, particularly as the Troubles deepened fault lines over the question of national self-determination. Elmer Kennedy-Andrews argues that modern and contemporary Irish poetry has been vital to articulating competing claims to land and country, from Yeats's projects of cultural nationalism that attempted to carve out a space for the besieged Anglo-Irish class to Heaney's mythological constructions of a Catholic indigenous connection to the land: "Poetry becomes an act of imaginative repossession, the recreation of community as synonym or synecdoche for the nation."[31] While Kennedy-Andrews is latitudinarian about such acts of "imaginative repossession," David Lloyd stridently criticizes these impulses in Heaney's poetry and accuses the poet of metaphorizing the land as a figure of unbroken historical continuity—and therefore fabricating a false sense of national community: "[Heaney] uncritically replays the Romantic schema of a return to origins through fuller self-possession, and accordingly rehearses the compensations conducted by Irish Romantic nationalism. But his poetic offers constantly a premature compensation enacted through linguistic and metaphorical usages which promise a healing of division simply by returning the subject to place."[32] What for Kennedy-Andrews is an act of "imaginative repossession" for Lloyd is a poetic sleight of hand in the service of empty cultural nationalism.

Since the rise and fall of the Celtic Tiger, however, it has become customary to speak of Ireland as caught in a moment when national identity is on the decline. In a scorching editorial for the *Irish Times*, Declan Kiberd accuses contemporary Irish artists of worshipping the ideology of "Europeanization" and "declar[ing] their embarrassment in the face of simple-minded notions of nation, faith and fatherland [and helping] to erode these forces."[33] But for Justin Quinn, the "disappearance of Ireland" ushers in an era of postnationalism that liberates Irish poetry from such nationalist constraints; rather than "mov[ing] in concert with a larger nationalist objective . . . [contemporary Irish poets] bear witness to the multitudes the island contains, and have extended its borders to include a fair piece of the known world."[34] Jefferson Holdridge and Brian Ó Conchubhair are more agnostic in their tellingly titled collection *Post-Ireland?* but nonetheless present a familiar argument: "Once, the larger threat was England, the United Kingdom, then America, now it is the European Union or globalization."[35]

While the scholars surveyed above represent a wide and sometimes conflicting range of politics, a familiar refrain echoes throughout their analyses of modern and contemporary Irish culture, where "nation, faith, and fatherland" have ceded ground to the realities of the globalized "new Ireland." Because Irish studies consolidated as a field at a time of intense intellectual infighting and during periods of partition and sectarian violence, the impulse has often been to divide scholarship along the fault lines of political and ideological affiliations—nationalist or revisionist, postcolonial studies or other critical theory. Although this disciplinary history should not be neglected, the attention on these fissures obscures how these scholars also tread shared ground.[36] Whatever their politics and whatever conclusions they draw, many periodizations of twentieth-century Irish literature rely on a pervasive tendency to read Irish modernism as split into two antipodal ideologies. According to such accounts, Revivalism is regarded as a holdover of nineteenth-century romanticism that is obsessed with Gaelic culture, Irish mythology, and the West of Ireland. Yeats is the quintessential representative of the Revival's fascination with peasant culture, especially in his early career as a proto-anthropological collector of Irish fairy tales and folklore. Modernism, on the other hand, is defined by its rejection of such cultural and national insularity. Instead, "true" modernists like Joyce and Beckett turned their backs on what they saw as the stifling provincialism of Irish nationalism and dedicated their careers (spent primarily on the European continent) to more innovative and cosmopolitan aesthetic practices. A similar binary underwrites the diagnostic accounts of postnationalism—whether Quinn's celebration of the "disappearance of Ireland" or Kiberd's more doleful outlook.

Rather than taking a side, I draw attention to how the concept of place has subtended these differing accounts of twentieth- and twenty-first-century Ireland. It is easy to discern that these periodizations rest on a spatialized teleology in which cultural nationalism subsides and is traded in for a more outward-looking cosmopolitanism. Indeed, by these accounts, the story of modern Ireland is a retreat from place and a move toward placelessness. But such a teleological view obfuscates the much more complex relationship between Revivalism and modernism that has characterized twentieth-century Irish culture.[37] It would be much more useful to reframe such dichotomies as instead dialectically linked cultural modes and to trace the ways that Irish writers have looked to the local in ways that can generate useful critiques of globalization as well as alternative forms of filiation outside the nation-state. This allows us to read the lingering centrality of place as something more than the residuals of nationalism or backward provincialism. Rather, Irish poets turn to place as a means of literally and figuratively grounding their critiques of the seemingly abstract and removed machinations of global capitalism, which are often seen as occurring offstage in some other corners of the Global North and South. As *Poetics of the Local* demonstrates, Irish poets confront the advent of globalization in Ireland not only through a repudiation of cultural nationalism but through a cultivation of the local.

III.

Irish poetry might not seem the most obvious archive to use in an analysis of globalization's effects on literary and cultural production. In addition to its seeming obsession with the "nation question," contemporary Irish poetry has often been occluded from larger critical conversations in poetry and poetics for its perceived formal—and correspondingly political—conservatism.[38] Additionally, poetry more largely has been more reluctantly folded into broader sociohistorical analyses, and still relatively little postcolonial and global studies scholarship centers on poetry when compared to the novel. This stems in part from a holdover notion that poetry is inherently private—an "utterance overheard," as John Stuart Mills famously described it—and therefore unsuitable for narrating the processes of nation-building, decolonization, and globalization. As Shira Wolosky explains, the concept of poetry as a "self-enclosed aesthetic realm . . . to be approached through more or less exclusively specified categories of formal analysis" emerged in the late nineteenth century and since then has governed the ways we read poetry today.[39] The result is that poetry criticism has often impeded rather than enabled newer modes of analysis for contemporary poetry. As Walt Hunter cogently argues, "knowledge of poetic devices serves as a border check for those interested in poetic criticism, slowing contemporary poetry's reception, inhibiting pedagogy, and operating like a canon of revealed truths."[40] Many scholars have sought to break open such hermetic modes of interpretation, as demonstrated by critical interventions such as Virginia Jackson and Yopie Prins's new lyric studies, Dorothy Wang's call to read together poetic innovation and race, and recent work on global poetics by Harris Feinsod, Hunter, Sonya Posmentier, Ramazani, and Anthony Reed, among others.[41]

Poetics of the Local learns from and works in concert with these scholars; in so doing, I hope to bring closer together poetics studies and Irish poetry criticism, as these scholarly conversations have sometimes been siloed from one another. One of the central aims in this book is to show how contemporary Irish poetry has much to contribute to emerging conversations in global poetics. For better and for worse, Irish poetry has served as a political battleground in the heated intellectual skirmishes waged between revisionist and nationalist scholars, which have both polarized and helped shape the field of Irish studies over the past half century. Irish poetry, then, has not been cocooned within a "self-enclosed aesthetic realm" but rather read against the backdrop of colonialism, decolonization, and partition. (To give one brief but telling example: when Heaney moved from Belfast to County Wicklow during the Troubles, his move was accompanied by multiple newspaper editorials, including one in the *Protestant Telegraph* that delighted in the departure of the "well-known papist propagandist.")[42] Margaret Greaves has pointed out the glaring omission of Irish poetry in new lyric studies, which she persuasively argues is a "missed opportunity" in that "nowhere in the postwar poetry world have poetics, politics, and history intersected with such concentration and with such investment in Anglo-American ideas about the lyric as in Northern Ireland."[43] Given its long engagement with histories of displacement and given Ireland's sudden global profile with the Celtic Tiger and now as the poster child of fiscal austerity and post-recession recovery, contemporary Irish poetry serves as a prime archive for understanding how poets can work within and intervene in discourses of globalization.

Alice Lyons illustrates how contemporary Irish poetry—and the landscapes it often sets its sights upon—is a rich site of engagement with globalization. In her poem "Developers," Lyons turns her gaze to her home in Cootehall in County Roscommon, one of the rural areas in Ireland that was targeted for real estate development during the Celtic Tiger and is now overrun with ghost estates.[44] In the poem, the speaker comes upon a vacant lot filled with discarded construction materials:

> O the places where pavement runs out and ragwort
> springs up, where *Lindenwood* ends but doesn't abut
> anywhere neatly, a petered-out plot of Tayto
> tumbleweeds, binbags, rebar, roof slates, offcuts
> guttering, drain grilles, doodads, infill, gravel!
> A not-as-yet nice establishment, possessing potential
> where we have no authorised voice but are oddly fitted-
> out for the pain it takes to build bit by bit.
> When the last contractions brought us to the brink
> of our new predicament, we became developers.[45]

In a collection that contains mostly concrete and experimental poems, "Developers" stands out in the ways Lyons transforms traditional poetic tropes and figures. (The poem was reprinted in the collection *The Breadbasket of Europe* but originally conceived as an experimental poem-film, in which Lyons's reading is juxtaposed with moving images of Roscommon's barren landscape.) An evocative signifier of the Great Famine, Ireland's most significant economic disaster, the potato field is reimagined as a "petered-out plot" strewn with Tayto chip bags. In an act of apostrophe,

Lyons uses the vocative exclamation "O" to call forth the deserted lot and lists in trochaic meter its "binbags, rebar, roof slates, offcuts" and other leftover debris. The abandoned property borders the already constructed ghost estates that forlornly await homeowners, their "doorbells, rows of them, glow[ing] in the night village / a string of lit invitations no elbow has leaned into."[46] The ghost estate is the most emblematic signifier of the boom period's excesses, which had been fueled not so much by credit default swaps (as had been the case in the US) but by property construction.[47] Terrence McDonough explains that while the 2008 financial crisis was a worldwide phenomenon, the "Irish *version* of financialization channeled a substantial amount of international credit into the property market" and led to unsustainable levels of construction.[48] At the height of the Celtic Tiger, the construction industry accounted for nearly 30 percent of total value produced in the Irish economy and over 10 percent of the Republic's entire GDP (though some economists claim it was closer to 20 percent). With much of employment centered on construction, the bursting of the property bubble led to both high vacancy and massive unemployment rates. (Unemployment rates climbed as high as 14.7 percent, and according to the 2011 census there are over 230,000 vacant dwellings in the Republic—a staggering figure if one considers that Ireland has a population of 4.5 million people.)

Recently novelists like Dermot Bolger, Anne Enright, and Donal Ryan have leaned on the mode of social realism to document the socioeconomic deprivations of the post-boom era. It may seem counterintuitive, and perhaps even unseemly, for Lyons to lyricize the barren landscape of Cootehall, especially as rural villages were arguably hit hardest by the construction craze. But in addressing and therefore giving voice to the absent, apostrophe has long been a crucial literary figure in political discourse. Barbara Johnson famously argues that apostrophe was a central figure in the legal language around abortion because it could make present what was absent, dead, and inanimate, and therefore extend the categories of personhood. For Johnson, apostrophe acts as a "form of ventriloquism through which the speaker throws voice, life, and human form into the addressee, turning its silence into mute responsiveness."[49] More recently, Margaret Ronda recalibrates Johnson's analysis in the context of ecopoetics, analyzing how postwar US poets mobilize apostrophe as a means of forging relations between the human and nonhuman, between a human speaker and seemingly distant environmental crises—melting glaciers, acidifying oceans, a depleting ozone layer. Apostrophe is a figure of both "intimacy" and "unreachability," an attempt to call forth environmental destruction that unfolds on the other side of the world.[50]

But why does Lyons apostrophize a ghost estate, which is not distant but decidedly local? (Lyons's text and film both focus on Cootehall, Lyons's home for fifteen years, and the poem's "we" is directly implicated as the village's "developers.") The ghost estate is also neither absent nor dead (despite what its name would suggest), as thousands still dot the Irish countryside more than a decade after the economic downturn. Rather, the "petered-out plot" is ghostly in a different sense: it is speculative, "not-as-yet nice" and "possessing potential"—what she earlier calls a "fake estate" that is the result of "cunning speculation." Of course, Lyons is mocking the language of development that underwrote the Celtic Tiger's runaway real estate development and the economic and ecological destruction it wrought.[51] Critics of financialization have often zeroed in on its immateriality and abstraction, fully deterritorialized from the concrete sites of production. As Fredric Jameson famously argues with unsettling prescience, "this free-floating capital . . . will begin to live its life in a new context: no longer in the factories and spaces of extraction and production, but on the floor of the stock market."[52] Joseph Vogl similarly describes the "spectral willfulness" of the global finance economy, whose immateriality and shadowy movements make it "unrepresentable": "Freed from the material manifestations of wealth, [finance capital] has installed itself in a 'time beyond geography and touchable money.' It dictates its own dynamics and standards of mobility, abandoning all local, social and political constraints . . . It embodies an economic sublime that manifests itself without taking material form."[53] For both Jameson and Vogl, the "economic sublime" of financial capitalism is at once all-encompassing and insubstantial, capable of catastrophe on a global scale and yet strangely invisible, built on liquidity and speculation.

But the legacies of financial crisis have taken on different forms and shapes in the context of Ireland, where the ghost estate has been its material and landed embodiment. (We might even pause to reflect on how the word "economics" stems from the Greek *oîkos*, or "house.") In her turn to apostrophize, Lyons points out the strange ontology of the ghost estate, which seems to hover between materiality and immateriality. The ghostly imprint of the "fake estates" is one not of post-industrial ruin and rubble but of empty lots of undeveloped construction materials. The litany of construction materials makes present what is absent:

labor and employment. For Lyons, apostrophe makes manifest what is local and yet not present, what is materially emplaced but also a fake estate. Ruth Jennison argues that poetry, with its emphasis on figurative language, is the genre most adept at confronting the seeming invisibility of financialization: "Since a crucial force of poetry resides in the figural and the unseen—metaphors, similes, line breaks, vast and micro fields of white space, allusions—it is . . . uniquely suited to represent a world financial system that is increasingly conducted in an invisible manner, through derivatives, currency trading, outsourcing, collateralized debt obligations, and so on."[54] Poetry, then, can attend to a key tension in representations of the financial crisis: recognizing the material conditions of unemployment and environmental violence while also appreciating how the movements of finance capital exceed the bounds of the local, particular, and material. Although the importance of landscape in the Irish literary imagination has certainly led to mythologizing and even nativist conceptions of land and identity, it also allows for materially grounded critiques of the apparently abstract and immaterial machinations of financialization.

New literary figurations are needed to represent the legacies of the financial crisis, and yet Lyons nonetheless returns to the classical figure of apostrophe and long tradition of landscape poetry. Such an impulse is not contradictory but rather reveals how contemporary Irish poets have revisited traditional poetic forms, tropes, and genres to make sense of Ireland's geopolitical landscape. As mentioned earlier, contemporary Irish poetry has often been cloistered from larger conversations in poetic criticism because of its formal conservatism. For David Lloyd, this insulation is willfully self-imposed; he argues that the tyranny of formalism and the "well-made poem" in contemporary Irish poetry has been a means of evading, rather than confronting, the advent of neoliberalism in Ireland.[55] Though I agree with much of Lloyd's sharp prognosis of the state of Irish poetry and share his frustrations (which I will further examine in the next chapter), I take distance from his claim that a meaningful engagement with global capitalism necessitates an absolute turn away from traditional poetic forms and genres.[56] The poets studied in this book often refurbish poetic forms both to draw on their deep literary history and also to show their limitations in a newly globalized Irish economy. Ronda argues for rethinking what she calls the "innovation paradigm" that has dominated discussions of modern and contemporary poetry and has often equated avant-garde poetics with revolutionary potential.[57] Such an unchecked celebration of innovation invests poetry in a problematic narrative of progress, which poets often seek to disrupt. "If these [poets] make it new," Ronda argues instead, "it is often by way of testing the capacities and limits of older genres, tropes, and recurring figures."[58] In Lyons's work, we can similarly see how the financial crisis and continued austerity measures (arguably the defining features of Irish society today) have transformed poetic figures like apostrophe. Contemporary Irish poetry, often insulated from broader conversations in poetry studies, is a privileged terrain in which the relations between place and globalization are staged and worked through.

IV.

Each chapter in *Poetics of the Local* centers on a different space mobilized by contemporary Irish writers to delve into and complicate notions of the local and global. In the opening chapter, I take as my local site both a geographic location and a poetic genre: Dublin and the occasional poem. Defined in terms of function rather than form, occasional poetry memorializes a specific event such as a death, wedding, or military victory. While critics often emphasize the temporality of occasional poetry, I read it as an also emplaced genre that locates itself in a specific place—specifically, in the case of this chapter, modern and contemporary Dublin. Occasional poetry is often disregarded as a minor genre because it openly relies on patronage, causing critics to cast doubt on its aesthetic and political autonomy. But as I argue, the occasional poem's overt lack of autonomy makes it an ideal genre to scrutinize poetry's relationship to public arts programs, arts councils, corporate philanthropy, and other cultural institutions. In the context of contemporary Ireland, the occasional poem's historic ties to patronage reveal how creative economy schemes (most notably the UNESCO City of Literature program and the Per Cent for Art Scheme) have come to shape the production and circulation of Irish poetry today. I begin by examining the early career of Thomas Kinsella, who established his own independent small press in 1972 in order to publish occasional poems that could circumvent the usual channels of the Anglophone publishing world. Then I move onto Paula Meehan, whose occasional poetry dramatizes the capitalist crisis of contemporary Irish literature, which has been transformed by Ireland's rapid financialization during the Celtic Tiger. In spanning from the 1960s to the present, the entirety of the historical period covered in *Poetics of the Local*, the opening chapter examines how poets reshape the same genre in varying ways to capture the different socioeconomic realities of globalized Ireland over the late twentieth and early twenty-first centuries. In so doing, I make the case that contemporary Irish poetry proves an exemplary archive in which to explore how the forces and conditions of neoliberalism and globalization have molded poetic innovation.

Over the following two chapters, I concentrate on narrower historical periods and on other sites that have been mobilized by contemporary Irish writers to interrogate the effects of globalization on their local places. In the second chapter, I investigate how contemporary Irish pastoral poetry registers the frictions felt in Ireland's sudden shift from agricultural to market economy in the 1960s and 1970s, particularly in the years preceding and following the country's accession to the EEC. I study political speeches and economic policies concerned with Ireland's global economic future alongside the work of Seamus Heaney and John Montague, who turn to the pastoral to give an alternative account to the celebratory narrative of what had been heralded as "the new Ireland." The pastoral has often been dismissed for what some scholars see as its idealization of rural life and inherently conservative ideology, but as Heaney and other writers have also argued, the pastoral has long engaged with histories of dispossession. For the poets discussed in this chapter, the pastoral acts as an incisive mode of economic critique that can grapple with the processes of uneven modernization that emerged during this turbulent period of Ireland's economic history. For Montague especially, the pastoral allows for a form of economic critique that moves beyond the pervasive political rhetoric that either depicted rural Ireland as backward and in need of development or sentimentalized it as the last remaining stronghold of nationalism and tradition. In directing my attention to representations of rural spaces, the chapter clears a space for a more diverse set of landscapes that have been occluded in scholarship on literature and globalization, which has primarily situated modernity within an urban framework.

I shift terrain in my third chapter and concentrate on the violent making and remaking of Belfast by city planners and paramilitaries alike, from the Thatcher-Reagan years to the so-called Peace Era of the present. The first half of the chapter focuses on Ciaran Carson, who is famed for his lifelong fixation on Belfast and celebrated for providing an intimate perspective into his home city. But while much has been written about the poet's exhaustive descriptions of Belfast's layered history, my chapter argues for reading Carson as more than simply a native informant of the city. I situate Carson's work within recent conversations on surface reading and the descriptive turn in literary studies, arguing that his writing pushes against familiar ways of reading topographical detail as simply offering a "sense of place." In particular, I analyze how Carson renovates the loco-descriptive poem (a genre that Samuel Johnson defined as "local poetry") to challenge understandings of locality, place, and belonging in a city caught in the throes of both military occupation and accelerated urban development. In the chapter's latter section, I trace the loco-descriptive genre as it is reworked in the poetry of Leontia Flynn, Alan Gillis, and Sinéad Morrissey, who established their careers in the wake of the cease-fire and 1998 Belfast Agreement. Although all of these poets' works are obviously shaped by the Troubles, the chapter focuses instead on how their poetries emerge out of a period when urban "revitalization" and "regeneration" schemes were and still are on the rise in the UK and other deindustrialized cities in the Global North. Such a reading shows how Northern Irish poetry should also be situated within the global processes of neoliberalism and the rising influence of the EU.

For the final two sections of the book, I change gears and contemplate a different though connected set of concerns, addressing the ethical questions that must be asked of Irish poetry that is produced in today's globalized world. My fourth chapter explores the work of Paul Muldoon, a poet who refuses to remain settled in a single place and instead experiments with the formal capacities of poetry to represent a global community. Muldoon is widely recognized for his poetry's breadth of varied cultural references, which range from medieval Irish history to Winnebago mythology to Chilean geography and beyond. Some scholars have regarded Muldoon's plethora of obscure allusions (particularly his recurring references to Native American culture and history) as a celebration of cross-cultural alliances made among disparate oppressed communities, while others have charged the poet with reckless cultural appropriation. I take a different approach and use Muldoon's poetry as an opportunity to meditate on the possibilities and limits of comparison in poetry. How can a poem make comparisons between disparate cultures and histories across the world? What are the poetic forms that emerge as contemporary poets make cross-cultural comparisons, which become all the more customary in an era of globalization? Given how questions of cultural and racial appropriation continue to remain pressing in poetry criticism, how might we imagine an ethical model of comparative poetry? I address these questions by analyzing Muldoon's use of the literary device of conceit, an extended metaphor that concocts similarities between the most dissimilar of things. With the figure of conceit, Muldoon theorizes the possible forms of comparison that can navigate the terrain of his poetry's juxtaposed geographies and cultures.

The book concludes with an extended coda that translates my project's conceptual framework to examine recent discussions in Irish geopolitics, which has often been characterized in spatial language, particularly in the recurring motif of soil. For instance, one of the great dangers posed by Brexit is the possibility of a "hard border" between Northern Ireland and the Republic, which could threaten the peace and stability brought by the Belfast Agreement. Or to take my coda's central example: Ireland was the last country in Europe to grant citizenship on the basis of *jus soli* ("right of the soil") until the 2004 referendum made citizenship determined by the nationality of one's parents. Soil has long been central to conceptions of Irish national identity since *The Nation*'s famed motto, "To foster a public opinion and make it racy of the soil." Recently, the precarity of soil as the sole basis of status and belonging has become especially fraught with renewed threats to end birthright citizenship in the US. Such seismic shake-ups demonstrate how the worldwide resurgence of ethnonationalism and xenophobia has been fundamental, and not simply ancillary, to contemporary Ireland's geopolitical landscape. Moreover, as shown in the previous chapters of *Poetics of the Local*, we must read such spatial language as more than just figurative and instead as revealing of the material relationships between locality, power, and citizenship. I conclude by offering a new reading of Heaney's infamous bog poems, which wrestle with themes of kinship, lineage, and soil, and yet are never analyzed through the lens of race. The coda, then, shows how the interconnections between place, race, and geopolitics have been and will continue to be crucial to Ireland's global identity in the decades to come.

Chapter 1

Occasional Poetry and the Creative Economy

I.

Although anxieties about the decline in poetry readership and altogether "death" of poetry have proliferated for decades now, there has been recent evidence that the state of poetry is not as dire as it once seemed. The Nielsen BookScan shows that sales of volumes of poetry in the UK have increased steadily over the 2010s and reached their highest rates in decades in 2018.[1] At the same time, a 2017 survey by the National Endowment of the Arts revealed that poetry readership in the US had nearly doubled since its previous survey period in 2012.[2] The resurgence of poetry is usually attributed to the rise of "Instapoets," who cultivate huge followings and share their work with millions on social media.[3] Literary critics therefore credit the growing sales of poetry to the broad dissemination afforded by digital platforms, though usually with much hand-wringing and pearl clutching over whether Instapoets have attracted new audiences for a genre on the decline or are, in fact, its death knell. But in this chapter, I focus instead on how the newfound popularity of poetry also stems from its turn to a much older and more traditional genre: the occasional poem.

In these think pieces, the poems cited are often occasional poems, praised for their timeliness and ability to deliver immediate responses to political crises and therefore speak directly to their audiences. For instance, a *Guardian* article mentions Tony "Longfella" Walsh's "This Is the Place," which the poet read on the steps of Manchester Town Hall the day after the 2017 bombing of the Manchester Arena; video of his reading was shared hundreds of thousands of times online and became instantly famous worldwide. Ben Okri's poem "Grenfell Tower, June, 2017," written and published in the *Financial Times* just days after the London fire killed seventy-two people, followed a similar trajectory.[4] In an article in the *Atlantic* (aptly titled "How Poetry Came to Matter Again"), Jesse Lichtenstein focuses on how a new generation of US poets of color, such as Danez Smith, Kaveh Akbar, and Chen, have found widespread success both in storied literary institutions like the *New Yorker* and the Poetry Foundation and on social media and nonestablishment literary tours. Lichtenstein's article ends with a laudatory analysis of Roy G. Guzmán's "Restored Mural for Orlando," a poem written and published days after the 2016 shooting at the Pulse nightclub in Florida:

> Forget William Wordsworth's "emotion recollected in tranquility": Guzmán's poem was an almost instant eulogy, and deeply affecting—Exhibit A of the power of the new lyric "I" to anchor a broad public response in the crosscurrents of complex, marginalized identities. Young poets are producing work that taps intimate veins, and responds to the headlines with impatience, nuance, compassion, and sometimes fury; with historical breadth and sharp critique; with unapologetic stabs at beauty; with ambition; and—above all—with the expectation of an audience.[5]

Instant eulogies, swift responses to national headlines, poetry written with a sense of urgency and a public audience in mind: such descriptions define not just a current generation's "new lyric 'I'" but the very genre of occasional poetry. In addition to an emergent cohort of poets and poetry readers, may we not also be witnessing a renaissance of the once seemingly moribund occasional poem?

In this chapter, I examine the reemergence of occasional poetry set in Dublin in the years leading to and during the economic boom of the Celtic Tiger. Rather than centering my study in the US or UK, where these critics have focused, I argue that contemporary Dublin, a space and period of rapid economic globalization and financialization, proves uniquely fertile ground for occasional poems, which are often conscripted into the many cultural tourism and creative economy programs that have come to dominate the fabric of literary life in Ireland.

At first glance, the two poets central to this chapter, Thomas Kinsella and Paula Meehan, seem to have little linking them, as they diverge in style and politics and establish their careers decades apart from each other. But Kinsella and Meehan share a preoccupation with how the processes of globalization and financialization in Ireland have shaped the relationship between poetry and place, especially in their home city of Dublin. I concentrate first on Kinsella's early and midcareer work in the 1960s and 1970s, the early decades of trade liberalization and direct foreign investment; then I move to Meehan's poetry, which was published when such economic policies came to fruition in the early aughts and the Celtic Tiger was fully underway and roaring. As I will argue, these poets were not just responding to a newly globalized Ireland but very much attuned to how the conditions of globalization have changed the very structures of poetic production—a shift in material relations that they examine in their experiments with the occasional poem.

Because occasional poetry is defined as commemorating an event such as a military victory or wedding, critics have often emphasized the genre's temporality. By contrast, I read occasional poetry as an emplaced genre located in a particular place. While the aforementioned poems are praised for their political exigencies, they also notably share an anchoring in place—whether in Guzmán's description of queer nightclubs like Pulse as spaces that "celebrate our bodies" but "also where our bodies / have been cancelled" or in Okri's haunting image of Grenfell Tower as a "burnt matchbox in the sky." Place has also been central to the twentieth century's most famed occasional poems. In "Easter 1916," Yeats sets his poem against the backdrop of "grey eighteenth-century houses," the august Georgian architecture that has become iconographic of Dublin's city centre. (Later in this chapter, I show how Yeats's poem casts a long shadow over Kinsella's and Meehan's works.) In Auden's "September 1, 1939," the speaker sits in "one of the dives / On Fifty-second Street" as he contemplates the onset of the Second World War in New York City. In fact, Auden's emphasis on setting—a Manhattan cityscape of "blind skyscrapers" and "buildings that grope the sky"—prompted the poem's recirculation in the aftermath of 9/11.[6] Returning to Walsh's "This Is the Place": the poem was originally commissioned in 2012 by Forever Manchester, a charity that raises funds for community events in the greater Manchester area. But Walsh's poem only catapulted to international fame when the poet recited it at a vigil for the victims of the Manchester bombing and video of the reading went viral.[7] The recirculation of Auden's and Walsh's poems demonstrates how place often trumps event in the long afterlives of occasional poems.

The little literature on occasional poetry often focuses on the tensions between the genre's public and private modalities. Stephen Wilson argues that occasional poetry is a specifically political genre in which the poet writes "not as a private individual but as a representative voice addressing the reader as a social being, a fellow citizen—as a political animal in the widest sense."[8] Auden argues that it was Yeats who modernized the occasional poem beyond its previous functions of "official performance of impersonal virtuosity or trivial *vers de société*" and transformed it into a "serious reflective poem of at once personal and public interest"—a feat that Auden would carry on in his own work, dedicating an entire section of his collection *Another Time* to "Occasional Poems."[9] Auden explains that the modern occasional poem "never loses the personal note of a man speaking about his personal friends in a particular setting . . . and at the same time the occasion and the characters acquire a symbolic public significance." The occasional poem seems to be an utterance at once overheard and also addressed deliberately to a public audience.

Without discounting these previous reflections, I argue that contemporary Irish poets have shifted the concerns of occasional poetry to matters aside from the union of poetry's public and private modes, and beyond the reconciliation of the public world of the occasion with the private world of the poet. For writers like Kinsella and Meehan, the focus is not so much on the public role of the poet as it is the socioeconomic dimensions of poetic production; specifically, their occasional poems reveal how the seemingly private, autonomous world of the poem is in fact structured by cultural and economic institutions that govern the writing and circulation of poetry. As these poets reveal, such institutions are inextricably tied to the accelerated processes of globalization at work in contemporary Ireland—especially the influx of multinational capital, much of which became channeled into both public cultural expenditures and corporate arts philanthropy. In their turn to occasional poetry, Kinsella and Meehan elucidate how globalization has transformed the metaphorical and literal landscape of Irish poetry, not in order to perform nostalgic laments for a bygone world but to reveal how globalization has altered the conditions under which they write poetry.

For these reasons, this opening chapter's methodology differs slightly from that of this book's other sections. Without discarding close textual analysis and broader histories of poetic genre and form, I also take a closer look at the institutional contexts in which poetry is often subsidized, particularly during the Celtic Tiger from the mid-1990s to 2008. Since the spectacular crash of the Celtic Tiger, more scholars have turned their attention to analyzing literary representations of the economic boom and its aftermath. However, less attention has concentrated on understanding how the boom period itself significantly transformed the literary and cultural marketplace.[10] Joe Cleary expresses his dissatisfaction with Irish studies scholars who treat literature as only a response to or reflection of the financial crisis. For Cleary, critics have missed the mark by seeing literature as a response to a capitalist crisis rather than understanding how a "crisis of Irish literature . . . must itself be grasped in terms of capitalist crisis."[11] James English makes a separate but related clarion call outside the context of Ireland, arguing that literary scholars would do well to take note of the "middle-zone of cultural space, a space crowded not just with artists and consumers but with bureaucrats, functionaries, patrons, and administrators of culture, vigorously producing and deploying such instruments as the best-of list, the film festival, the artists' convention, the book club, the piano competition."[12] While a comprehensive cultural materialist analysis of the scale that Cleary and English demand is outside the purview of this book, I make modest steps by analyzing how the genre of occasional poetry dramatizes the capitalist crisis of contemporary Irish literature and makes apparent this middle zone of cultural space, which was transformed by new schemas of public and private funding during the Celtic Tiger.

A seemingly outdated and minor genre like the occasional poem seems an unlikely vehicle for capturing the structural transformations wrought by globalization. Moreover, occasional poetry is an especially baggy and unwieldy genre, defined in terms of function rather than form and therefore seeming to dissolve into a number of other related genres like the elegy or ode.[13] I nonetheless turn to the occasional poem as the organizing framework of this chapter because it concatenates two different yet interlocking strands: the institutional dynamics surrounding the production of poetry, and the enduring affiliations between place and poetry. Specific genres register their historical moment; occasional poetry, with its dependency on patronage and its affixture to place, registers a moment when Ireland's landscape and its systems of cultural production were simultaneously being remade by the forces of globalization and financialization. One of this book's central drives is contesting the prevailing descriptions of globalization as fluid flows and scapes, and showing instead how Irish poets have emphasized the materiality of global capital and its (sometimes literal) concretization in place.

II.

Despite the popular attention that occasional poems have recently drawn, as a genre they have surprisingly attracted scarce attention from scholars. This is partly because occasional poetry has often been disregarded as a minor and even frivolous genre. While some occasional poems commemorate events of public import and therefore are regarded as "serious" works of art, many more are "trivial" poems written not for a public audience but for a private circle of friends, celebrating personal events like birthdays or weddings. But what most often disqualifies occasional poetry from the realm of serious art is the suspicion cast over its autonomy. Because occasional poems developed out of older systems of patronage and still are often commissioned, their aesthetic autonomy is often called into question.[14] William Wordsworth famously agreed to be the British poet laureate on the condition that he would not be required to write occasional poems. Andrew Motion, who held the laureateship from 1999 to 2009, retired from his post early, complaining that writing occasional poetry was "very, very damaging" to his career, as he was forced to churn out poems for the royal family's many special events. "I dried up completely about five years ago and can't write anything except to commission . . . The Queen never gives me an opinion on my work for her," Motion grumbled in an interview.[15] When Elizabeth Alexander was commissioned to write a poem for Barack Obama's first presidential inauguration and deliver it at the national ceremony, her "Praise Song for the Day" was widely panned by critics. One reviewer even went so far as to describe Alexander's poem as "bureaucratic verse" whose "weakness [was] precisely its consciousness of obligation. Her poetic superego leads her to affirm piously, rather than question or challenge."[16] While the dismissal of Alexander's poem as "bureaucratic" is unduly ungenerous, it reveals how occasional poetry is implicitly linked to literary and cultural institutions sponsored by the state. Whether in the context of poetry laureateships or one-off commissions, creativity and patronage are seen as mutually exclusive and by extension the occasional poem is often snubbed for being corrupted by the outside influences of the state.

On the other end of the political spectrum, poetry written in response to a political event and for a wider public audience is often dismissed as too didactic. For instance, while Okri's "Grenfell Tower, June, 2017" was widely shared in the aftermath of the conflagration, its reception by literary critics was much more tepid. One reviewer commends Okri's rightful fury but ultimately deems it a "directly documentary political" poem that relies on "clumsier and more trite imagery" to incite outrage from his audience.[17] Occasional poetry seems to be limned on two sides. It is either the product of patronage, commissioned by a private wealthy benefactor or the state and therefore bending to other wills and tastes; or it is mere protest poetry, written in haste and too "directly documentary" and overtly political. In both cases, occasional poetry is scorned for its contamination by the outside world.

The occasional poem also has a much longer genealogy that stretches well before the twentieth century and links it closely to place.[18] M. H. Abrams argues that what distinguishes Romantic poems from their Neoclassical precursors is their representation of a "determinate speaker in a particularized, and usually a localized, outdoor setting."[19] Works like "Tintern Abbey" are notable for being firmly located in a specific landscape and a specific time (a few miles above the Abbey, in the Wye Valley, during a tour on July 13, 1798, to be exact).[20] In other words, in Romantic poetry, poetic meditation is occasioned by both an event and an experience of place. Marjorie Perloff further argues that Romantic poems depend on an autobiographical authenticity: "It is a poem of experience, a dramatic lyric in which actual persons and places from the poet's own life and from the public life . . . that he knew become constituent parts of his drama."[21] In short, the occasional poem relies on a certain ontology of person and place.

Occasional poetry, then, has always rested on the tenuous division between poetry and the real world. More so than any other genre, it blurs the edges between the pages of the poem and the world beyond them. Hegel articulates the contradictory tensions within the reception of occasional poetry when he at once uplifts the genre for laying bare poetry's connection to the world and demotes it precisely for the same reason: "Poetry's living connection with the real world and its occurrences in public and private affairs is revealed most amply in the so-called *pièces d'occasion* . . . But by such entanglement with life poetry seems again to fall into a position of dependence, and for this reason it has often been proposed to assign the whole sphere of *pièces d'occasion* an inferior value."[22] For Hegel, occasional poetry breaks down the hermetic seal that insulates poetry from the world, but it is exactly this "entanglement with life" that subordinates the poem to the external world.

The occasional poem's "living connection with the real world" has made critics cast doubt on its aesthetic and political autonomy and designate it an inferior genre. But for the poets I study, occasional poetry's overt lack of autonomy makes it the ideal vehicle to highlight and therefore scrutinize the material conditions of poetic production. Especially because occasional poetry is often commissioned, it highlights questions of poetry's autonomy and its affiliation with cultural institutions such as arts councils, heritage programs, and universities. Robert Pinsky implicitly echoes such an understanding of occasional poetry when reflecting on his own experiences as a poet laureate and a poet writing on commission. For Pinsky, the occasional poem is at its heart a social piece of art, produced collectively: "The occasion, the challenge of a reality that falls into one's path, offers something like a collaboration—between the external world and the self, between language and intention—in the hoped-for event of the poem."[23] Although Pinsky is being more metaphorical in his language, we can take a literal interpretation of his words and understand occasional poetry as a "collaboration" between the poet and the "external world" of institutions that sustain the production and circulation of poetry.

Of course, in the context of contemporary literature, we know this collaboration between the arts and capitalism by another name: the creative economy.[24] The collusion between culture, capital, and governance that structures the creative economy has been incisively studied by Sarah Brouillette, who argues that literature has not so much offered a space of critique of neoliberalism as it has abetted it. While authors are often seen as autonomous, their creativity independent of the machinations of capitalism, it is precisely this false sense of autonomy that becomes the bedrock and engine of the creative economy, which depends on individuals, freelancers, and entrepreneurs rather than organized workers. In other words, the "value of culture's autonomy from capital" is in fact incorporated "*into* neoliberal capital."[25] For Brouillette, this becomes a central tension for contemporary British writers who must wrestle between two contradictory poles, "between the traditional veneration of artistic autonomy and the reality of conscription into proliferating state and corporate initiatives, and between the social production of culture and the lionization of the individual creator."[26]

For Brouillette, the genre that best dramatizes the contradictions of the creative economy era is the *Künstlerroman*, an offshoot of the *Bildungsroman* that traces the development of an artist. But occasional poetry proves an equally valuable genre in such conversations because it similarly revolves around the question of aesthetic autonomy—or to be more precise, its impossibility. Given its reception history, readers are predisposed to suspect occasional poetry as being nothing more than "bureaucratic verse"; unlike other genres, the occasional poem is never presumed to have any kind of aesthetic autonomy. This is not to argue that occasional poetry contains an inherent self-awareness that makes it immune to the forces of the creative economy and neoliberalism more largely. In fact, as I will point out, occasional poetry is often drafted into the innumerable cultural tourism and creative economy programs in Ireland. But because it openly relies on commissioning and other systems of patronage, occasional poetry makes explicit the poet's relationship to the cultural and political institutions that govern literary production. It therefore often serves as a genre with which poets can wrestle with questions of autonomy and poetic production.

Avant-garde art is often seen to trouble the lines between art and capital, whether with the Dadaists' play with ready-made art or the Situationists' practice of *détournement*. But one of this book's through lines is that there are archives outside the avant-garde and experimental traditions that can also elucidate how contemporary writers understand the complex relations between global capital and poetry. In what follows, I trace how Thomas Kinsella and Paula Meehan revitalize the occasional poem to challenge, however partially and even failingly, the processes of globalization and financialization that have shaped poetry in contemporary Ireland. Again, it is not my contention to valorize occasional poetry as a genre that resists being instrumentalized by the forces of neoliberalism. Instead, I bring together Kinsella and Meehan's occasional poems because they tell two stories about the conditions of Irish poetic production at two distinct moments in the closing decades of the twentieth century and the beginnings of the twenty-first. In so doing, I show how an attention to global economic conditions not only

34 | Poetics of the Local

brings to the fore a new periodization of Irish poetry but also changes our understanding of the genre of occasional poetry more broadly.

III.

Thomas Kinsella may be the poet whose personal life and career have been most intimately involved with the development of globalization in Ireland. For almost two decades over the 1950s and 1960s, the poet served as the private secretary to T. K. Whitaker, who was then the head of the Ministry of Finance and is still widely regarded as the chief architect of Ireland's economic modernization. With the support of Taoiseach Seán Lemass, Whitaker penned the landmark white paper *The First Programme for Economic Expansion (1958–63)*, which effectively ended Ireland's decades-long era of protectionism and promoted export-oriented manufacturing and foreign multinational investment. (Fintan O'Toole describes Whitaker as the "most important author of the contemporary Irish canon" and his white paper as "its seminal text.")[27] Throughout his career, Kinsella described their relationship in affectionate terms, even going so far as to dedicate one of his edited anthologies to "T.K. Whitaker / who gave the idea."[28]

But however amicable their personal relationship may have been, Kinsella was at best ambivalent about the processes of economic expansion and trade liberalization policies that were taking hold in the 1960s. In *Nightwalker*, a perambulatory poem set in the Dublin suburb of Dun Laoghaire, Kinsella makes evident his distaste for the "THE NEW IRELAND" (an all-caps headline emblazoned on a "soiled" newspaper) whose citizens now cater to foreign markets. The poem plays with the easy slippage between financial jargon and poetic language ("forms / Without principles, based on fixed ideas") and transforms Emma Lazarus's figure of the New Colossus into the figure of "Productive Investment," who opens Ireland to foreign investors: "Robed in spattered iron she stands / At the harbour mouth, Productive Investment, / And beckons the nations through our gold half-door: / Lend me your wealth, your cunning and your drive."[29] Suffused with financial language lifted from the *Economic Expansion*, the poem explicitly attacks Whitaker's plans to abandon economic protectionism and encourage direct foreign investment. But Kinsella does not shield himself from his own disdain and instead fixates on his own acquiescence in the new globalizing order. Not simply a passive bystander in a speedily modernizing Ireland, the speaker is a complicit member of the comprador class, comprising "native businessmen and managers" who solicit multinational investors by

> . . . show[ing] them our growing city, giv[ing] them a feeling
> Of what is possible; our labour pool,
> The tax concessions to foreign capital,
> How to get a nice estate through German.
> Even collect some of our better young artists.[30]

Kinsella's feelings of complicity do not only stem from his time as an employee in the Ministry of Finance. As the closing lines intimate, the poet feels himself interpellated by Productive Investment as an exploitable form of cultural capital. Indeed, a few years before the publication of *Nightwalker* in 1967, Kinsella becomes one of these collected "better young artists" when he quits the civil service to teach in universities in the US. In the increasingly export-oriented economy of the 1950s and 1960s, there was often an emphasis on culture as a potential resource that could draw tourism into the country and also be circulated abroad; this was especially true of the literary arts, given the international regard of Irish modernist literature.[31] As a native informant presenting "our growing city" and "a feeling / Of what is possible," Kinsella suggests the tenuous line between poetics and economics and articulates the sense of his own responsibility in ushering in the new Ireland.

Kinsella repeatedly expresses his anxiety over the exploitation and commodification of Irish poetry in the emergent decades of Ireland's globalization. "A Country Walk" is another perambulatory poem that traces the speaker's journey through a "martyred countryside" strewn with the ruins of crumbling aqueducts, empty barracks, and forgotten battlefields. At the grave site of an Easter Rising rebel, the speaker bitterly remarks how the city's "watchful elders" cursorily commemorate the grave each April only to return to their comfortable bourgeois lives: "chatting they return / To take their town again, that have exchanged / A trenchcoat playground for a gombeen jungle."[32] The poem takes an even darker turn when the speaker stumbles across the names of Yeats's Easter 1916 martyrs, who are now commemorated as the names of storefronts:

> Around the corner, in the Market Square,
> I came upon the somber monuments
> That bear their names: MacDonagh and McBride,
> Merchants; Connolly's Commercial Arms . . .
> I walked their shopfronts, the declining light
> Playing on lens and raincoat stonily,
> And turned away.

If Yeats can write it out in a verse and memorialize the Easter Rising leaders ("MacDonagh and MacBride / And Connolly and Pearse") in what Helen Vendler calls the "durable artifact" of poetry, Kinsella is less optimistic of what poetry can achieve in the new Ireland.[33] The line break brutally reveals that the "somber monuments" to the Easter Rising heroes are no more than the shop fronts of "MacDonagh and McBride, / Merchants; Connolly's Commercial Arms," and the ellipsis cuts short Yeats's poem, breaking away before it comes to the final name of Pearse. It is important to note that the collusion between poetry and economic globalization often materializes in the space of the city, namely the urban development of Dublin. (As I will argue later, this will be pertinent at another juncture in Kinsella's career, as well as in Meehan's poetry.) For Kinsella, the poetic memorialization of these national heroes is now synonymous with their commercialization. The modern state does not erase republican nationalism so much as absorb and regurgitate it in the form of a commodity.

Kinsella rearticulates such anxieties in a panel at the Yeats Centenary in 1965, when the then lesser known poet sat alongside the more senior and established Patrick Kavanagh, W. D. Snodgrass, and Stephen Spender to discuss the topic of "Poetry since Yeats." In the midst of a heated debate, Kinsella argues that the epicenter of midcentury poetry had shifted from England to the US, whose university system provided the main source of funding for poets and thus created a more open network of poetic collaboration and cross-pollination: "Since 1955 or so there has been some change, on the whole for the better. Economically, Ireland is taking her place among the nations of the West, and developing in the process a fine gombeen society—begot by the stallion of economic development on the mare of pietistic opportunism . . . But it is at least a more open society, where one's ignorance of, for example, contemporary American verse may be fairly said to be one's own fault."[34] In the panel discussion, Kinsella expresses a more optimistic outlook on the consequences of globalization on the state of poetry than he did a few years earlier in *Nightwalker* and "A Country Walk." The poet's inflamed rhetoric certainly disapproves of the "gombeen society" created by the expansion of foreign direct investment in Ireland, but he does not disavow the benefits he draws from the end of Ireland's economic and cultural isolationism. Such a revised perspective is perhaps unsurprising given how Kinsella personally benefited from this "more open society" and the particularly close cultural and economic ties between the US and Ireland: at the time of the panel, Kinsella held a writer's residency at Southern Illinois University and would later move to a professorship at Temple University, a position he occupied for the next two decades. Kinsella seems to prevaricate from the previous position he took in *Nightwalker*, which casts a distrustful eye over the special relationship between Ireland and the US.[35] But no matter the wavering of Kinsella's opinions, the poet always correlates the opening of Ireland's trade borders with the opening of a transatlantic literary network. Kinsella understands that, whether for better or for worse, the production and circulation of poetry—including that of his own—cannot be extricated from Ireland's economic globalization.

Of course, Kinsella is hardly the first poet to express apprehension over the commodification of poetry, but he uniquely turns to the occasional poem as a means of thwarting such co-optations of his work. In addition to his poetry, Kinsella holds a special place in Irish literary history for establishing his own small imprint, the Peppercanister Press, as a way of circumventing the pervasive control that London publishing houses held over the Irish literary scene.[36] But what's overlooked is the poet's corollary motivation for founding his own press: creating a venue that could quickly publish his occasional poems and bypass the need to submit to literary journals and be at the mercy of their editorial timelines. Kinsella's first four publications with Peppercanister Press were all occasional poems; of them, *Butcher's Dozen: A Lesson for the Octave of Widgery*, his first publication, earned the most notoriety.[37] In *Butcher's Dozen*, Kinsella denounces the Widgery Tribunal, which acquitted the British officers involved in Bloody Sunday who had shot and killed thirteen unarmed civil rights marchers in Derry in 1972. (A few months after the tribunal's exonerations and the poem's publication, the death toll reached fourteen when a final victim succumbed to his injuries.) The poem comprises mainly the imagined testimonies of the Bloody Sunday victims, whose ghosts arise to share their final living moments and now disgust over the tribunal's findings. (Sean O'Reilly describes it as a "horror-Aisling poem.")[38]

Butcher's Dozen earned the all-too-familiar criticism leveled at occasional poems that are seen as too overtly political. Trevor Joyce dismissed the poem as nothing more than "a piece of simplistic verse propaganda," while Denis Donoghue more sympathetically forgives Kinsella's "insistence upon unmediated rage": "It is natural for a writer to resent, on such a violent occasion, the admonition that his art is bound to be indirect in its effect and slow to act upon its cause. That poetry makes nothing happen is normally a tolerable fact; but there are occasions on which a poet feels that he must respond to one act with another similar in character and force."[39] Whether painted in critical or sympathetic tones, the critiques of *Butcher's Dozen* centered on its "unmediated rage" and rehearsed earlier dismissals of occasional poetry's too bald entanglement with life.

But Kinsella seems not bothered by such criticisms of *Butcher's Dozen*, going so far as to parrot his critic's complaints and describe his own poem as "immediate doggerel." For Kinsella, the occasional poem's artlessness is precisely its strength and purpose: "The pressures [of Bloody Sunday] were special, the insult strongly felt, and the timing vital if the response was to matter, in all its kinetic impurity . . . One changed one's standards, chose the doggerel route, and charged."[40] Julia Obert argues that *Butcher's Dozen* marks a pivotal moment in Kinsella's career when his emphasis on lyricism gives way to overtly politicized writing and a more cynical perception of place in Irish poetry: "As he engages more explicitly in the political, his poetry increasingly desanctifies place . . . 'Butcher's Dozen' acknowledges the ways in which Irish space and place are overdetermined by violence, a concession that necessarily coincides with another move away from the well-made poem . . . Bloody Sunday can perhaps be read as a formative trauma underwriting Kinsella's subsequent 'poetry of place.' "[41] Kinsella's turn from the well-made poem is made clear in both the tone of *Butcher's Dozen* (a blistering invective that condemns the "hard unnatural union grown / In a bed of blood and bone") and its form (rhyming couplets constitute the poem's entirety).

But while Kinsella may approach space and place with more trepidation and pessimism after the "formative trauma" of Bloody Sunday, his work remains fixated on locality. Like other occasional poems, *Butcher's Dozen* is tied not only to a specific moment but also to a specific place: Bogside, the Derry neighborhood where Bloody Sunday took place. The poem opens with the speaker touring through the urban blight of "that brutal place," where a "murder smell that stung and stained. / On flats and alleys . . . / on battered roof and wall."[42] *Butcher's Dozen* is one of Kinsella's many perambulatory poems but stands apart in its sparse rendering of space; unlike works in earlier collections like *Another September* or *Downstream*, there are no meditative asides of the poem's setting apart from some scant descriptions of the still lingering "murder smell." But while Kinsella refrains from any lengthy descriptions of cityscape or landscape, he nevertheless anchors his work at the site of the murders by framing the poem with the speaker's physical presence in the Bogside. *Butcher's Dozen* begins:

> I went with Anger at my heel
> Through Bogside of the bitter zeal
> — Jesus pity! — on a day
> Of cold and drizzle and decay . . .
> And when I came where thirteen died
> It shrivelled up my heart. I sighed
> And looked about that brutal place
> Of rage and terror and disgrace.[43]

At the poem's close, after the ghosts have dispersed, the speaker rouses himself from his haunted reverie and returns to the land of the living by touching one of the leftover barricades: "I stood like a ghost. My fingers strayed / Along the fatal barricade."[44] Patrick Crotty argues that the poem "puts physical place as firmly at the centre of its psychic geography as any of his other texts. What makes the speaker's moistened lips grow dry is his arrival at the actual site of the killings in the Bogside."[45] In other words, it is the poem's setting that gives occasion to Kinsella's embittered remembrance of Bloody Sunday and the Widgery Tribunal.

But if the Bogside acts as a site of witness and memorialization, Kinsella's poems of Dublin are more skeptical of the relationship between place and poetry. The poet expresses his distrust in another of his occasional poems, "Night Conference, Wood Quay, 6 June 1979," which was written during the protests over the construction of civic office buildings at Wood Quay in Dublin. (Wood Quay spans four acres in central Dublin and was one of the city's last remaining areas with pre-Georgian streets.) The protests were sparked when archaeologists unearthed the ruins of a tenth-century Viking settlement at Wood Quay, and Dublin Corporation (then the name of Dublin City Council) refused to postpone construction.[46] Tens of thousands of demonstrators marched to Wood Quay in an attempt to halt demolition; months later, as construction proceeded, a smaller group of fifty-two protestors—Kinsella among them—occupied the site. "Night Conference" depicts the protestors' ultimately futile attempts to stop the destruction of the Viking settlement site. Kinsella replicates the diatribe of his earlier occasional poems, rendering the protests an epic struggle waged between Dublin Corporation and the heroic preservationists on the battleground of the construction site ("half-dug pits and night drains brimmed with matter"). The city council members are ironically described as "white-cuffed marauders," who plunder the city of its rich archaeological history. The poem's setting is split between the two groups waging battle against one another: the inner circle of the protestors (whose "iron drum of timbers blazed and sparked / in rusty tatters at the mouth of the shed") and the bureaucrats and city planners, looking down from their offices ("At what window. / Visages of rapine, outside our circle of light").[47]

"Night Conference" is in keeping with many of the poet's other Peppercanister poems, which frequently take aim at Dublin's corrupt city planners and their destruction of the city's historic architecture. In a later poem, Kinsella takes another swipe at Dublin Corporation after its office buildings built at Wood Quay remained unoccupied for years because of mismanaged city funds, only to be eventually leveled for a parking garage: "shadow structures / that our city fathers, fumbling in their shadow budget, / beheld in vision for a while, pulverizing until the funds failed, / laying flat an enduring monument to themselves, / an office car park sunk deep in history."[48] Not only does Kinsella foreclose the accessibility of a "sense of place—an awareness of its mythological, historical, and familial associations," as Obert argues; his poems show how the history of place is expunged by the processes of urban development in Dublin.[49]

Throughout his work, the poet evinces a keenly prescient anxiety that poetry and place are readily co-opted into the apparatus of the new Ireland—a suspicion that becomes undeniable when we fast-forward to the twenty-first century in this chapter's next section. Many scholars have generated more optimistic interpretations of Kinsella's poetry, often incorporating his work within a tradition of *dinnseanchas*, or literature that recounts the origins of place-names in Ireland. In such readings, Kinsella's work acts as an archive of Irish place and history, a relationship that had become fractured by the country's colonial past. But as "Night Conference" shows and as Kinsella has pointed out repeatedly over his career, contemporary Ireland (and Dublin, in particular) does not passively suffer as the victim of globalization but rather welcomes it with open arms. This is not to say that Kinsella's writing is not entrenched in the intimate details of Dublin's cityscape or does not weave connections between Ireland's colonial history and the city's topography. But such readings are symptomatic of postcolonial scholarship that invariably reads for resistance; what's more, these interpretations overlook how Kinsella understands that poetry and place are in fact made perfectly serviceable for the machinations of multinational capital. As the poet bitterly points out, "MacDonagh and McBride Merchants" and "Connolly's Commercial Arms" are more than happy to be open for business.

But more than simply documenting the civic exploitations of a mercenary city government, "Night Conference" itself is an integral part of the protests' archives: the poem was originally published in the *Wood Quay Occupation News*, a small newssheet hastily put together and distributed by the protestors while they were occupying the construction site.[50] (The poem was later reprinted, in slightly edited form, through Peppercanister Press.) As with *Butcher's Dozen* and his other Peppercanister poems, Kinsella seeks alternative publishing venues in order to immediately distribute his occasional poetry and keep apace with the protests at Wood Quay. With his occasional poems, Kinsella attempts to combat at least the co-optations of his own work.

Of course, one could easily (and fairly) point out that Kinsella seems to reproduce naive notions of the aesthetic as a sphere of cultural production lying outside or offering a momentary reprieve from capitalism. In the emergent decades of Ireland's globalization, Kinsella expressed unease over his own role as one of the "better young artists" whose poetry might serve to usher in the new Ireland. Kinsella seeks to circumvent the commodification of his work by conjoining the autonomy of the small independent press and the immediacy of occasional poetry. Publishing through Peppercanister Press allowed Kinsella to write ripped-from-the-headlines poetry and instantaneously circulate it, avoiding the lag time that comes with the journal and magazine submissions process. As Kinsella puts it, the "immediate doggerel" of the occasional poem frees him to put aside the lyricism that preoccupied his previous work and to "charge" ahead instead. For Hegel, this is the downfall of occasional poetry: its subordination of poetry to the "entanglement with life." But paradoxically, for Kinsella the occasional poem's lack of autonomy—its "entanglement with life" and "living connection with the world"—allows him to stand outside the socioeconomic forces undergirding poetic production at this time. Kinsella turns to the occasional poem as a means of sidestepping the usual channels of literary production and shielding his poetry from the new Ireland that seeks to recruit the work of its better young artists. The next section analyzes the work of Paula Meehan, who writes at a later stage of global capitalism in Ireland when the occasional poem can no longer even appear to afford such autonomy.

IV.

If Thomas Kinsella's career begins during Ireland's nascent stages of globalization, much of Paula Meehan's work unfolds over its heyday, at the height of the Celtic Tiger. While Lemass and Whitaker ended economic protectionism and laid the groundwork for direct foreign investment in the late 1950s, their free-trade policies surged after the Irish government dramatically cut corporate tax rates in the 1980s: a tax rate of just 10 percent was introduced for all manufacturing in 1981, followed by a 10 percent tax rate for all financial services in 1987. (By comparison, the worldwide average corporate tax rate in the 1980s was 38.84 percent.) Additionally, Ireland had only a 6.25 percent corporate tax rate for revenue tied to intellectual property, making it even more attractive to research and development tech companies like Apple, Intel, and Dell. The lowered tax rates were bundled as part of the creation of the Irish Financial Services Centre (IFSC), a special tax incentive zone built in Dublin by the government with EU approval to house internationally traded finance services. The combination of corporate tariff breaks and the deregulation of financial laws in the IFSC made Ireland an effective tax haven for multinational corporations from the late 1980s to the present day.[51]

Such rapid financialization stimulated arts funding in both the public and private sectors in Ireland. From the mid-1990s to 2008, Arts Council funding increased fourfold, and the Department of Arts was made an independent agency in the Irish cabinet under the oversight of Michael D. Higgins, who was appointed its inaugural minister (and now serves as the president of Ireland). At the same time, a new tax exemption for Irish-based artists and the expansion of Ryanair into the European continent in the 1990s meant that Ireland, particularly Dublin, became an attractive hub for artists. But the increase in public cultural expenditures came coupled with the government's push for private corporations to simultaneously fund arts and cultural programs. Alexander Slaby explains that the aughts in Ireland saw the emergence of a new diversified creative economy, where the government would cease to be the exclusive source of arts funding and instead be one of several resources alongside private benefactors. For instance, in 2008 the Irish Arts Council launched the Partnership for the Arts, a program that helps arts organizations find sources of funding from the private sector, while a cabinet restructuring created a new Department of Tourism, Culture, and Sport that combined tourism with the formerly autonomous arts-and-culture department. As Slaby argues, the increasing privatization of cultural policy in Ireland demonstrates how the "economization of culture" is subtended by both government funding and corporate philanthropy, oftentimes operating in tandem. Since the recession, the "partnership" between government and private corporations has become a much more lopsided collaboration, with the latter subsidizing the lion's share of arts funding.[52]

A multitude of politico-economic factors transformed Ireland into a creative economy hotbed. In addition to its worldwide low corporate tax rates and deregulation of financial laws, Ireland also enjoys a unique status as an Anglophone member-state in the Eurozone and as a country with diasporic populations that gives it close ties to the US. The boom period and its collapse dramatically restructured arts funding, with private corporations now driving cultural policy. These factors, coupled with Ireland's internationally recognized literary heritage, made the country into a perfect laboratory for the creative economy.

The many cultural programs, schemes, and prizes housed in Ireland, particularly Dublin, attest to its newfound role as a hub as of the creative economy. For instance, the International Dublin Literary Award (formerly known as the IMPAC) is billed as the largest literary award in the world and was born out of a partnership between the Dublin City Council and an Irish American businessman, whose European consultancy offices were headquartered in Dublin. In 2016, on the centenary of the Easter Rising, Dublin joined the World Cities Culture Forum, an international cultural policy organization that conducts research on "the impact and importance of culture and creativity" in order to advise member cities on policies that support "the vital role of culture in their future prosperity."[53] Most notably, in 2009 Dublin launched a successful bid to become a UNESCO City of Literature and enter into its Creative Cities Network, which identifies cities that "recognize creativity as a strategic factor of their sustainable development" and helps them "make creativity an essential component of urban development, notably through partnerships involving the public and private sectors and civil society."[54] While such cultural policy organizations advertise themselves as at the service of their member cities, the relationship in reality is much more symbiotic. For instance, in return for receiving the title of City of Literature and rights to use UNESCO branding, Dublin's city government had to pledge to invest hefty amounts of its own money into building an extensive slate of cultural programming in 2010 and for years to come—a not insignificant commitment considering how the Irish government was at the same time slashing funds to social welfare and public services as part of austerity measures imposed by the IMF, European Commission, and European Central Bank. (Most Cities of Literature, including Dublin, do not receive any funds from UNESCO.)[55]

Oftentimes, these creative economy ventures capitalized on what they marketed as "literary Dublin" and the indelible ties between the city and its rich literary history. Ahead of the official decision, the head of the UNESCO City of Literature bid committee confidently asserted that Dublin's literary heritage would make it a shoo-in: "While it is not a foregone conclusion that we will receive the designation, our feeling is that with Dublin's vast literary wealth, we shouldn't have too much difficulty in gaining recognition."[56] (Tellingly, the UNESCO tagline for Dublin is "City of Words.") But it is not only the preponderance of place in the Irish literary imagination that drives an emphasis on site-specific cultural programing; there are material realities that explain why creative economy projects so often center on the space of Dublin and lean on the genre of poetry.[57] The explosion in real estate construction during the boom led to increased tax revenues that allowed local government agencies to develop public art programs such as the Dublin City Public Art Programme, which not only support local artists but also embed their artworks in specific places. Visual artists and art historians have long criticized how urban developers use public art as a means of increasing private property values in urban "regeneration" schemes, but less attention has focused on literature's vital role in these public art programs.[58] Poetry—with its compactness, emphasis on oral reading, and relatively low cost to produce and commission—makes it a genre especially amendable to cultural tourism and public art programs.

There are countless examples of creative economy projects that weld together poetry and place. As part of the Dublin: One City One Book Festival, the city council published *If Ever You Go: A Map of Dublin in Poetry and Song*, a literary guidebook that collates different poems and songs of Dublin and its suburban environs.[59] (Not so coincidentally, both Kinsella and Meehan are included among the book's poets.) Sponsored by the Department of Arts, Heritage, and Gaeltacht Affairs, *Dublin: A Year in Words* comprised a series of videos of poets reading their site-specific poems (which concentrate on different areas of Dublin) in different bookstores across the city. Poetry Jukebox, an interactive on-street installation that allows passersby to press a button and listen to prerecorded poems, gathered twenty works on the theme of "Hungering," which was selected by the EPIC The Irish Emigration Museum. The museum's director explained that the theme pays tribute to the Jukebox's location at the Custom House Quay, which once served as the departure point for emigrants during the Great Famine: "You can't pave over history. Like grasses and weeds, like buddleia cleaving to a building's rotting mortar, history notches itself into the empty spaces . . . Here, in the docklands, history stands its ground between office blocks and hotels."[60]

One could query the claim that "you can't pave over history," considering how the Custom House Quay is adjacent to the Dublin Docklands, some of the most expensive real estate in the city and home to the IFSC and headquarters for Facebook and Google. In fact, public arts projects can contribute to the historical amnesia of place as much as they purport to accomplish the opposite. To give one telling example: in 2013, the Poetry Project was launched as part of a cultural program celebrating Ireland's term as presidency of the Council of the EU. (The presidency rotates every six months among the EU member states.) A literary and visual arts program, the Poetry Project paired recordings of poems with short films and distributed them on its website. The poem-videos focused on the topography of Ireland, featuring films that panned over an array of urban and rural landscapes. One work featured Eavan Boland's "In Our Own Country," which had been published several years earlier and written in response to the construction of the Dundrum Town Centre, now the largest shopping complex in Ireland.[61] The poem draws from Boland's experiences living in Dundrum and her criticisms of the suburb's overdevelopment and displacement of its longtime residents. Boland articulates a now-familiar dread and suspicion over the prosperity promised by the "new Ireland" as the speaker watches her village being bulldozed by a "machine from the Netherlands or Belgium" that "break[s] apart the clay / in which our timid spring used to arrive."[62]

But more than taking aim at the new Ireland, Boland also sets her sights on a new Europe that she equates with global capitalism and a perversion of the EU's utopian founding principles (the "old Europe" and its "music, wars and treaties").[63] However, Boland's critique of the EU is belied by a more obvious point: the Poetry Project is part and parcel of the new Europe and in fact commemorates the fortieth anniversary of Ireland's accession to the EU. As part of its Council presidency, Ireland helped set the Council's six-month agenda and emphasized its new leading role as a "recovery country driving recovery in Europe."[64] This is not to accuse Boland of hypocrisy, as her poem was reprinted and divorced from its original context of publication. Rather, the recirculation of Boland's poem demonstrates how creative economy programs can mask their political purposes as much as they claim to pay homage to the histories and vicissitudes of place. What was once a strident critique of global capital is now repurposed as part of its armature of cultural programming. There is a bitter irony in the Poetry Project and similar arts programs, which are meant to restore a sense of place that has been eroded by the very institutions that subsidize their existence.

Such interpretations may seem overly cynical, nitpicking the rare sources of funding left for poets writing in a time of austerity and in a precarious literary marketplace. But what drives this analysis is not a faultfinding mission but a desire to broaden the ways we study how the processes and conditions of globalization have shaped Irish poetry and contemporary poetry more largely. How should we analyze contemporary Irish poetry in light of the dramatic structural changes wrought by Ireland's rapid globalization and financialization? As the Poetry Project demonstrates, we might begin by directing our attention toward a broader remit of poetry—poetry that does not only live in book collections or literary journals but in websites, public art installations, and promotional materials like bookmarks, plaques, or posters. There is little scholarship that examines the poetry and paratexts produced by these creative economy programs, which mainly reside in spaces like a jukebox on the street or a guidebook to "literary Dublin." What's more, literary and cultural critics should take a closer look at the "middle zone of cultural space," such as the strategic plans, monitoring reports, and grants guidelines that govern these projects. This is all the more important in a contemporary literary landscape that is increasingly underwritten by creative economy regimes and where readers often encounter literature outside the traditional contexts of books and journals.

This line of inquiry has become especially imperative in the wake of the Celtic Tiger. The brief period of prosperity not only increased funding for the arts in Ireland but also shaped the ways this capital was distributed. Although the economic downturn has led to severe cuts of public cultural expenditures, there has been a simultaneous push by the Irish government and international agencies like UNESCO to capitalize on culture as a means toward recovery from the financial crisis.[65] Given Ireland's international literary reputation, literature is marketed by the creative industries as an especially valuable tool that can salvage Ireland from the recession at a time when other industries have collapsed or fled the country. But for critics like Cleary, Ireland's enthusiastic embrace of neoliberalism has meant that the current generation of Irish writers has been defanged of any ability to criticize the global economic crisis in meaningful ways: "The whole vocation of the writer had become so uncritically identified with professionalism, entrepreneurialism, good Europeanism, and apolitical cosmopolitanism that it was taken as perfectly natural that successful figures like [Colm] Tóibín or [Neil] Jordan or [Colum] McCann should . . . gently remind political and corporate leaders of the importance of 'culture' and 'humanity' before standing in for photo ops, collecting their expenses, and returning to their desks or studios without creating any fuss."[66] Cleary's indicting words may read as harsh, but they are a judicious portent about the consequences of creative economies' deepening entrenchment in Ireland, which has made it more difficult for writers to critique the country's ever-accelerating neoliberal overhaul.

V.

What spaces of critique are available to writers given the ever-expanding dominion of creative economies and heritage tourism programs in contemporary Ireland? With their emphasis on site specificity and capitalization on "literary Dublin," how have these industries shaped the relationship between poetry and place? A sufficient response to such inquiries is beyond the scope of this chapter, but I begin a foray by examining an exemplary work that triangulates the complex relations between creative economy, occasional poetry, and place: Paula Meehan's sonnet sequence

"Six Sycamores." Commissioned by the Office of Public Works (OPW) in 2001, "Six Sycamores" is a work of occasional poetry that commemorates the construction of the OPW headquarters on St. Stephen's Green, the historic Georgian garden square in the heart of Dublin. At first glance, Meehan's work doesn't seem to fit the mold of the typical occasional poem. "Six Sycamores" comprises six sonnets interlaced with six short italicized interludes, all set around Stephen's Green. Rather than concentrating on a specific event or focalized through a single speaker, the sonnet sequence moves through different historical periods and perspectives. The sonnets shift from the Green's original construction in the late seventeenth century to its occupation by Irish republicans during the Easter Rising in 1916, from the perspectives of the exclusive district's wealthiest residents to those of the maintenance workers who have sustained its upkeep. Meanwhile, the interludes feature the voices of present-day Dubliners who traverse the Green: a pregnant woman on the way to her doctor's appointment, an unhoused person panhandling on the street, a night shift worker commuting home in the early-morning hours. In addition to the Green's human inhabitants, Meehan's poetry gives attention to the park's natural environment. The sequence's title comes from an agreement that the original leaseholders around Stephen's Green were required to plant six sycamores on the square, and the sonnets are often filtered through the trees' perspective over the centuries—what Meehan calls the "long patient witness of old trees."[67] In short, the center of gravity of "Six Sycamores" is not so much an event as a place.

But while "Six Sycamores" may not resemble a traditional occasional poem, it fits the genre's conventions in other ways. In addition to being commissioned, the poem is anchored around a specific place: two of the poem's titles, "Number Fifty-One" and "Number Fifty-Two," are the real street addresses of the OPW's headquarters on Stephen's Green.[68] Hovering in the background of Meehan's work is Yeats's "Easter 1916," which shares the same setting and also highlights the Georgian architecture that characterizes this area of Dublin. Meehan also makes reference to the Green's minor role in the history of the Easter Rising when insurgents established an armed base in the park's grounds. (Both Meehan and Yeats lived in nearby Merrion Square, another Georgian square a few blocks away from Stephen's Green.)

With "Six Sycamores," Meehan does more than simply allude to Yeats's occasional poem; she also expresses an awareness of the socioeconomic institutions that underwrite the production of poetry—including her own occasional poem—especially as they take shape during the Celtic Tiger. Meehan has been critical of Ireland's financialization since even before the crash, often describing it as a reformulation of colonialism: "After you're decolonized from one power, you're recolonized by another. It sometimes feels that in our case we're now just a part of the economy of the evil empire; transnational capitalism rules all."[69] For Meehan, the boom period's excesses stem from a much longer history—one that is embedded in the very architecture of Stephen's Green. She hints at this history in "Number Fifty-Two," which depicts David La Touche, the eighteenth-century banking scion who was a founding shareholder of the Bank of Ireland and who built the townhouse that now houses the OPW on Stephen's Green:

> . . . The new house on the Green
> is splendid, plasterwork sublime, furnishings divine
> and Angelica Kauffman turning up on a chance
> visit. Such a boon. He'll hurry to join
> her for tea before dark. He can already sense
> her copy of Guido's *Aurora* is a work of immense
> beauty. The way she's found in the early light
> of a Dublin dawn the exact tone for the dance
> of all that mythic flesh across his ceilings. She might
> well paint the grove's tender green from those sycamores.
> She's worth her weight in snotty stuccodores![70]

The sonnet caricatures the frivolous La Touche, afflicted with a "twinge of gout" and delighted by the prospect of commissioning the en vogue Swiss painter Angelica Kauffman for a mural for his new home. Meehan conveys a cynicism about art produced under such systems of patronage and demotes Kaufmann's paintings to the status of interior decor custom-made for the banker's pleasure palace, alongside the townhouse's "plasterwork sublime" and "furnishings divine." (Notably, it is the interior decorations that are deemed "sublime" and "divine" rather than the paintings.) The poem further equates the values of the visual arts and of interior design when La Touche asserts that Kauffman is "worth her weight in snotty stuccodores" and that her rendering of the "early light / of a Dublin dawn" might provide the perfect shade of paint for his home's ceilings.

As the poem suggests, the collusion between the arts and Ireland's financiers has stretched well before the contemporary moment. Since its original publication in 2001, the poem has taken on a more insidious undercurrent, as the Bank of Ireland was one of the major Irish banks that was responsible for the financial crisis and subsequently bailed out by the Irish government to the tune of 3.5 billion Euros. (The debt eventually was taken on by the troika of the IMF, European Commission, and European Central Bank, laying the groundwork for austerity measures for generations to come.) In an interview just prior to the collapse of the Irish banking system, Meehan voices her deep suspicions over the economic boom: "The global reality now is that we can't not be aware that events on the other side of the planet have a direct impact on us. Our boom here . . . was part of the movement of transnational capital which settled for a short time, as we knew it would, on the island, and then fucked off . . . Were we not saying that the multinationals would not develop loyalty to local community, would not prioritize local community when it came to decision making?"[71] In addition to their prescience, Meehan's words are remarkable for how clearly they articulate the challenges faced by Irish poets writing in an era of financialization. Financial capitalism is both capable of devastating the "local community" and yet fully deterritorialized from the concrete sites of production. How can poetry make sense of the shadowy movements of transnational capital that seemingly occur "on the other side of the planet" and yet nonetheless have very material and destructive consequences on the local? Such questions are all the more complicated in Ireland, whose rapid financialization situates the country within the Global North and yet is also a part of its postcolonial hangover.

    Meehan acknowledges her own work's imbrication within the networks of financialization that spurred the Celtic Tiger. Indeed, "Six Sycamores" was written and published during the height of the Tiger, and its very commissioning was made possible by the boom period's excessive real estate construction. Meehan's work was funded through the Per Cent for Art Scheme, a government initiative that earmarks up to 1 percent of publicly funded construction projects (including public buildings such as libraries and schools as well as infrastructural projects like roads and reservoirs) toward the commissioning of a work of art.[72] Although the Per Cent for Art Scheme differs from UNESCO and other international cultural policy programs, it is similarly tied to Ireland's economic globalization: the scheme was originally established in 1978 but only fully expanded in 1997 with the wealth brought in by the Celtic Tiger. In the decade between 1995 and 2005, the OPW commissioned and purchased over 4,600 works of art through the Per Cent for Art Scheme—more than quadrupling the number of acquisitions from the previous decade. This has incredibly transformed the OPW into one of the largest collections of Irish art in the world.[73]

Like many other creative programs in Ireland, the Per Cent for Art Scheme seeks out site-specific artwork. According to its guidelines, applications are assessed on the basis of how the proposed work "engages with a specific place or event" and "make[s] connections with the capital construction project and the environment connected with that project"; proposals must include an artist's brief that gives a "detailed description of the proposed context for the art project."[74] The head of the selection committee stresses that artists should not simply reflect the preexisting environment but develop new relationships between the site and its surrounding community. Therefore, OPW-commissioned artwork is unique for its embeddedness in and interactive relationship with its site. As the chair of the acquisitions committee explains, in the traditional arts museum, "art and its audience are the 'tenants' and are prioritized: the gallery space is expected to accommodate the optimum display of work." But the opposite is the case in Per Cent for Art Scheme artworks, which instead are "contributor[s] to the environment in concert with the building itself, as opposed to being the 'tenant.'"[75]

Given the strict parameters that govern projects under the Per Cent for Art Scheme, "Six Sycamores" might seem to be just another example of bureaucratic verse that pays lip service to the OPW and the architectural grandeur of St. Stephen's Green. But as shown by "Number Fifty-Two," Meehan does not shy away from painting an unflattering portrait of the financiers who built Stephen's Green. The poet explains that she feels both an attraction and a repulsion to the Green's architecture, having grown up in a tenement slum inside an old Georgian building: "I love those buildings; the intricacies of the craftwork, and the imagination, the ceilings, the stuccodoring work and yet what they stand for, the ascendancy class, the class privilege of the whole colonial adventure, I have real problems with. That tension between something I loved and something that oppressed me interested me, so I tendered for that commission."[76] Meehan uses spatial metaphors when explaining the sonnet's flexibility in accommodating a wide range of histories and experiences, comparing the poetic form to the very eighteenth-century townhouses on Stephen's Green: "The sonnet would be a good form to mirror something of the architectural complexity and the ornamentation of the houses themselves and how they had been shells for many different kinds of lives, for office workers now, for tenement families, for the rich, for the original owners of the houses, for the merchant and professional classes. I think of the sonnet as a kind of a shell in the literary tradition. Both house and poem are received forms that can be re-inhabited and are re-inhabited, that can be played with and changed." For the poet, the sonnet is an elastic "shell," able to house different socioeconomic classes over the centuries.

Meehan takes a similar approach to the occasional poem, using it as a genre that can accommodate the complex histories of art and capital in Ireland over the centuries. Since their construction, the Georgian squares of Dublin's city centre have acted as a synecdoche for the political and moneyed elite of Ireland. But throughout "Six Sycamores," Meehan emphasizes instead the custodial workers who have maintained Stephen Green's grand buildings and park over the centuries. The sonnet "Them Ducks Died for Ireland" opens with an epigraph quoting a report from the Green's superintendent about the maintenance work required to rebuild the park after the Easter Rising: " '6 of our *waterfowl were killed or shot, 7 of the garden seats broken and about 300 shrubs destroyed.*' " The poem raises a toast to the other unsung heroes of the Easter Rising:

> we'll salute the stretcher bearer, the nurse in white,
> the ones who pick up the pieces, who endure,
> who live at the edge, and die there and are known
> by this archival footnote read by fading light;
> fragile as a breathmark on the windowpane or the gesture
> of commemorating heroes in bronze and stone.[77]

Like much of Meehan's other work, "Six Sycamores" foregrounds the lives and experiences of Dublin's working class. The sonnets pay tribute to the invisible heroes of the Easter Rising—not Yeats's MacDonagh and MacBride, Connolly and Pearse, but the medics, nurses, and park maintainers "who pick up the pieces" with little recognition other than "this archival footnote read by fading light." Meehan purposefully makes ambiguous what exactly is "this archival footnote," which could refer to both the superintendent's report and the poem itself. The sonnet supplements the work of the OPW, offering poetic tribute to those who are not honored by being immortalized in "bronze and stone." But more importantly, "Six Sycamores" is also a tribute to the OPW's work as a government agency that undertakes the preservation of Ireland's infrastructure and built heritage. In other words, Meehan's poem is a commemoration of the labor of commemoration.

In so doing, the poet explicitly underscores the function of occasional poetry: its work of commemoration. Moreover, Meehan places on equal footing the custodial labor performed by the OPW and the work of poetry, often describing manual labor in the language of poetry. In the sonnet titled "all trades, their gear and tackle and trim," she borrows both a line and sprung rhythm from Gerard Manley Hopkins to "raise a glass and offer thanks" to the Green's custodians:[78]

> to the makers and minders of our material world.
> In their war against time: daemons fire them;
> St Joseph bear them; muses inspire them.
> Guild banner, lodge pennant, red flag of labour unfurled![79]

Both St. Joseph (the patron saint of workers) and the muses join forces to aid the "wielders of tools," the "makers and minders of our material world." Throughout "Six Sycamores," Meehan dissolves the differences between poetic and other forms of labor. In an earlier sonnet, the poet celebrates the "forms so crafty" of the Green's maintainers and their "common tools, / spade, rake, hoe . . . so sharp, so meet for the job."[80] Correspondingly, in interviews Meehan describes the poet as the "custodian of memory" and "professional rememberer," further dissolving the distinctions between manual and poetic labor.[81]

Of course, such comparisons can draw accusations of false humility or, worse yet, an elision of the class differences between a park maintainer and a poet (no less a successful one who can secure competitive arts grants). And indeed, an eyebrow should be raised about who exactly constitutes the "we" who will "raise a glass and offer thanks" to the park maintainers of Stephen's Green. But Meehan does not figure the poet as someone who can dig with the squat pen as a turf cutter might do with the spade. She does not seek to dissolve the material differences between different types of labor so much as highlight how poetry is a form of labor—one that has become ensnared in the growing creative economies in Ireland. As explained earlier, aesthetic autonomy has become fetishized in the creative economy. Not only that, but as Sarah Jaffe has persuasively shown, the rhetoric of the "labor of love"—the pernicious myth that certain kinds of work (including and especially that of the creative arts) are born out of passion and therefore do not count as work—is used to justify exploitative and low-wage labor conditions in a neoliberal economy. Building on the work of Raymond Williams and John Pat Leary, Jaffe writes, "'Creativity was a work of imagination, rather than production, of artistry rather than labor.' This split between art and work continues to mystify the work that goes into making art . . . Art is perhaps the ultimate fetishized commodity, where the work that went into creating it is almost entirely mystified, forgotten, wiped away."[82] But as "Six Sycamores" makes clear, poetry is often subsidized by cultural and arts programs like the Per Cent for Art Scheme and therefore no more outside capitalism than the construction of a "bronze and stone" statue or a public works building.

Meehan therefore posits a different purpose to the occasional poem than what was imagined earlier by Kinsella. For Kinsella, anxious of how his work will become subsumed within a rapidly globalizing Irish economy, the occasional poetry offers a reprieve outside capital and a means of critiquing the commodification of Irish poetry and landscape. But for Meehan, writing decades later when the creative economy has come to dominate the Irish cultural sphere, the poet is under no delusions that the occasional poem can furnish such aesthetic autonomy. Instead, Meehan turns to the occasional poem not to escape global capital but to stage a conversation about how poetry is enmeshed within systems of globalization and financialization. In "Six Sycamores," Meehan juxtaposes custodial and poetic labor not to craft some romantic notions of the working-class roots of poetry. Rather, she emphasizes how poetry is a part of the same neoliberal regime that underwrites the OPW and other cultural and heritage industries in contemporary Ireland.

VI.

What becomes clear by juxtaposing these two poets' work is that an attention to global economic conditions—whether burgeoning trade liberalization in the case of Kinsella or rampant neoliberalism for Meehan—transforms our understanding of Irish poetry. Such a vantage point allows a new history of Irish literature to emerge, which traces the transformations of a genre like the occasional poem under different stages of global capital in Ireland. It also situates contemporary Irish literature within the period of late capitalism, understanding how both Ireland's literary production and its politico-economic history (its accession to the EEC, the rise and fall of the Celtic Tiger, austerity) are shaped by these broader global flows.

At the same time, I want to emphasize an equally important reciprocal claim—that without attention to occasional poetry, we miss something central about the forms of capital investment in the arts in Ireland. As this chapter shows, the creative industries that were fueled by the Celtic Tiger have since been conscripted by both Irish politicians and international cultural policy organizations to rescue Ireland's economy after the financial crisis. The creative economy schemes that now dominate Irish cultural production have concentrated on welding together poetry and place, two of Ireland's most valuable remaining "commodities" after the crash. In other words, contemporary Irish poetry does not simply reflect and mourn the changes to the Irish landscape wrought by economic development and globalization—whether the bulldozing of an ancient archaeological site, the development of a massive shopping mall in a once-quiet Irish village, or the construction of new civic headquarters on a historic Georgian square. Rather, global capital has reshaped in tandem the Irish landscape and the conditions of poetic production in Ireland. Contemporary Irish poetry's continued preoccupation with place is not just nostalgia or the remnants of cultural nationalism that it cannot manage to shake off. The turn to the local, instead, is a strategy by which poets demonstrate how global capital inheres in and therefore can be made legible by place. Such an understanding gives new critical inroads into understanding the relationship between poetry and globalization in Ireland.

Chapter 2

Some Versions of Irish Pastoral

I.

In her work "Re-reading Oliver Goldsmith's 'The Deserted Village' in a Changed Ireland," Eavan Boland revisits the famed pastoral poem from the vantage point of her home in Dundrum in the early years of the new millennium.[1] At first, the eighteenth-century poem seems to mirror the realities of twenty-first-century Ireland during the heyday of the Celtic Tiger's real estate bubble. Just as Goldsmith condemns the Land Enclosure Acts that precipitated the decline of rural communities like Auburn, his poem's titular deserted village, Boland describes how the boom period's construction frenzy transformed Dundrum from a sleepy Dublin suburb into one of the costliest zip codes in Ireland. "The place was changing," declares Boland in the opening stanza, "That much was plain: / Land was sold. The little river was paved over with stone." While written centuries apart, both poems take aim at the privatization of public lands. (Boland's purposeful play on "plain" further reinforces the links between her work and Goldsmith's poem, whose first line reads: "Sweet Auburn, loveliest village on the plain.") But Boland also warns that Goldsmith's idealization of the fictional Auburn comes coupled with the erasure of the real Lissoy, the farming village where the poet spent his childhood and which is thought to be the model for his poem. Although Boland's work is titled a "rereading," the speaker never actually reads "The Deserted Village"; instead, she "let[s] Goldsmith's old lament remain / Where it was: high on my shelves, stacked there at the back— / Dust collecting on its out-of-date, other-century, superannuated pain." Rather than pulling down the book from off its shelf, the speaker "summons" the image of Goldsmith and watches as he "lay[s] phrase after phrase / On the island, the village he is taking so much care to erase." More a reappraisal—and perhaps even a reprisal—than a rereading, Boland's poem draws attention to the mystifying effects of "The Deserted Village" and the pastoral tradition more largely.

Although Boland discounts Goldsmith's poem as an example of outdated "other-century" nostalgia, her writing nevertheless demonstrates the pastoral's persistent presence in contemporary Irish poetry.[2] Boland is hardly the first writer to cast a sideways glance at the pastoral tradition.[3] The pastoral is often characterized by its aestheticization of the brutal realities of agricultural labor—what William Empson more graciously described as its "beautiful relation between rich and poor" and what Samuel Johnson more scathingly condemned as "easy, vulgar, and therefore disgusting."[4] But while rural retreat and the antinomian relationship between country and city remain indelible features of the pastoral, scholars have also explored the violent histories underlying its writing. The pastoral carries with it a long history of dispossession: Virgil composed the *Eclogues* in the wake of civil war, as lands in northern Italy (including the poet's own family farm) were confiscated and redistributed to veterans who fought in Octavian's armies. After Dryden's 1697 translation of the *Eclogues* and *Georgics* inspired a resurgence in the pastoral, poets like George Crabbe and Thomas Gray wrote in the midst of the Enclosures in eighteenth- and nineteenth-century England. Raymond Williams uses the image of an escalator moving backward and forward in time to describe the pastoral's many shifts in historical references, or what he calls its "problem of perspective": "What seemed a single escalator, a perpetual recession into history, turns out, on reflection, to be a more complicated movement: Old England, settlement, the rural virtues—all these, in fact, mean different things at different times, and quite different values are being brought to question. We shall need precise analysis of each kind of retrospect, as it comes."[5] With his metaphor, Williams does not argue for the pastoral's ahistoricity but demands that scholars accordingly recalibrate their perspectives and remain sensitive to the literary, political, and economic histories encoded within it. As I will argue, the pastoral is a fundamentally genealogical mode, and to invoke it so self-consciously in the contemporary moment is to engage with its history. Boland does so in her "Rereading," even if it is to dismiss the pastoral's romanticizing impulses. But even her poem concludes on an ambiguous note: "Hard to know which variant / Of our country this is. Hard to say / Which variant of sound to use at the end of this line."

For the writers discussed in this chapter, the pastoral represents more than just a simplistic idealization of country life; it serves instead as, to borrow Boland's words, the "variant of sound" that can best explore the ramifications of Ireland's sudden catapult into a globalized economy. This chapter concentrates on the period of the 1960s and 1970s when the pastoral mode becomes revivified in Irish poetry, just as Ireland was shifting from a primarily agricultural to a market economy and shedding decades-long policies of political and cultural isolationism. For the purposes of this chapter, my primary literary examples are the works of Seamus Heaney and John Montague, two poets who approach the pastoral as an engine of incisive political and economic critique. Montague, in particular, mobilizes the pastoral to engage with the discourses of economic development that dominated the Irish political sphere as the nation embarked on a series of trade liberalization reforms, leading up to the country's accession to the European Economic Community (EEC) in 1973. Although this same period of the late 1960s and early 1970s is widely regarded as the beginning of global capitalism by scholars like David Harvey and Vijay Prashad, Ireland has largely been left out of these analyses due to the country's position outside the financial powerhouses of the Global North and the extractive industries in the Global South. Neither part of NATO nor the Non-Aligned Movement, Ireland has long had a confounding political and economic identity, and its strange place within global geopolitics has only been magnified by the European debt crisis and Brexit. The decades of the 1960s and 1970s are of especial interest today, as these recent events have placed a spotlight back on the Republic and Northern Ireland's relationship to the European Union. By examining this period, we can better understand the groundwork that fomented Ireland's rapid globalization and situate Brexit within a longer history of the country's relationship to the EEC and Common Market.

In this chapter, I place poetry and economic discourse in closer dialogue than has been typical in studies of Irish literature.[6] While many scholars have focused on the political dimensions of literature during this period (particularly given the ratcheting violence of the Troubles in the 1960s), I steer my attention toward the dramatic changes in economic policy also underway at this time. Recently, a new wave of scholars has pushed to understand the close relationship between economics and literature and approach them as "coproducers of knowledge," as described by Patrick Fessenbecker and Bryan Yazell.[7] This is not to overstate the power of poetry to directly intervene in or shape economic policy at the state level. After all, as I argue in the previous chapter, there are many ways in which poetry can act more as complicit partner than as radical intervener in the machinations of neoliberal capital in Ireland. With its laments of bygone eras and of "Sweet Auburn," the pastoral is perhaps the aesthetic mode most amendable to capturing the vicissitudes of the local—and therefore also be most susceptible to (and indeed sometimes guilty of) conservative forms of nostalgia and place-belonging. But we can also read these poetries as more than just bad ideology and instead as opening up a language of economic critique that was unavailable in the Irish political sphere at the time. As Laura Finch argues, while literature and economics may be treated as coproducers of knowledge, the aesthetic also "offers a reminder that what appears as common sense is indeed an effect of hegemonic discourse, at base shaped by the needs of capital. In this way, the aesthetic is a form of knowledge that resists 'the stupidity of common sense' that privileges the visible, factual, and knowable, and allows access to knowledge discounted by the epistemic regime of capital."[8] The pastoral allows for these poets to reflect on the limitations of political and economic discourse, dominated as it was by proponents of modernization who derided the rural community as a space of backward nationalism or by conservative politicians who idealized it as a sanctuary of traditional values.

This chapter proceeds in two movements. In the first, I chart the pastoral's lasting legacy within contemporary Irish literature, centering on the critical suspicions aroused by Heaney's poetry. I also give a detailed account of Irish economic history in the 1960s and 1970s, showing how rural Ireland became crucial to conversations around the Republic's global economic future. Then I move on to examine Montague's collection *The Rough Field*, which takes a sharp look at these economic policies as they take shape in his home village of Garvaghey in County Tyrone. Montague and Heaney are acutely aware of the multiple ironies embedded within the pastoral, whose discursive power can reveal the contradictions in politico-economic ideology and cultural expression in modern Ireland. By reading their work against the backdrop of Irish economic history, we can see how a traditional literary mode like the pastoral registers the tensions felt when Ireland's identity on the global stage was in flux and transition, much as it is today.

II.

Arguably more so than any other contemporary poet, Heaney has engaged with the political and aesthetic legacies of the pastoral. From his inaugural collection *Death of a Naturalist* to his lyric sequence "Glanmore Sonnets" (modeled in part after Wordsworth's Grasmere poems) in *Field Work* to the eclogues in *Electric Light*, Heaney has consistently returned to the pastoral over the course of his career to the point where the poet's own life has been read as emblematic of the mode: when Heaney moved from his native Northern Ireland to the Republic of Ireland in 1972, many considered his departure as a betrayal of artistic responsibility—a pastoral retreat from the intensifying political (and urban) realities of Belfast and the Troubles.[9] The accusations of retreat were only intensified by the poet's relocation to Wicklow, a county south of Dublin nicknamed the "Garden of Ireland" for its famously picturesque landscapes.[10] One critic went so far as to say that Heaney's collections published after his relocation could have been more accurately entitled "Death of a Pastoralist," since in them "it is the notion of a pastoral, childhood Eden that actually dies."[11]

In certain ways, the critical reception around Heaney's poetry echoes the contested literary history of the pastoral. Heaney sometimes encourages the pastoralism of his biography, using images of rural labor as figures for the writing process, such as his famed metaphor of "digging" with his pen in the place of his forefather's spade. For Heaney, poetic and rural labor are historically intertwined, and he takes great pleasure in pointing out the etymology of "verse," which comes from the Latin *versus*, denoting both a line of poetry and a line of tilled earth: "the crunch and scuffle of the gravel working like a metre or a metronome under the rhythms of the ongoing chaunt . . . The poet as ploughman, if you like."[12] The question of Heaney's literary priorities—whether he privileges aesthetic form over political engagement or vice versa—has always been the focal point for critics of Heaney's work. For those who see Heaney's poetry as nothing more than aesthetic escapism, the poet's penchant for the pastoral has become a convenient whipping boy for what they consider his disengagement with politics and even reality. In a scathing review of *North*, Al Alvarez writes that "Heaney is not rural and sturdy and domestic, with his feet firmly planted in the Irish mud, but is instead an ornamentalist, a word collector, a connoisseur of fine language for its own sake."[13]

Heaney's detractors often pinpoint the pastoral as the literary embodiment of his political disengagement. But we can more profitably read the pastoral as instead the formal platform on which Heaney confronts the anxieties (including his own) around his engagement with the political. Although the pastoral is most closely associated with Classical and eighteenth-century British literature, it has proven to be a remarkably transportable genre. The pastoral's importation—particularly to Ireland and other postcolonial contexts—may seem surprising given the many critiques of its conservative ideology, especially as the mode often did endorse a comfortable status quo for the landowning class that had been the reading public prior to the nineteenth century. However, poets such as Rosanna Warren have offered more nuanced interpretations that read beyond the pastoral's scenic surface of green pastures and blissful shepherds. As Warren contends, pastoral literature always had the pressures of a larger, political world infringing on the edges of its Arcadian landscapes. The pastoral's very idealization of the landscape requires, as a corollary, the omission of political realities that constantly threaten to besmirch its unspoiled idylls. That is, pastoral literature dramatizes its own inevitable "contamination"; its very power relies on the precariousness of its withdrawal from the political realm.[14] The pastoral poet's task is to not mystify but instead emphasize what Heaney describes as the "ill fit . . . between the beautifully tinted literary map and the uglier shape that the reality has taken in the world."[15]

Moreover, Empson argues that the pastoral foregrounds a more fundamental crisis of representation—what he attributes to the "double attitude" or inherently ironic nature of the poet:

> Both versions [of the pastoral] are based on a double attitude of the artist to the worker, of the complex man to the simple one ("I am in one way better, in another not so good"), and this may well recognize a permanent truth about the aesthetic situation. To produce pure proletarian art the artist must be at one with the worker; this is impossible, not for political reasons, but because the artist never is at one with any public.[16]

In other words, the pastoral is no more or less ideological than other works of literature; it simply accentuates the inevitable disconnect between the writer and the community by embedding this divide in clear irony. Empson's oft-quoted description of the pastoral as a "beautiful relation between rich and poor" has been frequently misinterpreted as a confirmation of the mode's inherent conservativism when the scholar is in fact much more ambiguous about its political orientations. Writing in the midst of Stalin's promotion and eventual institution of socialist realism as state policy, Empson queries the status of realist aesthetics (what he names "proletarian literature") as the only authentic and truly communitarian literary mode:

> When communists say that an author under modern capitalism feels cut off from most of the life of the country, and would not under communism, the remark has a great deal of truth, though he might only exchange a sense of isolation for a sense of the waste of his powers; it is certainly not so completely true as to make the verse from Gray pointless to a man living under communism. The way this sense of isolation has been avoided in the past is by the conventions of pastoral with which I am concerned.[17]

Empson points out that all literature, whether a pastoral poem or work of socialist realism, suffers from a "sense of isolation" insofar as the author is always distanced from the audience and subject at hand. As he reiterates, "a representative is conscious that he is not the same as what he represents." While Empson does not dispute the disingenuousness of the pastoral writer's connection to rural life—it is "absurdly artificial," as he puts it—he nevertheless argues that the pastoral's purpose is to stage these relations, however contrived they may be.[18]

In "The Toome Road," Heaney experiments with the pastoral's conventions of irony and double attitude by transporting the mode's usual confrontation between landowner and peasant to war-torn County Derry. In the poem, the speaker confronts a convoy of British armored vehicles trespassing on her land, bringing to the fore questions of embattled ownership and the intertwined histories of colonialism and rural dispossession. "How long were they approaching down my roads," she demands, "As if they owned them?"[19] Colonial violence infects the very texture of poetic language as the British soldiers not only threaten proprietary rights but also pervert pastoral language: the usual "warbling" of birds is now the movement of the cars' slow advance, and the "turrets" of country estates like Thoor Ballylee now refers to the gun turrets of tanks. Not only the Irish countryside but the very space of the poem and poetic language itself are tainted by colonial occupation. The speaker expresses her outrage, listing her agricultural possessions in trochaic meter ("Silos, chill gates, wet slates, the greens and reds / Of outhouse roofs") as a way of insisting upon her now-contested "rights-of-way." As the tanks continue to encroach, she questions: "Whom should I run to tell / Among all of those with their back doors on the latch / For the bringer of bad news, that small-hours visitant / Who, by being expected, might be kept distant?" Left alone as the "whole county was sleeping," the speaker turns to no one and instead erupts into apostrophe, declaring that the rural community can withstand imperial invasion: "O charioteers, above your dormant guns, / It stands here still, stands vibrant as you pass."

Of course, such resistance is achieved only through the silence of an "invisible" and a "sleeping" community. In his descriptions of the speaker as the "bringer of bad news" and "small-hours visitant . . . kept distant" from the sleeping country that she dares not awake, Heaney uses the pastoral to foreground the disconnect between the poet and the rural community, between the apostrophizing speaker and the country that pays no heed to her. In Heaney's poem, rural Ireland is in equal turns defiant and mute—its defiance achieved only through its turn away from the impending forces of colonialism. What the pastoral offers, then, is a formal exploration of reciprocity and mutual recognition within the context of class difference and, in the case of Irish literature, ethnopolitical hostility. The submerged histories of violence that are primary to the pastoral—particularly those of dispossession—are also integral to the originary structures of colonial violence.

For Empson, the pastoral's double attitude is used to stage the disconnect between the artist and the community she attempts to represent—an aesthetic predicament that Heaney has interrogated throughout his career. But the pastoral's settings of shepherds and deserted villages are not incidental but essential to the work of Heaney and other Irish poets, who wrote during a set of unique capital configurations in Ireland at the midcentury. For much of the twentieth century, the countryside enjoyed a status that reflected the importance of agriculture to the Republic's economy, especially as farmers were regarded as Ireland's nation-forming class. After Ireland's entry into the EEC, however, the availability of huge subsidies for farming reshaped rural society and destroyed the remnants of small-farming communities. Heaney subtly hints at the submerged politico-economic tensions underwriting "The Toome Road" with the deliberate ambiguity of the word "country," which denotes both the rural countryside and the nation-state. Keeping both meanings in tension, Heaney points to the unique pressures placed upon the Irish pastoral, which must deal with the representation of both rural and national communities as an inseparable set of political and aesthetic concerns. (In "Re-reading," Boland plays with similar ambiguity when she remarks that it is "[h]ard to know which variant / Of our country this is.")

It is therefore imperative to understand the specific socioeconomic conditions of Ireland in the decades after independence, particularly the significant role of agriculture within discussions of Ireland's economic future. This is especially important because the discourse around economic nationalism was often coded in the language of pastoral. Take, for instance, Éamon de Valera's famous St. Patrick's Day speech, which he delivered on Raidió Éireann in 1943. In the radio broadcast, the then Taoiseach envisions the "Ireland that we dreamed of" as an idyllic landscape of "cosy homesteads," complete with the "laughter of comely maidens" and "fields and villages . . . joyous with the sounds of industry."[20] The speech did not simply reflect the rural upbringing or old-fashioned values (and dangerously fascist tones) of the Taoiseach. A general election was to be held three months after the speech, and de Valera had to contend with a new agrarian political group that threatened to lure the farming constituency from his Fianna Fáil party. The speech was a resounding success in its time (although it later became symbolic of what critics saw as de Valera's political naivete), and the Taoiseach's incumbent party won a majority of parliamentary seats even as the country was suffering from a serious economic slump.

However, de Valera's pastoral vision was more than just a ploy to secure the votes of the farming constituency; it was also a crucial component of his platform of economic nationalism. During his tenure, de Valera put into place a number of protectionist policies meant to shield the fledgling Irish Free State from competing in international markets. But the raising of tariffs on British imported goods, which was meant to counteract the fall in demand of Irish agricultural goods in the international market, set off the catastrophic Anglo-Irish Trade War (1932–1938), which resulted in a series of unilateral trade restrictions by both countries and devastated both the Irish agricultural and industrial sectors.[21] Economic isolationism was later compounded by cultural isolationism during the Emergency Era (1939–1946), when Ireland was effectively shut off from Britain and the European continent. During the Emergency, the Irish censorship board insisted on "balanced" accounts of the Allies and Axis (therefore blocking out much news about the war), and the state implemented wartime travel restrictions that limited movement between Ireland and Britain.[22] The consequences of these policies snowballed into the "Dark Decade," as the 1950s came to be known, which saw soaring employment rates, declining wages, and high levels of emigration. Over the course of fifteen years, nearly five hundred thousand people emigrated out of a country with a total population of less than three million. As farmers left the agricultural sector to seek employment in urban areas, they found industries that were unable to absorb the large influx of workers. By the close of the 1950s, the average British worker earned over 40 percent more than the Irish worker, and

Ireland's GDP per capita was just over half of the European median. De Valera's pastoral fantasy of economic self-reliance and "the Ireland That We Dreamed of" had completely fallen apart.

But, so the story goes, Ireland surfaced out of the Dark Decade under the stewardship of Seán Lemass and T. K. Whitaker, who implemented the historic white paper *The First Programme for Economic Expansion (1958–63)* and paved the way for trade liberalization and foreign direct investment (FDI). As explained in the previous chapter, the "Lemass era" saw the dismantling of protectionist acts that had prohibited foreign ownership of industries in Ireland; replacing them were policies that promoted FDI through a zero corporate tax on manufactured exports. By the 1990s, export-oriented FDI in manufacturing skyrocketed to almost 60 percent of all production, starting from nothing four decades earlier.[23] The narrative of the golden era ushered in by the Lemass–T. K. partnership has been complicated by many historians, who argue that Ireland's modernization was not simply an overnight affair orchestrated by two lone wolves.[24] But no matter the case, agriculture was central to the period's economic anxieties. The trade war made clear that the Republic, despite political independence, remained a satellite cloistered within the economic orbit of Britain, which was the largest market for Ireland's chief export of agricultural goods. Consequently, both major political parties greeted with open arms the reversal of economic isolationism and the shift toward European integration. Of particular allure was the Common Agricultural Policy promised by the EEC, which would provide significant dividends for the agricultural sector.[25] Lemass's Fianna Fáil party pitched economic liberalization as a means of severing the neocolonial economic link with Britain, framing potential EEC membership as symbolic of internationalism and economic prosperity under the aegis of Europe.[26] As one *Irish Times* commentator put it, "entry to Brussels may be one of the final steps in the establishment of Ireland as a nation, a further approach to the day when Emmet's epitaph may be written."[27] In so doing, Lemass and other proponents of European integration redefined the goals of Irish economic nationalism and political identity altogether.

Of course, Ireland's petition to the EEC was specifically timed so that it could join along with Britain, thus facilitating a smooth transition of their dependent economies, and the hypocrisy of Fianna Fáil's rhetoric was not lost on critics. Anti-integration activists argued that Ireland's joint entry with Britain would only cement the countries' neocolonial relationship—what one Sein Féin opponent deploringly described as "crawling in on England's coat-tails."[28] Opponents went so far as to claim that the EEC was merely another imperial entity seeking to replace Britain as Ireland's political and economic master. Such opposition efforts laid the foundations for anti-EEC responses from fringe socialist and republican parties who stressed the undemocratic nature of the EEC, which they argued would suppress the national sovereignty and independence of small states in the interest of the big ones. For these groups, the seat of power might have been shifted from London to Brussels, but the core-periphery dynamic remained the same. The accusations made in the 1970s have an uncanny similarity to those made in the wake of the 2008 EU debt crisis, when many political analysts (this time writing in mainstream newspapers and journals) made similar arguments about the patriarchal relationship between the large and small EU member-states, particularly between Germany and Greece.[29]

Depending on the perspective, European integration signaled either a pathway toward true economic nationalism or an absolute breakdown of it. But whether with de Valera's emphasis on self-reliance and protectionism or Lemass's formulation of the new European Ireland, economic determination was fundamental to conceptions of Irish national identity in the decades following independence. By understanding the 1960s and 1970s as a historical moment pivoting around Ireland's economic future and its transition from agricultural to market economy, we can develop a more nuanced analysis of the pastoral poetry that emerges during this period. Scholars often categorize Heaney and Montague (along with their respective forefathers, Yeats and Kavanagh) as oppositional poles of aesthetics, serving as the exemplars of romanticism and naturalism. For Joe Cleary, naturalism is the dominant literary mode in Irish culture during the decades between independence and the end of the twentieth century, flourishing in the work of writers like John McGahern and Tom Murphy. Disenchanted with the romantic idealism of the Revival, Cleary argues, naturalist fiction insists instead on depictions of the deprivations of rural life, which was in the eyes of these writers "the defining reality of Irish life. Irish naturalism was in its inception a dissident and reformist aesthetic: it measured the distance between the official state ideology of Irish nationalism and its tawdry reality."[30] Even Heaney, himself often subjected to these schematic categorizations, replicates such a bifurcated notion of Irish aesthetics: "on the one hand Kavanagh with his sense of 'home' and his almost extreme realization of the disobedience and peremptoriness of creative nature, on the other Yeats with his platonic rendition of 'heaven,' and of what can be made of this in terms of poetic rendition."[31] But by reading these poets against the backdrop of Ireland's complex economic history, we can see the aesthetics of naturalism/antipastoral (Kavanagh and Montague) and romanticism/pastoral (Yeats and Heaney) as perhaps dissident but not incongruent interlocutors in the conversations around Irish economic nationalism.

Raymond Williams and Leo Marx contend that the pastoral was generated from the tensions between city and country produced by the rise of industrialization in Britain and the US, respectively.[32] Postwar Ireland's lack of sustained industrial and urban development would therefore seem to make it inhospitable grounds for producing the usual tensions between rural and urban communities that give rise to the pastoral. Yet, as Oona Frawley points out, there was an outpouring of contemporary Irish pastoral poetry, whose resurgence was partly popularized by the publication of Heaney's *Death of a Naturalist* in 1969.[33] I argue that the Irish pastoral is generated by a different set of tensions—in this case, the frictions felt by a local economy catapulted into the global market. The traditional pastoral emerges out of situations of combined and uneven development within a domestic context, in which small industrial enclaves arose within a predominantly agrarian and preindustrial order. The Irish pastoral instead works through the tensions of emergent local economies entering the global market—in this case, the European Common Market. The pastoral, then, is not simply an inherited literary genre or a retreat from politics but a sophisticated reflection on the struggle over Ireland's economic future.

III.

If Seamus Heaney's life and career have been deeply entangled with the pastoral, then John Montague is another one of its most sophisticated contemporary practitioners, revitalizing the mode to interrogate Ireland's sudden economic transformation. "No Wordsworthian dream enchants me here," proclaims Montague in the opening sequence of his collection *The Rough Field*, originally published in 1972.[34] Comprising ten sequences interwoven with wood-block prints and excerpts of historical documents, *The Rough Field* centers around Montague's rural hometown of Garvaghey in County Tyrone, Northern Ireland. The poet repudiates the sublime landscapes of "glacial corrie, totemic mountain" and replaces them with "low hills and gravel streams / Oozy blackness of bog-banks, pale upland grass" that are more accurate of the countryside's topography. Such a declaration underlines Montague's turn from an aesthetics of romanticization to one of verisimilitude, a poetics literally grounded in the "gaunt farmhouses" and "plaintive moorlands" of the Northern Irish landscape. *The Rough Field* seems to work within a more naturalist tradition, bespeaking the impossibility of reconciling the scenic pastures commonly found in pastoral poetry with the socioeconomic realities of a depressed farming village in Northern Ireland. If the "essential trick of the old pastoral . . . [was] to imply a beautiful relation between rich and poor," as Empson famously argues, then Montague is intent on unveiling this obfuscation with his realist representations of the countryside.[35]

However, Montague does not outright abandon the pastoral so much as complicate it, and his work can only be fully appreciated if we analyze how his work engages with economic policies at the time. The preface opens the collection by describing County Tyrone as one of the "remote areas where the presence of the past was compounded with a bleak economic future, whether in Ulster, Brittany or the Highlands of Scotland."[36] While Northern Ireland's economy obviously cannot be collapsed with that of the Republic, it simultaneously entered a period of economic decline, albeit for a different set of reasons. After experiencing a short-lived postwar boom, the north's two major industries, linen and shipbuilding, faced severe and long-term falls in demand that had begun decades earlier in the interwar period. Similar to the Republic, Northern Ireland sought FDI to compensate for the declines in industry, and by 1990 over half of manufacturing jobs came from foreign-owned businesses.[37] (The next chapter delves into the details of Northern Ireland's history of deindustrialization.) And although *The Rough Field* concentrates on the landscape of Garvaghey, there are countless references to the economic histories of both Northern Ireland and the Republic. (Montague was personally associated with opponents of the EEC, such as the historian and archaeologist Liam de Paor, an ardent member of the anti-integrationist group the Common Market Defence Campaign.)[38] In one section, Montague goes so far as to question whether "our spiritual empire . . . at last relent[s] / With a trade expansion of 5 per cent," a financial figure directly lifted from Lemass and Whitaker's *Economic Expansion*.[39]

The poet's critiques come to a head in the "Balance Sheet" in "Hymn to the New Omagh Road," a caustic attack on the newly developed motorway connecting Belfast and Derry.[40] (See figure 2.1a–b.) Comprising "Loss" and "Gain" sections on facing pages, the "Balance Sheet" lists pro and con "items" supporting or opposing the Omagh

> I
>
> Balance Sheet
>
> # 𝕷𝔬𝔰𝔰
>
> Item: The shearing away of an old barn
> criss-cross of beams where pigeons moan
> high small window where the swallow built
> white-washed dry-stone walls
>
> Item: The suppression of stone lined paths
> old potato-boiler full of crocuses
> overhanging lilac or laburnum
> sweet pea climbing the fence.
>
> Item: The filling-in of chance streams
> uncovered wells, all unchannelled sources
> of water that might weaken foundations
> bubbling over the macadam.
>
> Item: The disappearance of all signs
> of wild life, wren's or robin's nest,
> a rabbit nibbling a coltsfoot leaf,
> a stray squirrel or water rat.
>
> Item: The uprooting of wayside hedges
> with their accomplices, devil's bit and pee the bed,
> prim rose and dog rose, an unlawful
> assembly of thistles.
>
> Item: The removal of all hillocks
> and humps, superstition styled fairy forts
> and long barrows, now legally to be regarded
> as obstacles masking a driver's view.
>
> [58]

Fig. 2.1a–b. "The Balance Sheet" from *The Rough Field*. The "Balance Sheet" mimics a ledger book with "Loss" and "Gain" sections, which respectively detail the disadvantages and advantages of the Omagh Road's construction in County Tyrone. Reprinted with kind permission from Wake Forest University Press and the estate of John Montague.

Gain

Item: 10 men from the district being for a period of time fully employed, their ten wives could buy groceries and clothes to send 30 children content to school for a few months, and raise local merchants' hearts by paying their bills.

Item: A man driving from Belfast to Londonderry can arrive a quarter of an hour earlier, a lorry load of goods ditto, thus making Ulster more competitive in the international market.

Item: A local travelling from the prefabricated suburbs of bypassed villages can manage an average of 50 rather than 40 m.p.h. on his way to see relatives in Omagh hospital or lunatic asylum.

Item: The dead of Garvaghey Graveyard (including my grandfather) can have an unobstructed view—the trees having been sheared away for a carpark — of the living passing at great speed, sometimes quick enough to come straight in:

Let it be clear
That I do not grudge my grandfather
This long delayed pleasure!
I like the idea of him
Rising from the rotting boards of the coffin
With his J.P.'s white beard
And penalising drivers
For travelling faster
Than jaunting cars

Road's construction: the "shearing away of an old barn" is, for instance, "balanced" by the highway's employment of ten men whose "ten wives could buy groceries and clothes to send 30 children content to school for a few months and raise local merchants' hearts by paying their bills." Unsurprisingly, Montague's balance sheet is tipped against the construction of the highway, which would wreck environmental havoc (eliminating "all signs of wild life" and literally flattening the landscape of blemishes like "chance stream / uncovered wells," "wayside hedges," and "all hillocks / and humps") for the convenience of faster highway speeds.

But *The Rough Field* also illustrates how Montague's deep ambivalences over the modernizing Irish economy cannot be contained within the neat bifurcations of a balance sheet. For all his displeasure with the construction of the Omagh Road, Montague acknowledges the profitable benefits of the highway that would facilitate ground transport and "mak[e] Ulster more competitive in the international market." An epigraph, set in italics and outside the neatly divided bounds of the balance sheet, adds the caveat, "*Let it be clear / That I do not grudge my grandfather / This long delayed pleasure!*" The poem's intertextuality—an arrangement of lyric, prose, travel narratives, and woodcut prints—is not only an instance of Montague's experimentation with the concrete poem. It is also a textual manifestation of the remainders, both material and affective, that are illegible within the tidy divisions of a losses-and-gains ledger.

In making visible these remainders, "The Balance Sheet" draws attention to the limitations of the language of economic policy while pointing to the possibilities afforded by poetry. Throughout *The Rough Field*, the voice of an interloping speaker interrupts the collection's many intertexts, and the mix of the modern and archaic elements points toward Montague's larger project of articulating the tensions between modernization and traditionalism, between concrete form and lyric. The concrete poem allows this lyric voice to be set aside not only grammatically, in its shift to first person, but also typographically. The itemized list form of the balance sheet mimics stanzas, but whereas the "Gain" section is composed in prose, the "Loss" section and epigraph are clearly set in verse. We should also consider the balance sheet's placement within the "Hymn to the New Omagh Road," which opens with a woodcut print and a captioning verse that details how the runoff from a nearby quarry chokes a stream with "slow-flowing mud / [in which] the mountain trout / Turns up its belly to die." Montague's bitterness reverberates through to the hymn's concluding stanza, which features the same italicized font and centered spacing of the earlier epigraph. The stanza announces in first-person:

> My sympathy goes out to the farmer
> who, mad drunk after a cattle mart,
> bought himself a concrete swan
> for thirty bob and lugged it
> all the way
> home
> to deposit it
> (where the monkey puzzle was meant to grow)
> on his tiny landscaped lawn.⁴¹

The image of concrete swans alludes to Yeats's Coole Park, which he references again when describing how a tourist "in search of a tradition" comes to find instead a dilapidated estate with a "lake / bereft of swans."⁴² Throughout *The Rough Field*, the mixture of lyric, prose, and image intimates Montague's complex relationship with the many legacies of the pastoral. (Indeed, the typography and wood-block prints in *The Rough Field* make it visually resemble another famous work of pastoral: Edmund Spenser's *The Shepheardes Calendar*.) He certainly faults certain strains of pastoral poetry—what he perceives as the incongruity of imposing "Wordsworthian mountains" onto the Tyrone landscape or the delusions of grandeur motivating a farmer to plant concrete swans onto his lawn. But Montague, in his invocation of these familiar tropes, also indicates that his critique of economic and ecological displacement must nevertheless be couched in the language of pastoral. While suspicious of the pastoral mode, Montague recognizes that he has inherited it in any case.

In fact, Montague's mixed feelings about the pastoral becomes a means of expressing his own ambivalence about Ireland's rapid modernization. As much as the poet disdains the Revivalists' naive romanticization of folk and peasant culture, Montague also mourns the displacement of the rural Northern Irish Catholic community (the "uncultivated pearls" and "shards of a lost tradition," as he calls them), which has been historically disenfranchised and is now part of an entirely illegible economic class: "The whole landscape a manuscript / We had lost the skill to read, / A part of our past disinherited."⁴³ Though the poet maintains a biting tone throughout *The Rough Field*, the collection often flits back and forth in its critiques, attacking both the "new Ireland" ushered in by economic modernization and those nostalgic for the socioeconomic deprivations of the past (the "gloomy images of a provincial catholicism").[44] The ambivalences of Montague's poetry reflect the contradictions within the economic debates at the time, particularly around Ireland and the UK's entry into the Common Market. Andrew Devenney explains that opposition campaigns against EEC integration never gained popular appeal because they were stuck in an impasse between radical forms of politico-economic critique and a traditionalism that sounded disquietingly similar to past rhetoric of protectionism and isolationism: "On the one hand, many anti-integrationists rested on a leftist critique of Irish society that sought to fundamentally change Ireland's socioeconomic structures, for instance, by removing the domination of big businesses and unscrupulous English industrialists and landlords. On the other hand, this was also a traditionalist vision, seeking to resist whatever innovations did not come from the Irish people themselves."[45] *The Rough Field* does not offer a straightforward politics, let alone a coherent economic platform; instead, the uneven affective register of Montague's poetry mirrors the uneven development in Ireland wrought by globalization. His ambivalence—the collection's restless oscillation between cynicism and nostalgia, experimental and traditional forms—problematizes the possibility of resistance in spaces like the rural communities in Northern Ireland and the Republic.

Montague poignantly articulates his poetics of ambivalence in the collection's epilogue, a rare moment when the poet's rancor relents. The concluding sequence describes a picturesque landscape of "lakeside orchards in first bloom" and "hawthorn with a surplice whiteness" as the speaker drives through County Cavan. However, the tone soon shifts to the elegiac as the poet contemplates the "changing rural pattern" of the countryside, now replete with modern agricultural machinery:

> A changing rural pattern means clack
> of tractor for horse, sentinel shape
> of silo, hum of milking machine:
> the same from Ulster to the Ukraine . . .
> Fewer hands, bigger markets, larger farms.
> Yet something mourns. The iron-ribbed
> lamp flitting through the yard at dark,
> the hissing froth, and fodder scented warmth
> of a wood stalled byre, or leather thong

> of flail curling in a barn, were part
> of a world where action had been wrung
> through painstaking years to ritual . . .⁴⁶

The stanza's assonance ("clack"/"tractor," "for"/"horse") and alliteration ("sentinel shape of silo," "milking machine") replicate the noise of farm machinery that drones on all the same from "Ulster to Ukraine." (However, the respectively short and long vowels of "Ulster" and "Ukraine" intimate how regional identities are not always assimilable under the generic bracket of "Europe.") Montague's anxieties tread familiar ground as the poet mourns the slow erasure of the unique textures of agricultural life: the "iron-ribbed lamp," "wood stalled byre," and threshing flail "curling in a barn." The poet even goes on to imply that at stake is the pastoral mode itself: "Palmer's softly lit Vale of Shoreham / commemorates it, or Chagall's lovers / floating above a childhood village / remote but friendly as Goldsmith's Auburn." Montague's specific details of the Irish landscape and everyday rural life stand in contrast to the abstract forces of global capital (the nebulous "international market" or "Gross National Product . . ." that trails off ambiguously with an ellipsis). The poet's detailed sketches of County Tyrone serve as a poetic record that preserves the "local grace" that he sees threatened by the impending forces of modernization, while they also recognize the futility of such attempts at preservation.

But it would be hasty to dismiss Montague's anxieties as only the product of a misguided nostalgia. Rather than seeing *The Rough Field* as closing with a backward gaze toward a pastoral past, we might consider how Montague's work exemplifies what Helen Tiffin and Graham Huggan term the mode's "spectrality," or its ability to hint at the submerged histories of violence. The pastoral's apparent political quietism, not to mention its reliance on European literary forms, makes it seemingly unamendable to postcolonial frameworks. But as Tiffin and Huggan argue, the pastoral rests on the tensions between affective belonging and property, which become all the more intensified in colonial and postcolonial contexts of dispossession and loss: "Pastoral, if it is anything, is an intrinsically ironic form . . . a spectral form, always aware of the suppressed violence that helped make its peaceful vision possible, and always engaged with the very histories from which it appears to want to escape."⁴⁷

Edward Said fully elucidates the spectrality of pastoral in his groundbreaking essay "Jane Austen and Empire," in which he outlines the method of contrapuntal analysis in his reading of *Mansfield Park*. Against accusations that his scholarship centered too exclusively on European culture, Said develops contrapuntal analysis as a methodology of "reading back" that could uncover the "submerged but crucial presence of empire in canonical texts" and demonstrate the text's "simultaneous awareness both of the metropolitan history and of those other histories against which (and together with which) the dominating discourse acts."[48] While Said's essay has since generated a corpus of rich contrapuntal readings that illuminate the specters of imperial unconscious hovering in the margins of literature, few have acknowledged the essay's work as an incisive analysis of the pastoral mode. Said begins by critiquing Williams's abbreviated analysis of the relationship between pastoral and empire in *The Country and the City* before moving on to highlight Austen's subtle references to the colonial capital (in the form of a sugar plantation in Antigua) on which Mansfield Park is dependent. Indeed, Said's model of contrapuntal reading suggests that the nineteenth-century novel can be read as a work of pastoral literature, in which the spectral residues of colonial violence not only haunt the English estate but also structure its very economic possibility: "*Mansfield Park* is a rich work in that its aesthetic intellectual complexity requires that longer and slower analysis that is also required by its geographical problematic, a novel based in an England relying for the maintenance of its *style* on a Caribbean island."[49] (The deliberate ambiguity of "style" subtly refers to both the landed aristocracy's way of life and the literary form of the novel.)[50]

Said perhaps gives too little credit to Williams, who does acknowledge the pastoral's revival in the work of postcolonial writers like Chinua Achebe and George Lamming. For Williams, the pastoral registers an emerging reconfiguration of global capital in the twentieth century.[51] As he argues, the pastoral was not simply imported to the Global South as an instance of colonial mimicry. Rather, the postcolonial pastoral mirrors the new international division of labor in which the Global South is effectively transformed into the rural hinterlands of the metropole: "The traditional relationship between city and country was then thoroughly rebuilt on an international scale. Distant lands became the rural areas of industrial Britain, with heavy consequent effects on its own surviving rural areas . . . It is the story of country and city in its harshest form, and now [thoroughly rebuilt] on an unimaginably complex scale."[52] Williams does not suggest that the Global South is a rural backwater lacking in the resources of urbanization (or, worse yet, unable to accommodate them). As he notes, the intense urbanization of colonial cities (which he dubs the "new metropolis[es]") has surpassed the development of metropoles in the Global North and begun to mimic a similar bifurcation of country and city, where rural locations are drained of their resources and capital accumulates exclusively in the state's urban areas. Instead, Williams enlists the city and country as a powerful metaphor for the neocolonial forces that exploit the Global South as appendages under the pretext of developmentalism. In other words, the city and country dichotomy is now encoded in the discourses of modernization that divide the globe according to "developed" and "undeveloped" cultures. Now mystifying the "beautiful relation" between rich and poor is the language of developmentalism that plots a teleological relationship between "industrialized" and "unindustrialized" regions.[53]

Williams's intervention has since lost some of the innovative luster it once had in its initial publication. But what's important to note here is how Said and Williams both pinpoint the pastoral as the mode that most saliently disrupts the language of developmentalism dislocating peripheral economies. If the spectrality of the pastoral is inscribed with the submerged histories of violence that have generated its own production, then it may act as a literary mode that problematizes the modernization discourses undergirding colonial and industrial rationale.

Throughout *The Rough Field*, Montague makes visually manifest the pastoral's spectrality in his collection's unique type settings. For instance, in the margins of "A Severed Head," the poet quotes an eyewitness account from an early-seventeenth-century British historian who expresses "unfeigned astonishment at the sight of so many cattle and such abundance of grain" in the Ulster countryside, overlooking how such bounty was part of an entirely export-oriented economy that exploited Ireland as an agricultural appendage to the industrializing British economy.[54] (See figure 2.2a–b.) In "The Hymn to the Omagh Road," the poet arranges on the page two staggered sets of stanzas of differing font sizes. (See figure 2.3a–b.) One set of stanzas offers a satirically pastoral scene of the Glencull Waterside, with ballad rhymes of "lambkins [at] sport and play" and "pretty feathered warblers . . . singing by the way." Meanwhile, the other series of stanzas describes the now-bulldozed valley as a "brown stain" and "smear of mud" leveled by the "crustacean claws of the excavator" in order to "resume new life as a plaint stream / of building material."[55] For Montague, the pastoral is defined neither solely by the romanticized scenery of Glencull nor the disillusioned description of its destruction; rather, the pastoral is made up of the staccato disjuncture between these two visions of the Tyrone countryside.

> To see a souldiour toze a Karne, O Lord it is a wonder!
> And eke what care he tak'th to part the head from neck asonder.
> John Dericke: *A Discoverie of Woodkarne*, 1581

> Sir Thomas Phillips made, a journey from Coleraine to Dungannon, through the wooded country . . . and thereupon wrote to Salisbury, expressing . . . his unfeigned astonishment at the sight of so many cattle and such abundance of grain. . . . The hillsides were literally covered with cattle . . . the valleys were clothed in the rich garniture of ripening barley and oats; while the woods swarmed with swine . . . 20,000 of these being easily fattened yearly in the forest of Glenconkeyne alone.
> George Hill: *An Historical Account of the Plantation in Ulster*

> Our geographers do not forget what entertainment the Irish of Tyrone gave to a mapmaker about the end of the late great rebellion; for, one Barkeley being appointed by the late Earl of Devonshire to draw a true and perfect map of the north parts of Ulster . . . when he came into Tyrone the inhabitants took off his head. . . .
> *Sir John Davies*

[32]

Fig. 2.2a–b. Pages from "A Severed Head" in *The Rough Field*. The margins in "A Severed Head" feature excerpts from various historical accounts of the Plantation of Ulster. Reprinted with kind permission from Wake Forest University Press and the estate of John Montague.

I

May, and the air is light
On eye, on hand. As I take
The mountain road, my former step
Doubles mine, driving cattle
To the upland fields. Between
Shelving ditches of whitethorn
They sway their burdensome
Bodies, tempted at each turn
By hollows of sweet grass,
Pale clover, while memory,
A restive sally switch, flicks
Across their backs.
                 The well
Is still there, a half-way mark
Between two cottages, opposite
The gate in Danaghy's field,
But above the protective dry-
Stone rim, the plaiting thorns
Have not been bill-hooked back
And a thick *glaur* floats.
No need to rush to head off
The cattle from sinking soft
Muzzles into leaf smelling
Spring water.
               From the farm
Nearby, I hear a yard tap gush
And a collie bark, to check
My presence. Our farmhands
Lived there, wife and children
In twin white-washed cells,
An iron roof burning in summer.
Now there is a kitchen extension
With radio aerial, rough outhouses
For coal and tractor. A housewife
Smiles good-day as I step through
The fluff and dust of her walled
Farmyard, solicited by raw-necked
Stalking turkeys
                 to where cart
Ruts shape the ridge of a valley,

2

    From the quarry behind the school
    the crustacean claws of the excavator
    rummage to withdraw a payload,
    a giant's bite . . .

'Tis pleasant for to take a stroll by Glencull Waterside
On a lovely evening in spring (in nature's early pride);
You pass by many a flowery bank and many a shady dell,
Like walking through enchanted land where fairies used to dwell

        Tuberous tentacles
    of oak, hawthorn, buried pignut,
    the topsoil of a living shape
    of earth lifts like a scalp
    to lay open

The trout are rising to the fly; the lambkins sport and play;
The pretty feathered warblers are singing by the way;
The black birds' and the thrushes' notes, by the echoes multiplied,
Do fill the vale with melody by Glencull waterside.

        slipping sand
    shale, compressed veins of rock,
    old foundations, a soft chaos
    to be swallowed wholesale,
    masticated, regurgitated
    by the mixer.

Give not to me the rugged scenes of which some love to write —
The beetling cliffs, o'erhanging crags and the eagle in full flight
But give to me the fertile fields (the farmer's joy and pride)
The homestead and the orchards fine by Glencull waterside.

        Secret places
    birds' nests, animal paths,
    ghosts of children hunkering
    down snail glistering slopes
    spin through iron cylinders to
    resume new life as a pliant stream
    of building material.

[60]

Fig. 2.3a–b. Pages from "The Hymn to the Omagh Road" in *The Rough Field*. In "The Hymn to the Omagh Road," Montague staggers the stanzas' arrangement on the page and uses different font sizes in order to visually represent two conflicting portrayals of the Glencull Waterside. Reprinted with kind permission from Wake Forest University Press and the estate of John Montague.

These scenes bring recollections back to comrades scattered wide
Who used with me to walk these banks in youthful manly pride;
They've left their boyhood's happy homes and crossed o'er oceans wide
Now but in dreamland may they walk by Glencull waterside.

                     A brown stain
seeps away from where the machine
rocks and groans to itself, dis-
colouring the grass, thickening
the current of the trout stream
which flows between broken banks
— the Waterside a smear of mud —
towards the reinforced bridge
of the new road.

3

My sympathy goes out to the farmer
who, mad drunk after a cattle mart,
bought himself a concrete swan
for thirty bob, and lugged it
all the way
home
to deposit it
(where the monkey puzzle was meant to grow)
on his tiny landscaped lawn.

The spectral residues in *The Rough Field* intimate the poet's awareness of the complex ironies and histories of violence carried within the pastoral mode. The collection's ambivalence, its mixture of nostalgia and disgust, can make it frustratingly difficult to pinpoint its politics. For John Goodby, sections like "The Hymn" excoriatingly attack modernization in Northern Ireland, and so Montague's "absence of a constructive vision of modernity can mean a lurch towards nostalgia, a vacillation between two polar opposites, the archaic/traditional and the commercial."[56] Richard Kirkland similarly argues that the collection's creative energies oftentimes dissipate into a "creative and political dead end, a road to nowhere."[57] But while Montague elegizes the loss of "local grace" in rural Northern Ireland, he also admits that the technological innovations in agricultural labor have undoubtedly reaped material benefits for farmers. Montague grants that it would be grossly foolish to lament the backbreaking labor and seasonal unemployment that burden agricultural workers ("the labourer hibernating / in his cottage for half the year / to greet the indignity of the Hiring Fair"); he acknowledges that "Only a sentimentalist would wish / to see such degradation again." As the poet concedes earlier:

> To worship or destroy beauty—
> That double edge of impulse
> I recognize, by which we live;
> But also the bitter paradox
> Of betraying love to harm,
> Then lungeing, too late
> With fists, to its defence.[58]

On the one hand, *The Rough Field* is in keeping with the traditional pastoral as it looks back to a bygone era; on the other, the poem's backward gaze is troubled by the author's recognition of the debased conditions of rural life and his reluctant resignation to the inevitable advancement of modernization. The complexity of pastoral lies in its mingling of contempt and nostalgia, which encode the larger economic tensions in Northern Ireland and the Republic—tensions that are always sliding toward the dyadic and abstract. The pastoral, then, with its double attitudes and its desire for a certain concreteness, is an effective antidote toward the pull of abstraction even as it is caught up within it.

IV.

It certainly is not my intention to impose Williams's story of country and city onto Irish literature, which invariably escapes such strict narratives. Instead, I argue that Irish poets like Montague and Heaney have exploited the pastoral's spectrality and genealogical nature as a means of confronting the complex political and economic transformations at work in the Republic and Northern Ireland. What best unites my analysis of these poets is my emphasis on the multiple ironies and spectral forms of pastoral, which complicate conventional readings of landscape poetry. There is often a temptation within analyses of pastoral (and "nature poetry" more generally) to read local landscapes as the guarantors of authenticity. Such interpretations rest on the premise that locality is obvious, that its affective power flows automatically out of direct experience and face-to-face encounters.

In many ways, Heaney and Montague offer this intimacy of place in their detailed depictions of the Irish landscape. But to see Heaney and Montague only as native informants who give ethnographic "access" to their local places would be to underread their poetries' complex negotiations of place and history. We can even detect these complexities at work in the titles of their two collections, *Field Work* and *The Rough Field*, which entice us to think of "field" in both its spatial and discursive connotations. If we return to "The Toome Road," we see how Heaney suggestively hints at the transnational and transhistorical dimensions of the pastoral when he transforms the scene of British occupation into one of Roman imperial invasion. The trespassing "charioteers" and "untoppled omphalos" allude to the Classical origins of the pastoral—an allusion cemented by Heaney's punning of "Toome" with hecatomb, the Greek and Roman sacrifice of a hundred cattle to the gods. Heaney's densely wrought invocations of the pastoral's long genealogy demonstrate how the apparent immediate experience of local spaces is actually mediated by a wider set of historical and economic relations.

To circle back, then, to this chapter's opening: like Boland, Montague rereads Goldsmith's "The Deserted Village." In his essay "Oliver Goldsmith: Sentimental Prophecy," Montague cites the eighteenth-century poem as a primary influence on his own work, arguing that "The Deserted Village" is a proto-modernist precursor (a "sort of rural *Waste Land*") that directly correlates the downfall of rural life with the rise of imperial expansion. While many scholars have debated the real-life analogue of Auburn, Montague insists instead on reading "The Deserted Village" as a "universal village," which tracks a genealogy of dispossession in rural England and Ireland that stems from imperial expansion and a globalizing world economy:

> It is not merely that villages, like Auburn, are being dispossessed, but that this dispossession is part of a whole pattern of economic greed which will in time, destroy society . . . It is this vision of decay consequent upon imperial expansion and excessive trade, which haunted Goldsmith throughout his career: like the Roman Empire, like the commercial oligarchies of Venice and Holland, Britain will sink into obscurity, destroyed by her "rage of gain." *The Deserted Village* is one of the first statements of a great modern theme, the erosion of traditional values and natural rhythms in a commercial society: the fall of a whole social order.[59]

Though Montague's essay predates *The Country and the City*, it articulates a similar description of the pastoral's "problem of perspective." Rather than being calibrated to a specific historical and economic crisis, Goldsmith's poem acts as a historical continuum of the pastoral's grievances, not only alluding to the ancient Roman agricultural crises of Virgil and Horace but also foreshadowing the ecological concerns of modernist writers: "It looks forward to Wordsworth; even, to Lawrence and Pound, and to Faulkner's protest against the destruction of the Big Woods." For Montague, Auburn serves as both allegory and microcosm, representing the "fall of a whole social order" and exemplifying the crisis of a rural village threatened by the encroachment of global capital that it is also bitterly forced to sustain. The deserted village was, in fact, always a global village. Or, as Montague drolly puts it earlier, Goldsmith is simultaneously "country bumpkin *and* cosmopolitan."[60] Auburn, Garvaghey, even Faulkner's Mississippi: all, in Montague's estimation, share a homologous colonial history. Montague proposes that the spectral form of the pastoral can uncover these roots of paralleled rural exploitation and track their permutations in the contemporary moment. Such a comparative analysis opens new avenues of imagining cross-cultural literary affiliations that operate outside the usual networks of cosmopolitanism that move exclusively amongst urban centers—that is, a form of cosmopolitanism without a polis as its organizing unit of structure.

Heaney and Montague reveal how the pastoral works in several different registers. First, the pastoral is a literary tradition that stretches well before the twentieth century but finds itself revivified in new directions at a time when Ireland undergoes significant shifts in political and economic identity. More importantly, the pastoral is at its heart a genealogical mode whose spectral form can uncover roots of paralleled rural exploitation and track their permutations. Its genealogical nature is all the more appreciable when it is invoked in the twentieth century by writers like Heaney and Montague. In other words, the home of the country bumpkin proves a vital site in baring the complex circulations of global capital. The pastoral, then, is a form that lends itself to triangulating the complex relationships among place, economics, and poetics.

Chapter 3

The Loco-descriptive Details of Belfast

I.

There has long been an obsession with detailed descriptions of place in modern and contemporary Irish literature. James Joyce famously boasted that if Dublin were to disappear from the earth, *Ulysses* could be used as a blueprint to rebuild the city. Hugh Kenner revels in the novel's "detailed actuality," from the meticulous descriptions of Bloom's house (which Joyce modeled on real floor plans) to the streets of the city: "[Joyce] catalogued for future scholars the furniture of a Dublin house and the contents of a Dublin kitchen cabinet (not omitting the moustache cup) and two Dublin dresser drawers. These pages might some day be key to a kitchen midden, as other pages, indicating which street intersects with which, might afford the clues to an excavator's map."[1] The fixation on detail and place continues into contemporary Irish literature, from Tim Robinson's cartographical studies of the West of Ireland to Thomas Kinsella and Ciaran Carson's celebrated translations of *The Táin*, the most famous example of *dinnseanchas*, or early Irish onomastic poetry that recounts the histories of place-names. Like Kenner, critics often invest these literatures with a restorative capacity, an ability to recover the textures of the Irish landscape that have been lost in the processes of displacement and linguicide wrought by first colonialism and then later globalization. More often than not, these literatures' recuperative possibilities stem from their exhaustive detailing of place. One typical reading of Robinson's work commends the cartographer for his painstaking topographical surveys of the Aran Islands: whereas the Ordnance

Survey "ignored the many particularities of local landscapes, emptying the landscape of colour, texture, details of habitation and crops," Robinson embarks on a "quest for greater detail" and creates geographic surveys that "resurrect as far as possible their historic territorial structure."[2] It seems that if an archaeologist in the distant future were to unearth the ruins of Ireland, she could resurrect the entire island inch by inch from the "excavator's map" of these literary blueprints.

In the context of Irish literature, perhaps no poet has been more closely affiliated with a specific city than Ciaran Carson, a writer famed for dwelling in and dwelling on his home of Belfast. In this chapter, I examine how Carson and then a later generation of Northern Irish poets have renovated the loco-descriptive poem, a genre that has often been regarded as the most "local" of poetries in its sustained attention to the topographical details of particular places. (Samuel Johnson, when applauding John Denham's "Copper's Hill" for inaugurating a new "species of composition," notes that this genre would be more accurately "denominated [as] *local poetry*.")[3] While a comprehensive genre history is outside the scope of this study, I trace the loco-descriptive poem primarily in Carson's writing, particularly his collections published in the 1980s and 1990s, and secondarily in the work of the "Peace Poets," who established their careers after the IRA cease-fire in 1994 and the Belfast Agreement in 1998 and include writers such as Alan Gillis, Leontia Flynn, and Sinéad Morrissey. As I will argue, these poets all draw out a version of the loco-descriptive that derives from Romantic tendencies but is substantially reformulated under the socioeconomic conditions of deindustrialization, sectarian violence, and urban regeneration in Belfast. The previous chapter argued for reading the pastoral as a genealogical mode that can trace global networks of rural dispossession; this chapter takes a similar route and explores how the genre of loco-descriptive poetry also carries a deep literary history that reverberates in the work of contemporary poets. The conventions of loco-descriptive poetry—its attention to the details of landscape, as well as its shifts between elevated and on-the-ground perspectives—take on new significance as they reshape the genre to fit the sociopolitical architecture of Belfast.

This chapter reads the works of these Northern Irish poets within the context of the ideologies of urban redevelopment in the UK, from the 1980s to the present. After decades of destruction waged by the British military and Republican and Loyalist paramilitary groups in the 1960s and 1970s, city planners sought to remake Belfast through several urban redevelopment campaigns, in hopes of erasing the memories of sectarian divisions and mitigating their ongoing violence. Inspired by downtown revitalization programs in other deindustrialized cities across the Global North, planners and politicians looked to urban regeneration as a way of overcoming the socioeconomic deprivations and ethnoreligious segregation caused by the Troubles. Belfast's neoliberal makeover would eventually come to fruition in the post–Peace Process era, as signaled by the opening of the Victoria Square Shopping Centre in 2008 and the Titanic Quarter in 2012. These forces of urban development, alongside deindustrialization and the advent of neoliberalism, gathered with the earlier agents of sectarian violence to transform Belfast's cityscape.

Of course, loco-descriptive poetry calls to mind the picturesque landscapes of ruined abbeys and sunlit horizons, and it may seem inappropriate to transplant the genre to a city with such a scarred history. But more than simply offering unmediated representations of the local, loco-descriptive poetry emerged in the eighteenth century as writers pondered new ways of representing place at a time when the Land Enclosure Acts and rise of global trade were dramatically reorganizing conceptions of space. As scholars like John Barrell have argued, the genre has long lingered on questions of dispossession at moments in history when the portrayal of place was politicized and increasingly fraught.[4] The poets in this chapter highlight the capacity of a genre like the loco-descriptive poem to register the frictions of representing place at a time of politico-economic upheaval. My goal is not to make a classificatory argument about whether these poems would be more properly labeled as loco-descriptive. Not only have scholars fruitfully situated contemporary Irish poetry within literary traditions like *dinnseanchas* and regionalism, literatures of place have always drawn from constellations of overlapping genres and other discursive frameworks.[5] To attempt to pin down these poetries to one "proper" genre would be to ossify what are fundamentally fluid and porous aesthetic categories.

Rather, I argue that Carson uses the loco-descriptive poem as a means of testing the limits of poetic description in a city overwhelmed by the maelstrom of sectarian conflict and urban redevelopment. A rich outpouring of scholarship has analyzed Carson's representations of Belfast during the Troubles, especially in the collections *The Irish for No* (1987) and *Belfast Confetti* (1989) and the experimental memoir *The Star Factory* (1997). Critics often celebrate the poet's detailed descriptions of Belfast, which give an insider's perspective on the city that can countervail the militarized surveillance technologies that enveloped it. Carson's careful attention to the details of place is seen as necessarily emancipatory; his intimate knowledge of the city affords him the ability to escape the claustrophobic confines of Belfast's surveillance state and British occupation. But I take a different approach and argue that Carson's experimentations with the loco-descriptive poem reveal how topographic details do not always offer a comforting sense of place but instead can be appropriated by state and paramilitary forces and yoked to violent ends.

Writing in the wake of the Agreement, poets including Flynn, Gillis, and Morrissey continue to explore the relationship between place and detail as Belfast attempts to recast its image into that of the "post-conflict," global city of the twenty-first century. The Peace Poets write at a strange moment in Belfast's history when urban policies articulate inconsistent and contradictory strategies for rehabilitating the city. After the cease-fire, city planners began developing new arts-and-culture quarters and luxury mixed-use buildings as a means of attracting tourism and "neutralizing" the city's downtown, which had once been the locus of paramilitary violence. But at the same time that some traces of the Troubles were being expunged, other spatial markers of sectarian violence were proliferating as part of the same tourism economy: Black Cab tours of Nationalist and Loyalist murals, military and industrial museums, repurposed historical sites like the Crumlin Gaol, the once notorious "Alcatraz of Europe" that reopened in 2012 as a conference center and event venue. Like Carson, the post-Agreement poets express a deep skepticism over the fetishization of place, which becomes either effaced from Belfast's cityscape or subsumed within place-branding strategies. In the final section of this chapter, I read together the works of Carson and Gillis to show that the loco-descriptive poem—and along with it, the genre's preoccupation with topographical detail—stretches across these generations of Northern Irish poetry. Taken together, the works of these poets interrogate the very function of topographic detail in a city where the notion of place is never neutral or stable.

In reading these Belfast-centric works, this chapter reconsiders some of the assumptions that implicitly govern analyses of place and poetry. Jim Cocola argues that loco-descriptive poetry is no longer relevant to the work of modern and contemporary poets, who depend "less and less upon strictly descriptive effects or strictly local engagements"; quoting Charles Olson, he contends that "art does not seek to describe but to enact."[6] While Cocola compellingly analyzes the concept of place-making in twentieth-century US poetry, I query his dismissal of the "local," which has again and again been seen as something that needs to be transcended by the modern. One of this book's overarching arguments is that the transcendence of the local is so essential to the definition of the modern and the contemporary that we may need to see them not as diametric opposites but as discursive siblings.

There also seems to be an undisputed, if largely uninterrogated, fellowship between the local and the descriptive—one that becomes central in criticism of the loco-descriptive poem. After all, Samuel Johnson argues that such "local poetry" is defined by its scrupulous attention to "some particular landscape, to be poetically described."[7] Olson, and by extension Cocola, dismisses the "strictly local" alongside the "strictly descriptive," which is denigrated as secondary and even antithetical to poesis. Olson is not the first to diminish description as frivolous and inconsequential. Yeats classifies modernism in opposition to description, defining modernism as a "revolt against [the] irrelevant descriptions of nature" that he finds characteristic of Victorian poetry. The depreciation of description is not limited to poetics. For Georg Lukács, narration and description are the two opposing modes of the novel; he belittles the latter as a monotonous mode that transforms active readers into passive and lifeless observers.[8] In her feminist analysis of detail in Western aesthetics, Naomi Schor traces how detail has been treated with "suspicion if not downright hostility" since Neoclassicism, which privileged a masculinized ideal over a femininized particular. Schor quotes as evidence Sir Joshua Reynolds's *Discourses of Art*, widely regarded as the bible of Neoclassical aesthetics: "The whole of beauty consists . . . in being able to get above singular forms, *local* customs, *particularities*, and *details* of every kind."[9] There is a familiar echo between the gendered discourse around description and that around the local, which is often associated with domestic, private, and natural spaces in contrast with the abstract and fluid movements of the global. For the same reasons that description has been often dismissed in poetics and narrative theory, the local has been denigrated as minor and inconsequential in comparison to the machinations of the global.

Recently, however, scholars like Sharon Marcus, Stephen Best, and Heather Love have made a bid to recover description from its degraded status within literary studies. They argue that scholars often overlook description because it seems insufficiently critical in comparison to interpretation; description is seen as a "dull accountant" that "simply repeats what anyone can see or hear."[10] This chapter does not seek to champion the "descriptive turn" in literary studies or to intervene in the debates around critique and postcritique, especially as this book would certainly be deemed a prime example of the suspicious reading that these aforementioned scholars criticize.[11] But while demurring at the polemics of postcritique, I take away from Marcus, Best, and Love their revivification of description. If description is not derided for its supposed dullness and tedium, it is then panned as necessarily inadequate, seeking to capture in language a world that invariably escapes its grasp. But Marcus, Best, and Love contend that a "better description" can do the opposite and "embrac[e] rather than den[y] the problems of reference and incommensurability that have long preoccupied scholars and thinkers, but with an important difference. Incommensurability can motivate description not as something to be overcome but as a way to build the uncertainty of any attempt to describe into description themselves."[12] Or as the poet Sarah Manguso puts it more bluntly, "nothing is more boring to me than the re-re-restatement that language isn't sufficiently nuanced to describe the world. Of course language isn't enough. Accepting that is the starting point of using it to capacity. Of increasing its capacity."[13] In other words, a better description would recognize the gap between the world and the word. It would not act as an excavator's map but instead shows the discrepancies between the blueprint and its site.

In what follows, I trace how contemporary Northern Irish poets offer a better description of Belfast at a time when the city's identity was being reimagined by a number of different political and economic actors. How do contemporary Northern Irish poets transform the loco-descriptive poem under the unique set of pressures at work in Belfast in the closing decades of the twentieth century and in the new millennium? How can a poet depict a city that has so many competing visions of its past, present, and future? In answering these questions, this chapter not only rereads these poets' works in the context of late capitalism; it also rethinks the many presumptions that underlie understandings of place and poetry.

II.

Carson's lifelong fixation on Belfast has earned him the unofficial designation as the city's poet laureate. (Sinéad Morrissey was officially awarded the title of the city's inaugural poet laureate in 2013.) An obituary, published after his untimely death from cancer in 2019, describes how the poet had "Belfast lore and topography at his fingertips"; another pays tribute to the poet's "inventive and roomy imagination [that] found a way to write about Belfast which made the city uniquely his own, street by street."[14] Belfast acted as the center of gravity for much of the poet's oeuvre as well as his own life; unlike most of his peers, Carson never left the city to relocate to the Republic, Britain, or the US. In his best-known collection *Belfast Confetti*, Carson describes what he calls the "subjunctive mood" of his home city, whose shifting ground had been destroyed and remade by IRA bombings, deindustrialization, and Thatcherite urban planning.[15] Even when Carson wanders outside Belfast, he is quickly drawn back in by the city's strong gravitational pull. In the introduction to his translation of Dante's *Inferno*, he explains how the geography of Belfast ("claustrophobic, cramped and medieval") informed his portrayal of the "Byzantine world of Florentine politics."[16] In the poem "Schoolboys and Idlers of Pompeii," set in New York's Alphabet City, the common signifiers of urban blight ("barricaded liquor stores, secretive tobacco shops") evoke the feel of Belfast for the poet, and he even spots a piece of graffiti that spells in "three-foot-high black letters, saying BELFAST, with the cross-stroke of the T extended into an arrow pointing east, to Belfast."[17] Carson confesses, "I cannot help but see bits of Belfast everywhere, Berlin, Warsaw, Tallinn, New York, to name some, have Belfast aspects."[18]

While Carson does not shy from shining a light on Belfast's underbelly, he remains murky about exactly where he stands politically, stressing that his poetry is not a condemnation of any one party but of the mistakes he sees committed by the British army and Republican and Unionist paramilitary organizations.[19] The poet acknowledges the hands of all sides in destroying the city, and his poetry depicts Belfast as a space pockmarked by guerilla warfare ("Belfast confetti" is the nickname for homemade explosive devices filled with nails, bolts, and other bits of shrapnel) as well as botched Thatcherite city planning that often exacerbated, rather than relieved, the city's deindustrialized rot and ethnic divides. William Neill terms 1970s Belfast the era of "Fortress City," which included the construction of the infamous Peace Walls and major motorways such as the Westlink, which were used to divide West and North Belfast from the city's commercial core and reinforce segregation between Catholic and Protestant enclaves.[20] In "Revised Version," a prose poem made up of archival records, Carson sees such city planning as a part of a much longer history of failed urban development schemes ("glimpses of what might have been," a "grand never-to-be canal," and "intended streets") that have long plagued Belfast:

> what are we to make of this earthern rampart built in 1642, already partly obliterated at its north end? Obliterated? Never finished? Proposed? And do we trust this improvement made out on the strand?
>
> Improve, wipe out, begin again, imagine, change: the map appended to the Parliamentary report of 1859 *shows very clearly the improvements effected by the making of Victoria Street and Corporation Street . . .*[21]

In Carson's rendering, the city is overwrought with polluted waterways, empty junkyards, and ring roads that lead nowhere—a dismal visualization of malignant city planning and the accompanying delusions that such urban "improvements" could act as a panacea for deindustrialization and sectarian violence. Carson presents Belfast as continually made and remade by city planners and paramilitaries alike, who are not dueling antagonists so much as twinned players simultaneously grasping for spatial control of the city.

Carson's preoccupation with Belfast unfolds over the most turbulent periods of the city's history. As with other British cities like Leeds, Liverpool, and Manchester, Belfast was shaped by postwar deindustrialization, when manufacturing industries that had once flourished during the Victorian period began to collapse following the Second World War. The city's two major industries, linen and shipbuilding, disintegrated with the end of the postwar boom, the rise of competition from cheaper international markets, and the growth of aviation. Belfast sank into an economic nadir in the 1970s, when it was grappling with the most intense periods of the Troubles' bombing campaigns after the introduction of Direct Rule in 1972 as well as a worldwide recession in the wake of US and British withdrawal from the Bretton Woods accord.[22]

However, Belfast's deindustrial plight was distinctive in that it received massive subsidies from the British government as part of an effort to alleviate the socioeconomic deprivations plaguing the city. By 1992, these subsidies accounted for 23 percent of Northern Ireland's GDP, though some surveys calculate the figure at closer to a third of the region's total GDP.²³ In an effort to assuage anti-British sentiment in Northern Ireland, the Thatcher administration increased spending in both city planning and manufacturing and public sector jobs in Belfast, even while it cut such expenditures everywhere else in the UK. Between 1982 and 1985, almost 86 million pounds were invested in Belfast's downtown area; by 1989, over two-thirds of Northern Irish employment was concentrated in public sector jobs such as education, health, and social services. (To give a sense of comparison: over the course of the 1970s, public services employment expanded by 52 percent in Northern Ireland, while in the UK as a whole it increased by only 22 percent.)²⁴ Meanwhile, improvements in public housing became a priority for Belfast Corporation, which tore down and rebuilt unpopular tower blocks like the Divis Flats (the site of the first child casualty of the Troubles, whose top floors were occupied by the British army and transformed into a surveillance station).²⁵ Northern Ireland, and in particular Belfast, was an exceptional site in an era defined by Thatcherite policies of fiscal conservatism and large cutbacks in public expenditures.

The mammoth public investments in Belfast were justified by politicians as a means to peace and reconciliation, and were part of a broader strategy of neutralizing sectarian violence with economic cooperation.²⁶ In 1965, Taoiseach Sean Lemass signed a free-trade treaty with the UK and met with Prime Minister Terence O'Neill to create a Dublin-Belfast trade corridor. Economic development was presented by both nationalist and unionist politicians as a salve to the persistent differences between Catholics and Protestants in unemployment rates and overall living standards, which had sparked the 1960s civil rights campaign and culminated in the implementation of the Fair Employment Act of 1989. But despite the British government's substantial public expenditures, the revitalization of the downtown area and rehabilitation of public housing did little to prevent residents from abandoning the city in droves. Continued threats of paramilitary violence meant that Belfast transformed into a ghost town at sundown when people commuted home to their segregated suburban communities. Between 1970 and 1980, nearly 20 percent of municipal Belfast moved from the inner-city areas to the suburbs; from 1971 to 1991, Belfast lost a third of its population.²⁷ The result was a city filled with shops and restaurants but depopulated of residents.

Because public funding was funneled into rehabilitating Belfast's urban environment, there was an unusual alliance welded together between the promises of commercial real estate development and a sense of civic duty. An illustrative example is the story of the Castlecourt shopping center, which began construction in 1984 and was completed in 1990.[28] By building the shopping center on Royal Avenue in the city center, developers hoped that Castlecourt would transform the downtown area into a desegregated and "ethnically neutral" area that could serve as a leisure space for residents and visitors and also provide much-needed employment to both Catholics and Protestants in the nearby working-class neighborhoods in west Belfast.[29] Richard Needham, the Northern Irish environment minister and chief architect of the rehabilitation for Belfast's downtown, insisted that the building's facade be built completely in glass—a bold and seemingly misguided decision considering how the edifice had been barricaded in anti-rocket screens in the previous decade. (In actuality, the building's windows were nontransparent and supported by concrete blocks to protect them from bombings, which the center did sustain several times during and after its construction.) Needham saw the glass-enclosed facade as evidence of the government's triumph over a sustained paramilitary campaign designed to deny the normality of urban everyday life; in his words, the shopping mall signaled the "defining landmark of the city's new confidence" and the task of "rebuilding Belfast" was a "battl[e] for peace."[30] As William Neill explains, real estate projects like the Castlecourt shopping center were an "invitation to leave behind sectarian space with its antagonistic ethnic identities and to identify with the 'anywhere' of postmodernist space."[31] (As I will discuss later, these kinds of architectural strategies carried over after the cease-fire and continue to inform urban regeneration schemes in post-Agreement Belfast.)

Of course, not everyone welcomed the "'anywhere' of postmodernist space" that papered over the city's downtown, often at the expense of the historic Victorian streets and buildings that had characterized the area's architecture. Gerald Dawe calls Belfast a "centre-less city (grossly abused by bombers and then crassly re-imagined by history-less architects)," sarcastically pointing out that the city's replication of other downtowns in the UK and the Republic means that "we all live, more or less, in the same post-modern heaven."[32] Such criticisms are not unique to Belfast but ring familiar in the work of geographers such as David Harvey and Anthony D. King, who have critiqued globalization's homogenization of the built environment, particularly within city centers.[33] The construction of Castlecourt seems to be an early instance in Belfast's later makeover into a global city, as developers seek to make downtowns more attractive to corporate tenants and wealthy local residents by constructing similar mixed-used buildings with upscale office spaces and expensive retail shops.

Carson's indexing of the spatial and historical particularities of Belfast—its deserted side streets, facades of ruined buildings, abandoned architectural plans—seems to serve as a bulwark against these various forces of demolition and homogenization. In "Travellers," a young boy relies on his firsthand knowledge of the city ("his personal map") to snake through an encampment on the "waste ground that was Market Street and Verner Street" in a city that constantly "Tore itself apart and patched things up again."[34] The poem "Hamlet" recounts the urban myth of a slain British officer whose ghost once could be heard rattling like a tin can on Raglan Street, the site of his murder, but now has gone quiet since the street was demolished along with large swaths of west Belfast in the 1970s: "The sleeve of Raglan Street has been unraveled; the helmet of Balaklava / Is torn away from the mouth. The dim glow of Garnet has gone out, / And with it, all but the memory of where I lived."[35] In his poetry, Carson "tr[ies] to piece together the exploded fragments" of Belfast with his encyclopedic cataloging of its now-disappeared streets and districts.

In fact, critics credit the poet's fastidious attention to topographical detail as the key to his poetic success. Patricia Craig asserts that Carson has written the "best book" of Belfast because he is able to "make Belfast into an unreal city, which is at the same time strikingly real, with every detail in place," while Paul Muldoon attributes the "territorial aspect of [Carson's] achievement" to his ability to "[take] in the rubble and rumpus and riddling of day-to-day life in Belfast."[36] This is the case as well when scholars focus on Carson's perambulatory speakers, who meditate on Belfast's complex history as they anxiously navigate the divided city. Scholars often claim that walking offers a more intimate, grounded view of the city's details, a counterbalance to the inadequacies of cartography and the militarized surveillance technologies that menacingly monitor the city's residents. (The poet cautions, "No, don't trust maps, for they avoid the moment: ramps, barricades, diversions, Peace Lines."[37] In another poem, he warns even more baldly, "*Be paranoid.*"[38]) For instance, John Goodby argues that the pedestrian perspectives in Carson's poems present a closer look at the city than do the aerial views provided by maps, helicopter patrols, and security cameras.[39] Similarly, Neal Alexander reads Carson's speakers as Benjaminian flaneurs who immerse themselves in the city's "minutiae and marginalia" and prefer "active engagement in the writing and rewriting of the city-text" to positions of "detached objectivity." For these scholars, the perambulations in Carson's poetry offer moments of escape, however temporary, from the panoptic gaze of military occupation.[40]

For Eric Falci, the contrast between the bird's-eye view of maps and surveillance technologies and the flaneur's immersed perspective creates a set of "splintering visuals" that place the reader on unstable footing and undercut any sense of a stable lyric "I."[41] The two recurring viewpoints comprise competing fields of vision that appear throughout the poet's oeuvre. Notably, they also reflect the two major subgenres of loco-descriptive poetry: prospect and peripatetic poems. Inspired by seventeenth-century landscape painters, prospect poetry features a speaker atop a promontory who gazes down over a wide stretch of landscape. The elevated perspective is crucial to the prospect poem because it creates distance between the landscape and the speaker, who reflects on the terrain below but nevertheless remains removed from it. John Barrell underlines the nefarious purposes of prospect poetry, whose detached perspective affords the poet the ability to survey, organize, and therefore control the landscape at a moment when the Land Enclosure Acts were consolidating large tracts of land. More importantly, the elevated vantage point allows the poet to dictate topographical detail—to decide which hillocks, rivers, and fields to include and which to exclude: "The features of the landscape are . . . so thoroughly controlled by the poet's eye that they cannot impose themselves on him or demand any more of his attention than he is prepared to concede."[42] Adam Potkay explains that this suppression of detail is the key to the genre's violence: the poet accomplishes the ideological work of the Enclosures and subsequent extension of metropolitan control over the countryside by "extirpating or glossing over local forms of life, and inculcating the abstract, occlusive, and seemingly disinterested point of view of the gentleman connoisseur."[43] Similarly, Bonnie Costello argues that rather than fixating on "local detail and enargeia," the prospect poem is guided by an "impulse . . . toward the grand 'surmise' of the supernatural truth in or beyond the natural world."[44] Prospect poetry, then, is defined not by an all-encompassing gaze that includes every facet of the landscape but by the poet's stifling of certain local details.[45]

On the other hand, the peripatetic poem is often celebrated for its careful appreciation of the textures of the physical environment. The subgenre emerged when walking transformed from a laborious necessity of rural life to a recreational activity for the middle and upper classes in the late eighteenth century, including Romantic poets like Wordsworth.[46] Robin Jarvis argues that the immersive experience of pedestrianism makes the poet more aware of the particularities of the landscape, disallowing the usual abstractions of the prospect poem: "Walking . . . is capable of fostering resistance to any idealizing aesthetic tendencies the traveler may start out with, and of countering the generalizing and abstracting mentality inherent to all travel."[47] For Jarvis, the physical act of walking encourages a more egalitarian relationship between the pedestrian and the environment; the leisurely pace and grounded perspective allow a walker to dwell on the topographical details rather than succumb to the abstracting tendencies of the prospect poem. This has meant that pedestrianism has become associated with ecologically minded and radical forms of thinking, ranging from John Thelwall's eighteenth-century treatise *The Peripatetic* to the Situationists' concept of psychogeography. Even more recently, Harryette Mullen echoes Jarvis's claims when she reflects on how walking remedied the alienation she felt from her Los Angeles surroundings and became a vital component of her poetic practice that allowed for a "different kind of attention to surroundings . . . I became a bit more aware of my environs."[48] (Notably, the peripatetic poem reappears in Carson's final collection, *Still Life*, which depicts the poet's daily walks through North Belfast with his wife Deidre. I will return to *Still Life* in this book's coda.)

It is not my intention to vilify prospect poetry as the ideological instrument of capitalism or to venerate peripatetic poetry as a tool of political resistance, as such broad-sweeping interpretations are invariably reductive.[49] Instead, I draw attention to the centrality of detail in both of these subgenres. Loco-descriptive poetry is defined as having either too little detail (suppressed under the objectifying gaze of the prospect poet) or an overabundance of detail (that is savored by the pedestrian). In other words, the loco-descriptive poem is limned on two sides by these opposite poles of seeing and sensing place: it is either distant and removed from the landscape, or completely immersed and swallowed within it.

Carson certainly does delight in savoring the details of Belfast, which many critics see as part of the poet's attempt to carve out a space of liberation in the city's constricting landscape of checkpoints, observation towers, and Peace Walls. Scholars often envisage the poet's strolling speakers as Debordian psychogeographers who disrupt Belfast's panoptic networks by forging new pathways through the city.[50] But such readings belie how the peripatetic mode is also associated with the movements of British military troops in Carson's work. In "Queen's Gambit," the helicopter's aerial view joins forces with the movement of army officers' boots on ground: "the windswept starry night, through which a / helicopter trawls / Its searchlight. Out there, on the ground, there's a spoor of army boots."[51] In "Army," a "duck patrol" unit of British officers cautiously inches its way down enemy territory on Raglan Street:

> Frere Street. 47. 45½. Milan Street. A grocer's shop.
> They stop. They check their guns. 13. Milton Street. An
>   iron lamppost.
> No. 1. Ormond Street . . .[52]

The frequent caesurae and clipped fragments echo the staccato rhythms of the officers' apprehensive steps as they "waddle" down block by block, the street numbers slowly descending from 47 to 45½ to 13 to finally No. 1 Ormond Street. Certainly, the peripatetic perspective reveals the particularities of Belfast's cityscape as Carson traces the very street numbers of Raglan and all its intersecting cross streets. But while such topographical details may demonstrate an engrossed attention to the city—the poem certainly elicits a "participatory rather than disinterested experience," as Jarvis would argue—it is only because they are carefully weaponized by British military and paramilitary groups.[53] The pedestrian point of view may grant an intimacy of place, but that intimacy can quickly become co-opted by the forces of the state and paramilitary groups. The immersive experience of place, then, is not necessarily an appreciation of the city's textures but instead can be drawn into the battle over spatial control of Belfast.

Carson hints at how an intimate knowledge of place can become weaponized in the context of sectarian Belfast. At first glance, the prose poem "Question Time" seems to offer a moment of respite when it opens with the speaker's "harmless spin on the bike" through the city's suburbs.[54] The bike ride's easy movements give way to the speaker's reverie over childhood memories of the "familiar territory" of the Shankill Road and Falls Road neighborhoods. The carefree mood is reflected grammatically in the poem's shift to simple declarative sentences, which mirror the biker's linear movements: "I come to the Shankill Road Library"; "I see the green cupola of Clonard Monastery"; "I turn idly down Mountjoy Street"; "I come to the other side of the Peace Line." But the speaker's easygoing ride grinds to a sudden halt when he is apprehended by IRA paramilitaries, who haul him off his bike and begin interrogating him:

> *You were seen. You were seen.*
> *Coming from the Shankill.*
> *Where are you from?*
> *Where is he from?*
> *The Falls? When? What street?*[55]

Although the interrogators are members of the IRA, they nonetheless participate in the surveilling of city; they are clearly monitoring the speaker's movements. ("*You were seen*" is repeated four times.) The hostile cross-examination continues for dozens of lines, and the questions' sharp one-sidedness (which are "snapped at [the speaker] like photographs") are emphasized in italics and with frequent caesurae and line breaks. The grilling interrupts the very structure of the poem, which otherwise is prose. Indeed, the interrogation scene is the only section of "Question Time" set in verse, which suggests how loco-descriptive poetry can be appropriated for violent purposes. The IRA paramilitaries probe the speaker for his knowledge of place, pummeling him with questions of the neighborhood: "*Where was that? Mooreland? / Where is that? Stockman's? Where is that? / What's next? Casement? Right. What's next?*" In a city riven by territorial contestations, topographical details do not offer a sense of place or comforting nostalgia; rather, they become instrumentalized for the purposes of information-gathering. When describing his violation, the speaker describes himself as a map "which they examine, checking it for error, hesitation, accuracy." In one sense, the dissection of the speaker recalls Allen Feldman's argument that Belfast's surveillance state imposes "compulsory visibility" onto its citizens and invades their private lives and very bodies: "The visual staging and technological penetration of the body by cameras, high-velocity bullets, or digitized bombs . . . unite both seeing and killing, surveillance and violence in a scopic regime."[56] But as Carson suggests, it is more than the speaker's body that is violated; by underscoring the exploitation of the speaker's intimate familiarity with the city (his childhood memories of the Shankill Road Library, Clonard Monastery, and Mountjoy Street), the poem suggests that the very knowledge of place becomes absorbed into the city's scopic regime.

Belfast seems to contaminate all forms of loco-descriptive poetry, whose local details are drafted as tools of violence by paramilitaries and

British security forces alike. But Carson does not mold the loco-descriptive poem simply to fit Belfast's architectures of violence and reveal the toxic ground of his home city. Rather, he uses the genre to revise long-standing assumptions about the relationship between place and poetry. There is often a presumption that an intimacy with place can serve as a guarantor of authenticity or even an antidote to the alienating experiences of life under globalization. Daniel Weston, for example, argues that Carson's poetry upholds a "practical 'knowledge' of place" and "more personal register of place," which allows for "a reconfiguration of knowledge itself away from a panoptic conception associated with the map, and towards knowing 'by foot' from a street-level perspective."[57] But as suggested by my analyses of Carson's poetry, a "street-level perspective" does not necessarily equate to utopian practices of resistance and instead can be seized for violent ends and even weaponized against those who possess a "personal register of place."

While Carson's work abounds with intricate descriptions of Belfast, the poet evinces little patience for nostalgia, for the longing over the loss of place, which he sees as especially futile given the city's constantly changing landscape. In his poem "The Exiles' Club," a group of Belfast émigrés gather weekly in an Australian bar to wax nostalgic about their home city and resurrect it from their collective memories:

> After years they have reconstructed the whole of the Falls
>   Road, and now
> Are working on the backstreets: Lemon, Peel and Omar,
>   Balaklava, Alma.
> They just about keep up with the news of bombings and
>   demolition, and are
> Struggling with the *finer details* . . .[58]

The poet paints the exiles as a pathetic bunch, more eager to recreate the city's "finer details" that they left behind than to try to make themselves at home in their new country. But the poem is also a self-directed cautionary against any poetic attempt to resurrect a now-gone Belfast by obsessively cataloging its backstreets, pawnshops, schools, and cafés. To circle back to this chapter's opening: Carson forecloses any claims that poetry can act as an excavator's map and help recover a city that has been destroyed by colonialism, partition, and now globalization. For Carson, the recourse to poetic detail is ever only a fruitless effort.

III.

In her poem "Leaving Belfast," published a decade after the Agreement, Leontia Flynn presents a vision of the "post-conflict" city's future: "it will bury its past, it will paper over the cracks / with car parks and luxury flats, it will make itself new—or perhaps / become the place it seemed before you lived here."[59] After decades of sectarian violence, Belfast finally seems to emerge out of the Troubles a fully fledged global city like any other, gleaming with newly constructed luxury apartment buildings and shopping centers that offer "concerts and walking tours (Friendly! Dynamic! Various!)" to propel a thriving tourism economy.[60] Now replete with "arcades, mock-colonnades, church-spires and tapas bars," Belfast seems a far cry from the fractured city of military checkpoints and Peace Walls depicted by Carson and other poets of the Ulster Renaissance.[61] Urban revitalization plans accelerated in post-Agreement Belfast as the cloud of the Troubles dissipated, allowing the city to attract more external investments. Beginning in the late 1990s and continuing through the twenty-first century, inner-city Belfast underwent a series of urban restructuring schemes that reorganized sections of the downtown into different cultural quarters—part of a larger trend in deindustrialized cities in the UK and the US to use revitalized downtowns to solicit creative industries, stimulate foreign investments, and generate new tourism markets. These redevelopment schemes were part of larger policies of "normalization," a term coined in 1994 by British prime minister John Major to refer to the dismantling of military infrastructure in Northern Ireland, including watchtowers, roadblocks, and checkpoints. While it originally connoted demilitarization, normalization evolved into a catchall term for the regeneration of downtown Belfast—once the epicenter of Troubles-related deaths and territorial battles—into "neutral" spaces through means of commercial real estate development. As Catherine Switzer and Sara McDowell explain, normalization became a means of "making the city look more like any other city" with the hope of "eradicating evidence of the Troubles from the city centre, and thus effectively writing the conflict out of its history."[62] In Belfast, then, urban revitalization is often seen as not only breathing life into formerly dead economic zones but also fostering a new sense of civic inclusion and multiculturalism.

Yet, as Flynn warns, such cosmetic architectural updates merely "paper over the cracks" rather than providing any substantive change. For Flynn and her post-Agreement peers, "neutral" Belfast offers less a resolution and more a perpetuation—albeit in shinier forms—of the long-simmering ethnic divisions and class inequalities that had underlain the Troubles. Belfast's seeming prosperity is far from being evenly distributed, and the emphasis on real estate development in the city's reimaging has failed to remedy other forms of socioeconomic deprivation, particularly in historically low-income neighborhoods, which remain as segregated as they were in the decades since the Agreement (or, according to some studies, have become even more segregated).[63] Remarkably, Belfast is home to more multimillionaires per capita than any other city in the UK aside from London and Aberdeen, which are the region's respective financial and oil capitals; at the same time, Northern Ireland ranks second lowest in average annual income.[64] Brendan Murtagh describes contemporary Belfast as a "twin speed city," in which much of the inward investment, employment, and government-assisted projects have concentrated almost exclusively in prosperous areas, leaving behind the working-class neighborhoods of the city that were hit hardest by the Troubles.[65] For Aaron Kelly, the explosion of expensive waterfront properties and revitalized arts districts does not signal a new era of peace and prosperity but instead papers a shiny veneer over the deep class, ethnic, and gender inequities that still continue to fester in Northern Ireland: "Although the names have changed—from the Troubles to the Peace Process—it is the same rubric of historical enclosure that once viewed bombs, killings and roadblocks as immutable which now regards with consonant certainty the unshakeable ineluctability of multinational capital, corporate re-branding and consumerism . . . As Glenn Patterson says in regard to urban gentrification and redevelopment strategies: 'the opposite of all that went before is not this.'"[66] (Kelly's forewarnings take on a more prescient edge with the recent reignition of Loyalist paramilitary violence over the fallout from the Brexit Northern Ireland Protocol.) Alan Gillis puts it more frankly: "although the war is over, / the Party of Bollocks and the Party of Balls / are locked in a battle for the City Hall."[67]

Despite—or perhaps in reaction to—the policies of normalization, post-Agreement poets have not turned away from representing the intricate details of Belfast's cityscape but instead have retrenched their poetries in them. In his exuberant, almost hallucinatory portraits of the city, Gillis juxtaposes the old Belfast (with "walls guarding jinkered / cul-de-sacs, siderows, bottled sloganlands") alongside the new ("the multinational malls' slicker / demarcations, their Xanadu of brands").[68] Similarly, for

Flynn, Belfast may have "now found a kind of continental glamour," but it nonetheless remains weighed down by a fetid "whiff of old atrocity / still hung like sulphur low over its sky."[69] In her ekphrastic poem "Photographs of Belfast by Alexander Robert Hogg," Sinéad Morrissey depicts the titular Edwardian photographer's detailed documentation of the city's slum districts: "a yard / on Little York Street" with "its ruin of toppled bricks / and broken guttering," the terraced housing with "crumbling masonry / and dark for doors."[70] As this book shows, the ushering in of globalization has not led Irish poets to stray far from place and locality. The opposite holds true, as clearly demonstrated by Flynn, Gillis, and Morrisey; their poetries do not transcend the local but instead remain mired in the details of place. How does this newer generation of poets see and sense place in an era driven by neoliberal globalization as Belfast seeks to transform itself into a twenty-first-century global city?[71]

The discourse around Belfast's redevelopment is unique in how it amends some of the common notions about globalization, which is often seen as a threat to the local, as prompting the erasure and "McDonaldization" of once-distinctive cultures, peoples, and places. But in Belfast, city planners pitched urban homogenization as a potential salve for the segregation and other ethnic divisions that had become literally cemented in the city. What may seem to be unsightly examples of "urban cloning"—the proliferation of the same retail shops, mixed-used buildings, and revitalized arts quarters common to cities across the globe—are seen from another angle as modernizing and neutralizing spatial remedies to sectarianism. In one telling interview conducted by urban studies scholars, a local resident commends the rehabilitation of the Titanic Quarter, which was designed, via the costliest urban regeneration project in Belfast, to resemble other high-end European waterfront properties: "Yes, it's like a neutral environment with an 'I'm happy to go there' mentality. As you would in any other city."[72] (In fact, Belfast's cultural quarters were modeled after other gentrified districts in the U.K. such as Manchester's Northern Quarter and Glasgow's Merchant City.) In other words, urban redevelopment has often been welcomed in Belfast and hailed as a curative blank slate to the Troubles' sectarian divisions that have torn the city asunder. As John Nagle argues, the arrival of "shops and arcades selling Crème de la Mer face creams and Joseph trouser suits" were seen to "'normalize' the city center by making it into a commercial 'shared space' for Catholic and Protestant consumers . . . a facade to subvert and mask the injustices of segregation and socio-spatial exclusion."[73] Therefore, the ability of global capital to efface the local remains especially alluring in Belfast.

The poetry of Gillis, Morrisey, and Flynn thus shares with Carson's work an impasse, a term familiar to anyone acquainted with the many political deadlocks that have encumbered the peace process in Northern Ireland, particularly after the collapse of the power-sharing arrangement in 2017. On the one hand, Belfast has been razed to the ground by both paramilitary violence and overambitious urban planners, and so there is a desire to counter these destructive forces and preserve its cityscape. But on the other hand, the fetishization of place could potentially retrench sectarian divisions, and urban preservation and restoration projects can easily be rolled over into neoliberal urban branding. How can Northern Irish poets register the processes of displacement without regressing into a nostalgia for the past, which is especially dangerous in a city still riven by ethnonationalism and sectarian divide? Moreover, how do these poets see their own roles within this culture, given that their works also participate in the making of place in Belfast?

I answer these questions by tracing the loco-descriptive poem across the works of Carson and Gillis. As explained earlier, loco-descriptive poetry centers around the detailing of place. The elevated perspective of the prospect poem allows the speaker to dictate which details of the landscape are worthy or not worthy of description; meanwhile, in the peripatetic poem, the speaker strolls through a landscape and becomes engrossed in its details. An obsession with topographical detail also underpins the discourses around urban regeneration in Belfast—whether in the anxiety that globalization will foment the erasure of the local or in the optimism that such erasure can offer a curative and "normalizing" blank slate. Therefore, the genre of loco-descriptive poetry is especially amendable to capturing Belfast's complex, often contradictory relationship with place and place-making.

Even as Carson and Gillis seemingly seek to catalog every street corner and alleyway of their shared home city, their loco-descriptive poems also disclose an uncertainty about whether their works can in fact detail Belfast and about their poetries' own limited lines of sight. The prospects in Carson's poetry, for all his preoccupation with the surveillance technologies that unceasingly patrol Belfast and its denizens, are often obstructed, their views obscured. In "Ambition," the speaker ascends Black Mountain, the large hill overlooking Belfast, but the city vista is cloaked in "sfumato air": "Now that I've climbed this far, it's time to look back. But smoke obscures / The panorama."⁷⁴ If not shrouded in smoke, the landscapes in Carson's poetry extend just beyond the poet's field of vision. In "Auditque Vocatus Apollo," the speaker climbs to the top of Parnassus only to be confronted by yet another mountain: "You think you've reached the summit when another distant crest / Appears to challenge you."⁷⁵ A similar fate befalls the poet again in *The Star Factory*, where Carson recounts another time when he climbs the "celestial summit" of Black Mountain with his father and listens to him point out the city's various landmarks:

> . . . he'd light up a Park Drive cigarette and point it towards the *various details* of the urban map spread out below: the biggest shipyard in the world; the biggest ropeworks; the green cupola of the City Hall; the biggest linen mill; Clonard Monastery; Gallaher's tobacco factory; my school; the GPO, and in between the internecine, regimental terraces of houses and the sprawled city-wide Armada of tall mill funnels writing diagonals of smoke across the telescopic clarity of our vision.⁷⁶

A few points of reference lend us some sense of the layout of the "urban map," such as the terraced housing projects that sit "in between" the city's more recognizable buildings, but for the most part Carson's father presents the city as an unordered list of "various details." In an interview, Carson explains that his obsession with Belfast comes from his father, whose career as a postal carrier made him an expert on the city's streets and history: "He would take us on family walks around town, point out places, tell the stories behind them. Why this street was called that, an art gallery, museums . . . So the whole sense of exploration, the webs of buildings, streets, factories, shops was there from early on."⁷⁷ But for someone who worships his father's exhaustive knowledge of Belfast, Carson shares nothing substantive of his father's stories of the city's geography or history. The "telescopic clarity of our vision" and the abundance of details it allows, in fact, reveal little of the city.

The poems' obscured views deviate from the usual conventions of loco-descriptive poetry, in which the poet uses her ascents to mountaintops or walks through lake districts as opportunities to ruminate on the surrounding landscape. John Wilson Foster argues that loco-descriptive poets inherit from landscape painters a desire to create a "three-dimensional space": in lieu of visual elements of background and foreground, poets use spatial language like a set of "stage directions" so they can place different parts of the landscape in relationship to one another.[78] But Carson often omits such stage directions, and his poems can read like laundry lists of different sites either within Belfast or beyond the city limits. For instance, when reminiscing about his childhood hobby of philately, the poet muses about the many places where stamps are "salivated on by thousands of tongues" and pasted onto envelopes: "All of this takes place in boudoirs, public houses, studies, cafes, libraries, ports, railway stations, hotels, aerodromes, schools, surgeries, pleasure gardens, post offices, garages, on piers and esplanades, on board trains and boats and planes."[79] Many of Carson's poems are crowded with similar kinds of topographical lists. In "Intelligence," even the high-powered searchlights that expose Belfast's every corner nonetheless give little sense of the city:

> bread-vans, milk-carts, telegraph poles, paving-stones, lime trees, chestnuts, hawthorns, buses, tyres, fishing-lines, prams, JCBs, coal, shopping-trolleys, cement-mixers, lamp-posts, hoardings, people, sand, glass, breeze-blocks, corrugated iron, buckets, dustbins, municipal waste-bins, scaffolding, traffic signals, garden sheds, hedges, milk-churns, gas cylinders, chimney-pots, snow, oil-drums, gates, crazy paving, orange crates, fences, weighing-stands, camera tripods, ladders, taxis, dismantled football stadia, bicycles.[80]

The standalone paragraph acts like a literary landfill filled with industrial detritus ("corrugated iron," "municipal waste-bins," "scaffolding," "oil-drums"), and at first glance the passage seems to be further evidence of the urban blight that characterizes so many depictions of Belfast. But upon closer examination some items seem misplaced in a landfill: pastoral greenery ("lime trees, chestnuts, hawthorns") and glimpses of suburban life ("garden sheds, hedges, milk-churns") as well as simply "people." The list does not so much portray Belfast's deindustrialized decay as offer a miscellany of the entire city. More importantly, the passage lacks any directional signposts that would give some sense of how these topoi relate to one another; aside from the commas, it lacks syntax altogether. Carson's prospect poems, then, deliver not a coherent panorama of Belfast but a hodgepodge of unanchored locales with no relation to one another, seemingly set adrift in space. As argued earlier, loco-descriptive poetry is defined by either its suppression or surplus of detail. But Carson's loco-descriptive poems enact a different relationship to detail. While his poems certainly brim with topographical details, they also withhold the stage directions that offer any sense of relationality and create an intelligible representation of place. The effect is paradoxical: a poem ostensibly filled with place and yet totally unmoored.

It is no coincidence that these scenes of topographical miscellany also recur throughout the work of Gillis, who has been crowned as Carson's heir apparent and the new "lover-laureate" of Belfast.[81] Gillis's poetry often delights in alliterative and onomatopoeic language that details the city's bountiful flotsam. (Naomi Marklew describes how the poet's use of alliteration and "nonsensical diction" makes his work "distinctly surreal" and even lends it a "sense . . . of drunkenness.")[82] For instance, in the peripatetic poem "Laganside," the speaker strolls along the newly developed river walk and describes the flora and fauna that populate "this laminate lagoon": "buckeyes and rose of Sharon bushes occupy / snowberry banks, restharrow and gillyflowers / garland bamboo trunks and sapodillas . . ."[83] But lest he paint a too-pastoral scene, Gillis soon follows with a list of the debris lurking beneath the river's "bokey fudged mulch":

> a Black & Decker angle grinder, outstanding
> debt reminders, buckled pushchairs, threadbare
> pink and olive striped deckchairs, moustachioed
> schoolmasters, startled newscasters introducing
> shots of headshots, roadblocks, deadlocks,
> English cocks and Irish jocks, mutilated livestock . . .

As with Carson's miscellany, there is only the barest whisper of stage directions organizing the list of random, sometimes fantastical debris submerged in the Lagan. Gillis strings together the heterogeneous list with scarcely any syntax and instead peppers the lines with playful instances of internal consonance, assonance, and internal and end rhymes. (The poem also includes "bullies, trolleys, satanic creepy crawlies" and a "timer's tick-tock, confused with the cistern's drip- / drop . . .") The effect is a stanza that reads less like a landscape or cityscape and more like a chaotic soundscape of poetic devices. In the prose poem "Traffic Flow," Gillis presents another panorama of Belfast's residents, who are linked together by the city's matrices of streets and telephone lines: "Byron steers his bright red van, dreaming of Sara in Economy Place, whose handheld has just gone dead," while "Katie from Downhill texts Conrad, lingering in Joy's Entry."⁸⁴ But while "Traffic Flow" is loosely organized by a network of streets and telephones, Miriam Gamble describes how the poem creates a "groundless state," less a unified and cohesive community and more a "disparate collection of 'somebod[ies], somewhere'" set afloat in the city.⁸⁵ As in many of his other works, Gillis depicts Belfast as a city barely strewn together, where people may be "scampering under the same weather, crossing lines," but without ever "coming together."⁸⁶

In part, Carson's and Gillis's poems bespeak the alienating experiences of life in Belfast, a city that has yet to escape the long shadow of partition and sectarian violence. But these two poets' recourse to the loco-descriptive poem, particularly their revisions of the prospect poem, also charts a different kind of poetic vision that emerges in Belfast. In "Intelligence," Carson depicts the militarized surveillance technologies that menacingly monitor Belfast's residents, but at the poem's conclusion he offers a reprieve when he recollects another time when he and his father climb Black Mountain and look over the cityscape below, straining to point out "the tiny blip of our house that we both pretend to see":

> down there, in the Beechmount brickfields, I can nearly see James Mason squatting in the catacomb of a brick kiln where I played Soldiers and Rebels, these derelict cloisters half-chocked with broken brick and brick-dust, that are now gone, erased, levelled back into the clay, like all this brick-built demolition city, like this house we strain our eyes to see through the smog, homing in through the terraces and corner shops and spires and urinals to squat by the fire—coal-brick smouldering and hissing—while my father tells me a story . . .⁸⁷

Carson refuses to indulge in outright nostalgia, but in "Intelligence" he reminisces about the Beechmount brickfields, once a setting for his childhood games and now razed to the ground like so many other areas of Belfast. The father-and-son duo squint at the panorama below, their eyes "homing in" like security cameras but still struggling to "nearly see" the landscape beneath them. The poem's slow zoom into the brickfields is reproduced grammatically in the series of adjectival and adverbial clauses, which penetrate deeper into the recesses of Beechmount, into the "catacomb of a brick kiln," the "derelict cloisters," the "terraces and corner shops and spires and urinals." The series of clauses propels the reader forward in anticipation of a grammatical and spatial closure, but the poem closes with an ellipsis that withholds the father's story and gestures toward an ever-receding horizon slipping out of vision. The defining characteristic of the prospect poem has always been the expansiveness of its poetic vision, made possible by its elevated perspective. But here Carson points to how some places—especially those obliterated by deindustrialization and urban development—remain out of sight even under the prospect poem's sweeping gaze.

Gillis demonstrates a similarly strained line of sight in his work, questioning whether the loco-descriptive poem is still a viable genre in Belfast today. The collection *Somewhere, Somebody* opens definitively, "This is not about burns or hedges. / There will be no gorse," and goes on to reject the very prospect of prospect poems: "this is not about horizons, or their curving / limitations."[88] (Indeed, the poem reads like Gillis's take on the famous withering first lines of another Carson poem: "Forget the corncrake's elegy. Rusty / Iambics that escaped your discipline / Of Shorn lawns.")[89] Later, Gillis tempers his tone and imagines ascending to a mountaintop ("You could watch the sun leak into horizons"), but he ultimately refuses the spectatorial control and reflective respite that was once afforded to the prospect poet: "for you could see / the world from here, *if* it would only stop / curving."[90] The recurring image of the earth's curvature—and the all-encompassing view that it forecloses—shows how Gillis extends (figuratively, literally) the prospects found earlier in Carson's poetry. In Carson's works, the poet's gaze often mimics the surveillance technologies that envelope the city and penetrate into its recesses, only to reveal a disordered spread of topographic miscellany. But Gillis's works are guided by a poetic vision that is pointed outward at the world beyond Belfast—only to be obstructed by the globe's very curvature, its "curving limitations." For both Carson and Gillis, the horizon does not provide a focal point for poetic contemplation but rather gestures toward an ever-receding world beyond that escapes the poet's field of vision. Walt Hunter argues that contemporary poets have transformed the prospect poem, which no longer guarantees an "imperial position . . . of superior knowledge of personal and historical time or receptive intimacy with the natural world."[91] Rather than the sublime steeps of Mont Blanc or the craggy summits of the Alps, Hunter argues, the more modest hill in contemporary prospect poems becomes reimagined as a "location for staging the dilemmas of the 'global citizen.' "[92] For Gillis specifically, the prospect poem stages the global citizen's inability to envision the world before her, the impossibility to "see the world from here."

Despite his initial hesitations, Gillis does pen a prospect poem with "The Mournes," which takes as its Parnassus the humbler Mournes mountain range in County Down, about an hour's drive south of Belfast. The poem opens with a speaker and her companion who, disillusioned with modern society, "lose the city for the russet rills" and take a day trip to the titular mountain range.[93] Reaching their destination only to be trapped in a parking lot filled with tourists and "the crush of bumper-to-bumper cars," they quickly make their way up the mountains. But even after arriving at the peak and "look[ing] over the Silent Valley," the speaker realizes her field of vision can only go so far:

> . . . the Slieves sloping, as ever before,
> down to the wave-lipped and blue-burst
> sea of trawlers, yachts, dinghies, and, too far
> out for us to see, the milk-drops of dolphins,
> cruisers, carriers, frigates gathering for war.[94]

As in Gillis's other poems, the horizon extends "too far / out for us to see" and suggestively closes with the image of "cruisers, carriers, frigates gathering for war," intimating at the Iraq War unfolding outside the edges of the poem. Gillis includes other references to the US and UK's "special relationship" that facilitated the invasion of Iraq: earlier in "The Mournes," the speaker encounters children wearing "George and Tony masks" in the tourist parking lot, and another poem references news coverage of the Iraq War and makes a dig at "Little Britain merchandise, / made in China."[95] (In 2003, after a controversial parliamentary debate, the British House of Commons voted to approve the invasion of Iraq; only one of the eighteen Northern Irish MPs opposed the resolution.) Gamble points out that Gillis rewrites the popular folk song "The Mountains of Mourne," which imagines an Irish emigrant in London who yearns for the home he left behind in County Down. Gillis reverses the emigrant's longing gaze toward his homeland, and "The Mournes" closes with the speaker looking out onto a horizon that ebbs away into the distance: "Instead of viewing, from the sea, the indisputable boundaries of home—the line where water cedes to land—Gillis' poem works from the land outwards, marking the point at which the assured coordinates of island status blur, meet the shifting morass of water which touches on, and acts as transport between, innumerable and murkily related contexts."[96] The poet certainly troubles the boundaries between home and abroad, situating Northern Ireland within the wider orbit of global wars and economies. But the poem does not transport the speaker so much as highlight its own nearsightedness and representational incapacity. Like a GPS that has stalled and cannot fully load, Gillis's work teases but withholds what is "too far out for us to see."

Carson and Gillis turn the loco-descriptive poem on its head, amending the genre to accommodate the quagmire of political and socioeconomic pressures that crystallize around the urban development of Belfast. Although these poets painstakingly detail every facet of Belfast, their works push against customary ways of reading place and poetry, particularly the notion that detail is somehow always recuperative or ameliorative. Their poems do not paint a coherent portrait of the city but instead point to their own inability to describe place altogether. In so doing, they upend the presumption that poetry can act as a blueprint to Belfast, an archive of the streets, neighborhoods, and architecture lost to sectarian violence and urban development. The task of the poet cannot simply be to catalog the erasure of the local; as Carson especially suggests, is it neither productive nor wise to long for the past given Belfast's "subjunctive mood" and violent history. Rather, contemporary Northern Irish poets must grapple with the susceptibility of place to both valorization and erasure, acknowledging the local itself as a representational problem. These poets offer partial, uncertain poetic descriptions of Belfast, which lay bare the problems of the fissures between the blueprint and the site, between the poem and the city in crisis that it attempts to describe.

Chapter 4

Paul Muldoon and the Difficulty of Comparison

I.

One cannot discuss Paul Muldoon's poetry without first acknowledging its difficulty. Whether lauded as a demonstration of the poet's erudition or denigrated as nothing but pretentious wordplay, Muldoon's poetry is consistently described as unwieldy, sprawling, and most of all, difficult. As one typical book review reads, "we expect elusiveness, technical wiliness, sly humour and a wide-eyed amazement at the world: we also expect a quite unusual degree of difficulty when it comes to elucidation."[1] The obsession with Muldoon's elusiveness has generated a corpus of criticism that centers its praise or scorn on the poet's difficulty. Rajeev Patke preemptively apologizes for the poet's opacity, insisting that underneath all the postmodern play beats the heart of an old-fashioned romantic: "Beneath the fun and games, beneath the modishly postmodern and post-structuralist disavowal of agency sits a poet who is not all that different from the Arnold, Auden, and Heaney that Muldoon castigates."[2] (That said, it is questionable whether Muldoon actually reproaches any of these poets.) A *New York Times* profile of Muldoon is more ambivalent about the poet's ultimate worth: "Depending on which critic you listen to, Muldoon is 'one of the five or so best poets alive,' 'the most significant English-language poet born since the Second World War' and a serious contender for the Nobel Prize, or else he is a victim of 'pyrotechnical autism' who writes 'artificially enriched, overinformed doggerel.'"[3]

While Muldoon does include a dizzyingly wide range of cultural and historical allusions in his poetry, critiques of his work's alleged difficulty are often motivated by a presumed horizon of expectations for Irish poetry—one that the poet purposefully violates. The outcry over Muldoon's difficulty is especially suspicious given T. S. Eliot's dictum that "poets in our civilization, as it exists at present, must be *difficult*."[4] A quick glance at the work of Muldoon's peers—the dense and allusive poems of Cambridge poets like J. H. Prynne, or the linguistic experimentations of the Language poets—demonstrates that his work is by no means exceptionally difficult. Instead, the hyperbolic attention on Muldoon's difficulty is the product of an implicit assumption that Irish poets must descend from and therefore inhere within a certain tradition of lyric poetry. In other words, Muldoon has been expected to inherit Heaney's mantle and act as the poetic spokesperson of Northern Ireland and the Troubles, and the poet's clear discomfort with this role has only fomented allegations of political disengagement. As Robert Archambeau explains, "if the nation of Ireland was created by writers, it's also true that our idea of the Irish writer—especially the poet—has been the product of Irish nationalism. That is, the received idea of the Irish poet is that of a public figure, speaking to a national audience on questions of nationhood—someone altogether different from the self-obsessed garret dweller we imagine when we think of poets in Paris or New York."[5]

This expectation of the poet-as-spokesperson is made manifest in the reception of Muldoon's work, which is still almost exclusively discussed within the purview of Irish poetry even though he has spent the majority of his career in the US and enjoys a celebrated international reputation, having served as the poetry editor of the *New Yorker* and the founding chair of Princeton's Lewis Center for the Arts. In his joint review of the Muldoon's *Maggot* and Heaney's *Human Chain*, Dwight Garner points out the not-so-coincidental simultaneous publication of the two collections: "It's surely time to give up the Heaney/Muldoon analogizing. These are men whose poems—in terms of texture and structure, tactics and tone—could not be more dissimilar. But here they are, each with new books, issued within a two-week span by the same publisher. What's a wide-awake couch potato to do but read them side by jowl?"[6] Not only is Muldoon marketed and studied as an Irish poet, but his work is also expected to operate within the confines of a strict literary tradition, and in turn the poet has become marked as difficult in nearly every critical assessment of his work. The burden of representation—the responsibility to act as, as Trinh Minh-ha describes it, the "sender and bearer of a message, to serve the people and to come off the street"—weighs heavily on Muldoon's shoulders, as it does on those of other Irish poets.[7] Muldoon's "difficulty," then, exposes a contradictory tension in the reception of his poetry. On the one hand, Muldoon seems to inaugurate a post-Heaney generation of Irish poets whose work cannot be confined within national borders. And yet contemporary Irish poetry continues to be read within a national framework, and poets of Muldoon's international stature are especially demanded to speak on the "nation question." The poet's difficulty is defined not so much by its opacity but by its recalcitrance and resistance to such schematic categorizations.

Because Muldoon's "difficulty" is often reduced to the obscurity of his allusions—culled from Irish history and language, Native American mythology, transatlantic literary history from the Romantic to the Language poets—there can be a tendency to react by providing informative glosses to his omnivorous poetry's many references. But Fran Brearton notes how the advent of Internet search engines has done little to resolve the poet's elusiveness: "What left many readers 'high and dry,' and what provided plenty of fodder for the academic, has been transformed by the Internet . . . The great virtue of that change is not the ease with which Muldoon is now 'elucidated'; rather, we can now shortcut to a recognition that such elucidations and explications . . . don't really help that much at all."[8] As I will further discuss, Muldoon does stack an overwhelming surfeit of cultural and historical references that are seemingly random and meaningless. However, his work is not simply difficult for the sake of difficulty, transnational for the sake of transnationalism; instead, the poet stretches the possibilities of cross-cultural comparison in poetry by turning to the figure of conceit. In threading purposefully tenuous connections among Muldoon's heterogenous references, conceit operates as the key literary device for testing the limits of comparison.

As with the other sections of this book, this chapter shows how poetry contains its own set of formal resources in representing the transformations wrought by globalization. The peregrinations of Muldoon's poetry make his work a fruitful site for analyzing the kinds of poetic strategies and figures that emerge in a more and more globalized Irish literary scene. Rather than settling in a particular locale, Muldoon's poetry flits among a multitude of places, all within the compacted space of a stanza or even a line. For instance, within nine short lines in "Yarrow," Muldoon freely skips from the Appalachian territories of the

Hatfields and McCoys to an early medieval Irish settlement to a port in Valparaiso to Transvaal.[9] Foucault argues that the postmodern episteme (what he terms the "age of the simultaneous") is not simply a "plurality of histories juxtaposed and independent of one another" but rather the preoccupation with the forms of relation that accommodate these varied histories and geographies.[10] Muldoon's work is not only symptomatic of the "age of the simultaneous" but also an exploration of the poetic forms that can navigate this "plurality of histories." The novel has often been the predominant genre in scholarship on literature and globalization, but scholars like Jahan Ramazani and Walt Hunter have argued for the formal capacities of poetry in representing a globalized world. What poetry lacks in its world-building abilities, Ramazani contends, it makes up for with its "globe-skipping form" and "rapid-fire transnational jumps": "Traveling poetry proceeds more quickly and abruptly, through translocational juxtapositions, which by their rapidity and lyric compression typically prevent us from believing that we are entering an *alternative space* and, instead, foreground the negotiations and fabrications of imaginative travel."[11] I emphasize Ramazani's point that traveling poetry refuses to create for the reader points of entry into an "alternative space." Postcolonial literature is often read as ethnographic, offering the reader admission to other cultures and opening a window onto unfamiliar terrains. As discussed in the previous chapter, a similar expectation falls on loco-descriptive literature, which is appraised on the "sense of place" that it provides for the reader, the intimacy with place it affords with its detailed descriptions of landscapes and cityscapes. But as I will argue, Muldoon's difficulty is a purposeful poetic strategy that withholds such an intimacy of place and refuses to act as a cultural broker for the reader. Thus, whereas this book's other sections foreground specific local sites, this chapter seeks to understand a poet who not only refuses to remain grounded in one place but also forecloses the experience of place altogether.

This final chapter therefore takes a slight detour from the work of the preceding sections, which analyze in tandem both how the forces of global capitalism have shaped the production of Irish poetry and also how contemporary Irish poets attempt to capture the rise and consolidation of globalization in Ireland. In this chapter, I instead concentrate on the ethical questions that arise as Muldoon negotiates the messy cross-cultural connections made in his itinerant poetry. If contemporary Irish poetry can be profitably analyzed under the framework of global poetics, as I have been arguing in this book, what new questions do we need to ask about how Irish poets relate to and represent peoples and cultures outside Ireland?

To work through these questions, I situate Muldoon's work within the nexus of two conversations that are preoccupying poetry scholars today and yet are seldom discussed in conjunction: the questions of comparative poetics and cultural appropriation. Virginia Jackson and Yopie Prins pinpoint what they see as a central contradiction within comparative studies of lyric poetry: even as scholars attempt to distinguish distinct lyric traditions through cross-cultural comparison, their comparative analyses nevertheless rely on a protocol of "lyric reading," or the critical tendency that misrecognizes all poetry as lyric and reads it as a disembodied and ahistorical voice speaking to itself.[12] "The more we try to differentiate lyric through cross-cultural comparison, the more it appears to be a universal phenomenon," Jackson and Prins argue. "Since that norm [of lyric reading] continues to allow so many critics to read across cultures, across periods, across disciplinary divides, and across so many other critical points of departure, it is unlikely that we will give it up anytime soon."[13] That is to say, the more we compare, the more lyricization stays the same, collapsing disparate poetic traditions under a single mode of lyric reading. However, Eric Hayot pushes against Jackson and Prins's polemic, arguing that their work forecloses the study of non-European literatures under the guise of "respect" for cultural difference and historical rigor: "It is in the name of 'respect' for Chinese *shi* or Arabic *ghazal* that one omits them from the category of the lyric—they are not different types of lyric poetry but different types of poetry (but do the Chinese have a concept of poetry?), departures from the lyric. If we do not include them, if we do not permit them to interfere with our thought, it is because we honor their difference so much."[14] Such "historical fundamentalism," as Hayot terms it, serves as a critical straitjacket that constricts the horizons of comparative literary studies.

The discussions surrounding comparative poetics revolve around the axis of cultural difference versus cultural sameness—an axis that has also guided the debates around cultural appropriation in poetry criticism. Whether in regard to Yeats's reworkings of Noh theatre, Ezra Pound and Ernest Fenollosa's backhanded exaltation of the Chinese language in their theories of Imagism, or Sylvia Plath's use of Holocaust imagery, questions of cultural appropriation have long preoccupied poetry scholars, particularly in the twentieth and twenty-first centuries. Some critics reproach such poets for either exoticizing and overemphasizing the otherness of non-Western cultures (one thinks of Fenollosa's description of the Chinese pictogram as completely "other" and "illogical") or flattening the differences of what are singular cultural and historical experiences (the accusation leveled at Plath's much maligned line that "I think I may well be a Jew"). Still others have countered by claiming that such critiques rely on problematic discourses of authenticity and deny the transnational influences that inevitably occur within literature.[15] Such conversations pinpoint the dilemma of comparison in global poetics, in which poets seem doomed to censure whether they claim cultural difference or sameness. Jacob Edmond argues that scholarship in comparative literature has remained stymied by the binary of cultural sameness versus cultural difference: "Global theory, comparative literature, and modernist poetics all orbit around the mutually constituting and reinforcing poles of linguistic and cultural sameness and difference. This binary reflects deep-seated habits of thought that continue to shape our understanding of literature and culture at the very moment when they seem to have outlived their usefulness."[16]

If the debates around cultural appropriation have had a long-standing presence in poetry criticism, they were fervently reignited by the outcry over the controversial works of the conceptual poets Kenneth Goldsmith and Vanessa Place. In a 2015 performance at Brown University, Goldsmith read aloud one of the official autopsy reports of Michael Brown, the unarmed Black teenager who was murdered by police in Ferguson, Missouri. A few weeks later, Place set up a Twitter account with the avatar of Hattie McDaniel as Mammy from *Gone with the Wind* and began tweeting sections from Margaret Mitchell's original novel. It is easy to oversimplify critiques of Goldsmith's and Place's projects, reducing them to territorial battles over identity politics and whether a white poet is "allowed" to represent Black suffering. But as Chris Chen and Tim Kreiner argue, while Goldsmith and Place conceived of their projects as confronting anti-Black racism, they in fact reproduced a binary between racial content and aesthetic form, in which "race is primarily imagined in terms of raw material 'grabbed, cut, pasted, processed, machined, honed, flattened, repurposed, regurgitated, and reframed'" through "formal strategies conceived elsewhere, in race-neutral terms."[17] In other words, Goldsmith and Place's poetry reduces race from a complex and ever-evolving matrix of sociohistorical relations to "the fixed content of identity categories." The danger of appropriation lies not in white poets' engagement with racist material but in the transformation of race into a static category that must be reimagined by (white) avant-garde techniques.

This chapter situates Muldoon's poetry at the intersection of these critical conversations of comparative poetics and cultural and racial appropriation. Although postcolonial theory has been a central mode of analysis in Irish cultural criticism for decades now, there has been less emphasis on critical race studies in scholarship on Irish poetry.[18] (This book's coda further takes on this topic.) Muldoon's poetry, particularly his sustained interest in Native American history, demands a critical engagement that goes beyond cursory arguments about the poet's cross-cultural solidarity. I place pressure on the moments when the poet "plays Indian," the term coined by Rayna Green to describe performances of Native American identity by non-Natives.[19] In such instances, Muldoon's poetry exemplifies how poetic comparison does not so much build cross-cultural alliances as it does contribute to the erasure of Indigenous peoples. Rather than glossing over or attempting to recuperate the troubling moments in Muldoon's work, I argue that these failures of comparison are an essential part of—and not something ancillary to—his experiments with comparative poetics.

At the same time, the itinerancy of Muldoon's work provides productive ground for exploring the possibilities and limitations of poetic comparison, which is particularly vital in the context of contemporary Irish literature. As I will discuss, there has been a critical tendency in Irish studies scholarship to compare Ireland's anticolonial struggles with those of other countries in the Global South, particularly during the field's formative years in the 1980s and 1990s. In fact, I would suggest that it is not coincidental that much of Muldoon's engagement with Native American history and culture occurs in his early and midcareer collections, such as *Meeting the British* and *Madoc: A Mystery*, which were published during the same time period. An analysis of Muldoon's poetry, then, offers an opportunity to assess how cross-cultural comparison has long percolated in Irish studies and reassess how it might operate today in the field.

This chapter centers around the question, how does poetry compare? To put it another way, how does a poem make comparisons between disparate cultures across the world? What poetic figures, if any, can negotiate the cross-cultural encounters that characterize the conditions and experiences of global modernity? Such questions revolve around not only what we can compare but how much we can compare; that is, what are the limits of comparison in an ethical model of global poetics, especially at a time when poetry scholars have rightfully had to contend with accusations of cultural and racial appropriation? This chapter traces how Muldoon theorizes forms of poetic comparison that attempt to relate the seemingly most unrelated of peoples and places without eliding their differences. While metaphor is often regarded as the poetic figure most central to comparison, Muldoon instead turns to the figure of conceit to press on questions of commensurability and compatibility. In my analysis, I recall Adrienne Rich's predicament when she attempts to imagine an infinitely inclusive collective women's movement: "Two thoughts: there is no liberation that only knows how to say 'I.' There is no collective movement that speaks for each of us all the way through."[20] I dwell on the latter half of Rich's aporia, examining how poetry deals with the inevitability of communities that cannot represent "us all the way through." This emphasis on both the potentialities and failures of comparison in poetry is integral to my chapter's arguments.

II.

"The Mudroom" is an archetype of a difficult Muldoon poem. (Indeed, the poem's title is a playfully slant anagram of the poet's name.) In it, the eponymous mudroom is stuffed to the beams with the jumbled "dreck and clutter" of the newlywed speaker and his wife. The poem reads like a miscellany of incongruous items: household objects half unpacked ("cardboard boxes from K-mart and Caldor, the Hoover, the ironing board") alongside biblical imagery ("the ram's horn on which Moses called to Aaron") alongside personal ephemera ("a pair of my da's boots so worn it was hard to judge where the boots came to an end and the world began"). The poem commemorates Muldoon's marriage to the novelist Jean Korelitz, and the sundry juxtapositions in "The Mudroom" are mainly the result of the couple's different cultural backgrounds, particularly his wife's Jewish heritage. (The poem describes walls that are lined with "jars of gefilte fish and garum" and ceremonial accoutrements of past Seders and Shabbat dinners.)[21] The cultural landscape of the poem, however, sprawls beyond Judaism, as the speaker's apparently free-associating thoughts digress to everything from twentieth-century painters ("Hopper, Magritte, Grant Wood") to classical literature (Virgil's *Georgics* sits next to Plato's *Dialogues*) to even a self-referential dig at a stack of unsold remainders of Muldoon's poetry ("the stack of twenty copies of *The Annals of Chile* [$21 hardback]"). As the speaker journeys through the mudroom's bric-a-brac to search for a refrigerator at its opposite end, he is guided by recurring visions of a goat from the sacrifice of Isaac:

> Yet again something had come between
> the she-goat poised on a slope on which the cattle batten
> and ourselves, that rivulet
> or blue-green fault
> between the clabber of morn and the stalwart even-clabber . . .
> It was time, I felt sure, to unpack the Suntory
> into the old fridge, to clear a space between *De Rerum Natura*
> and Virgil's *Eclogues*,
> a space in which, at long last, I might unlock
> the rink, so I drove another piton into an eighty-pound
> bag of Sakrete and flipped the half door on the dairy cabinet
> of the old Hotpoint . . .[22]

The practice of reading Muldoon requires an informative gloss to his many esoteric allusions. Suntory (a Japanese whiskey) and Hotpoint (a home appliance company) may be more familiar brand names, but Sakrete is a lesser-known business that makes concrete and mortar. The "clabber of morn and the stalwart even-clabber" refers to the process of making Morbier cheese, which consists of a layer of morning milk and evening milk divided by a line of blue-green ash. (An Anglicization of the Irish word *clábair*, "clabber" refers to a traditional Appalachian milk dish imported to the American South by Ulster Scots, perhaps a winking reference to Muldoon's own move to the US.) As in all of Muldoon's writing, frequent consultations of the encyclopedia are needed for a basic understanding of the poem, let alone for an elucidation of its sly etymological jokes.

However, it is not simply the obscurity of such references that unsettles critics; rather, the preoccupation with Muldoon's difficulty centers around the cultural and historical range of these references. A language of excess pervades descriptions of Muldoon's poetry. One critic breathlessly describes how the cavalcade of images in Muldoon's poems results in "chaos: a maddening whirl of incidents and images, references and recherché allusions . . . Huge lists of things are strung through its stanzas—of poets, novelists, their books, their characters, places, saints, food, drink, weapons, modes of transportation."[23] Even a positive review of *The End of the Poem*, a compilation of Muldoon's lectures delivered during his post as Oxford Professor of Poetry, ends with a tongue-in-cheek nod to the difficulties of following the poet's many trains of thought: "Yet however obscure Muldoon can be, there is a strong emotional and intellectual pulse to every poem that allows a reader to get the gists and piths of sense even when some specifics slide by. And there's always Google."[24] The consensus of critics is that Muldoon demands much of his readers: extensive knowledge of Irish history and language, Native American mythology, transatlantic literary history. Clair Wills outlines the frustrations with Muldoon's wide range of references and the challenges it imposes on different audiences of readers: "There is undoubtedly something maddening about such references. It's not just that they are obscure, but that they are totally idiosyncratic. Irish readers may be familiar with the resonances of the bittern and the curlew, but at a loss compared with Americans when it comes to 'Decatur' (while English readers possibly fare worst of all). The references mirror not only the contemporary cultural patchwork which is the subject of the poem, but the writer's own obsessions."[25] Wills pinpoints the major difficulty of Muldoon's work not in the poet's overabundance of references but in the wide range of these "idiosyncratic" sources. Notably, Wills describes Muldoon's idiosyncrasy along national borders, or rather explains how it refuses to fall neatly within them. While Irish readers may recognize the indigenous bittern and curlew that are foreign to others, the reference to Decatur, a suburb of Atlanta, Georgia, will likely be familiar only with US audiences. (All of which is to say nothing of the beleaguered English reader, as she points out.) Muldoon traffics freely in a variety of cultures and histories, and his work defiantly refuses to adhere to expected geographical and historical boundaries. The inaccessibility of Muldoon's work is further underlined when we consider that this quotation comes from an academic monograph and not a review in a popular journal or magazine. Wills goes so far as to suggest that Muldoon collapses into moments of solipsism, insinuating that only the poet himself could possibly track his own tangled web of references: "It's almost as though we are required to become the poet in order to follow his logic fully." Robert MacFarlane likewise observes that Muldoon includes so many personal anecdotes in *The Prince of Quotidian* and *Moy Sand and Gravel* that the poet's linguistic playfulness can be read as a "sustained effort to privatize language."[26] Muldoon's difficulty does not simply stem from the obscurity of its allusions; the poet purposely renders his poetry unknowable. Another reviewer hints at the elusive elements of Muldoon's work, adding that even the most "highly qualified reader" needs knowledge beyond the university library: "If you knew everything Muldoon has ever known (and half forgotten), had met everyone Muldoon and could make every mental connection Muldoon has ever clicked on, you'd be in the running to qualify . . ."[27] It seems that even Google is not enough; one must be privy to all knowledge, both public and private, in the poet's mind.

But an exclusively annotative gloss to Muldoon's poetry would overlook the parataxis at work in his writing. For instance, threading together the sprawling clutter of "The Mudroom" is the "blue-green" line of a wheel of Morbier cheese, which the speaker and his wife follow through the room and which ultimately leads them to the refrigerator. The blue-green ash line—described as a "schism," "ditch," "ravine," and "crevasse"—comes to represent the difficulty of negotiating the couple's different cultural heritages, and throughout the poem the ash line threatens to divide the speaker from his wife as they journey through the perilous junk of the mudroom. While notoriously reticent about his political position on the Troubles, Muldoon sneaks in a reference to his Northern Irish background when the speaker stumbles upon a "hubcap from a Ford Sierra blown up in—yes, siree—a controlled explosion in Belfast." (Moreover, the American inflection of "yes siree" impersonates the colloquialism of a gun-toting cowboy in the Wild West, further linking the US with Northern Ireland.) The speaker's treacherous journey through the mudroom's disarray—"weighed down" and "struggling for a foothold"—parallels the reader's struggle through the mishmash of historical and cultural references in the poem. The clutter overwhelming the mudroom is more than the sum of the couple's possessions; it also represents the cultural histories that come to define and possibly also separate them. In "The Mudroom," parataxis does not simply juxtapose disparate historical and cultural references without explaining their connection; it suggests that the gulf between different cultures is sometimes unbridgeable.

Muldoon's difficulty is not merely a flashy display of poetic pyrotechnics but rather a literary strategy that purposefully evokes these feelings of distancing and estrangement in the reader. Rather than exclusively approaching difficulty as intrinsic to literary form, we should also understand it as an affect, a word encoding the feelings of exasperation and even anger that characterize almost all criticism on Muldoon. A contradictory tension is at work in Muldoon's poetry. On the one hand, the wide range of the references forecloses the possibility of comprehensive understanding and alienates the reader with its impenetrability. It is not only that Muldoon culls from different sets of cultural knowledge in his far-ranging references, whether to a small suburb in Georgia or to a brand of Japanese whiskey. Rather, the itineracy of Muldoon's poetry seems to pull the very carpet from beneath the reader's feet by withholding any stable ground altogether. The poet himself admits that his work's careening trajectories void place altogether: "If the poem has no obvious destination, there's a chance that we'll all be setting off on an interesting ride."[28] On the other hand, the variety of references creates different communities of readers who have access to specific sets of knowledge. That Wills divides these readers along lines of nationality hints at the political dimensions of Muldoon's global "idiosyncrasy." Muldoon's work therefore contemplates the relationship between knowledge and communities—specifically the processes by which knowledge can foreclose and also create communities. Readers do not simply feel uninformed or unqualified; they also realize that the limits of their knowledge are delineated along cultural lines and that their subject-positions are defined within communities of reading. Though such ideas have been explored in reader-response and reception theory, nowhere are the feelings of irritation as acute as they are in the experience of reading Muldoon's work, which is evident by the many incensed book reviews that the poet has generated. Much of the anger underlying these reviews is indignation: after all, if a professional reader (journalist or academic) cannot understand Muldoon, who possibly could? Even the most "qualified reader" is nonetheless confronted with the limits of her knowledge.

Because Muldoon's idiosyncratic style traffics in a wide range of cultural and literary references, his poetry is often felt as exclusive rather than as inclusive. Muldoon's poetry enacts a feeling of "dissimilation," as described by Natalie Melas in her study of comparison in postcolonial literary studies. Dissimilation occurs when the act of interpellation does not usher the subject into a community of shared subjectivity but instead excludes her from it. In instances of dissimilation, it is the experience of exclusion rather than inclusion that forms subjectivity. Melas cites as an example V. S. Naipaul's experience reading of *Heart of Darkness* and observes how the writer's subjectivity is created not through an identification with the novel's colonial paradigms but through his difference from them:

> Naipaul begins as a subject confident in the fixity of the colonial world, and is interpellated into the political panic of partial vision . . . Dissimilation is not an experience of pure difference, but of boundedness—a recognition of cultural and historical limits, precisely because these limits are uncertain or ambiguous . . . Dissimilation is an interpellation into dislocation . . . What I have in mind with dissimilation is an interpellation that instead of assimilating the subject to a social whole dissimilates him from it and provokes an experience of difference, of being outside.[29]

An "interpellation into dislocation," dissimilation is the feeling of groundlessness experienced when postcolonial subjects are made simultaneously aware of a "given system" and their exclusion from it. I glean two important arguments from the concept of dissimilation. First, Melas describes dissimilation as a specifically postcolonial condition characterized by the trauma brought on by the colonized's dissociation from a "social whole"—what she calls the "panic of partial vision" and the feeling of "boundedness" and "being outside." Second, Melas emphasizes dissimilation as the "effect of a mode of reading," describing Naipaul's feeling of unfixity as the result of his reading experience. The frustration expressed in the critical assessments of Muldoon's work underlines how the experience of dissimilation is unsettling (in both figurative and literal meanings of the word). "Difficulty" is not simply the frustration of parsing the many historical and cultural allusions in Muldoon's work; it is also the experience of confronting the "cultural and historical limits" that delineate the "boundedness" of one's reading community. The literary text is not only descriptive of the postcolonial condition but also inscriptive—producing and reinforcing the reader's subjectivity.

But while Muldoon's work does produce the alienating experience of dissimilation, his poetry's difficulty also has more generative impulses. The mobility of Muldoon's work—not just its excursions to various geographies but also its movements between seemingly unrelated thoughts—points to the specific ability of poetry to showcase and celebrate the most tenuous of connections. Another poet famed for his impenetrable writing, J. H. Prynne, argues that difficult poetry allows for this flexibility more so than prose does. The density of poetry, in which semantic and syntactic links are often absent, welds together dissimilar concepts and allows for the reader to contemplate with "rich uncertainty . . . [the] many possibilities crowded together":

> Not only is poetry characteristically condensed, so that some semantic links may be cut out or completely absent, but also a diversity of apparently incompatible references is often deliberate and a valued feature of complex poems . . . Poetry allows for more interconnections made amongst words than prose does. In prose, though not all prose, there is generally a quite closely defined channel or corridor of sense-making . . . which is not distracted by word-sounds or by excess of side-meanings—incidental or accidental semantic possibilities that lie outside the main channel. But in certain types of "difficult" poetry this corridor of sense is much wider and more open . . . with many loops and cross-links of semantic and referring activity which extend the boundaries of relevance . . .[30]

As Prynne asserts, poetic difficulty is produced not by the obscurity of references but by their heterogeneity and apparent incompatibility. His description of poetry as a complex semantic network ("corridors of sense-making," "loops and cross-links," possibilities of meanings "outside the main channel") celebrates the sprawling trains of thoughts characteristic of Muldoon's poetry, which can be generated and then turned away by any segue—whether a shared etymological root, slant rhyme, or playful figure of speech. For both Prynne and Muldoon, difficult poetry has the unique capacity for forging interconnections between what are seemingly unconnected or even incompatible things.

III.

But what happens when such interconnections are based on cross-cultural comparisons, as is the case with Muldoon's repeated pairings of Native American and Irish histories? One of Muldoon's earliest portrayals of Native Americans comes in the poem "The Indians on Alcatraz," which juxtaposes the Troubles with the 1969–1971 occupation of Alcatraz ("this island . . . forever the destination / Of all those dwindling bands") by a group of ninety Native Americans from different tribes ("brilliant beautiful guerilla fighter[s]").[31] In the long poem "The More a Man Has the More a Man Wants," a Sioux man travels to Belfast to murder the descendants of an "Ulsterman who had some hand in the massacre at Wounded Knee."[32] Muldoon continues exploring the roots of British colonization of North America in *Madoc*, which portrays an imaginary pantisocratic society founded in Virginia by Robert Southey and Samuel Taylor Coleridge. Muldoon draws on the legend of Madoc, a Welsh prince who sailed to America and later settled with Native Americans and established a "white" tribe who spoke a hybridized Gaelic language. (Madoc's voyage supposedly dated hundreds of years before Columbus, and the myth was used to justify British occupation of North America over rival claims made by Spain and Portugal.)[33] *Meeting the British*, his last published collection before his move to the US, depicts Pontiac's Rebellion, the uprising of a confederation of Native American tribes from the Great Lakes region from 1763 to 1766.

Scholars have often cast Muldoon's references to Native American culture as the celebration of cross-cultural alliances made across disparate colonial and postcolonial communities.[34] Omaar Hena sees in Muldoon's cross-cultural encounters an example of the postcolonial solidarity possible between Native American and Irish cultures and an allegory for the globalized nature of identity today: "Muldoon's investment in American Indian cultures and figures clearly demonstrates how the globalization of cultural identity is not always equivalent to cultural imperialism. Instead, globalization can foster 'global imagined communities' linked together through their common disempowerment and resistance."[35] Elizabeth Butler Cullingford similarly argues that the Irish identification with oppressed communities (including African Americans and Native Americans) can generate a "politics of imaginative solidarity with the potential for practical action."[36] Luke Gibbons extrapolates from these moments of "imaginative solidarity" a tradition of "lateral mobility" in the history of modern Irish thinking, which stems from Edmund Burke's theories of the "sympathetic sublime," an attempt to engage with colonial cultures rather than consigning them to the dustbin of history according to Enlightenment theories of progress.[37] In his survey of postcolonial theory in Irish studies, Eóin Flannery describes the Northern Irish political murals that borrow images of revolutionary figures like Che Guevara and Nelson Mandela and make allusions to Palestine, South Africa, and Cuba as examples of an "ethics of oppressed solidarity" and "spectres of comparison."[38]

While Muldoon's writing may assemble together various colonial and postcolonial cultures, terms like "cross-cultural encounter," "lateral mobility," and "spectres of comparison" suggest a mode of comparative analysis that examines their synchronic similarities but ultimately holds them in separation from one another. But Muldoon's poetry inhabits a different form of comparative thinking, envisioning instead an infinitely interconnected global history in which all cultures are imbricated, both synchronically and diachronically, in the fabric of imperialism. When questioned about his poetry's repeated turns to Native American history, Muldoon answers that he at first was drawn to its "fairly crude parallels with the Irish situation." However, he goes on to argue that such comparisons have a long history, stemming from the use of Ireland as a "testing ground" for colonial practices in North America: "[There was] an association between Native Americans and the Irish, both of whom the British found so wild and primitive . . . They treated the Indians according to what they learned in Ireland. I say mine is a crude comparison, but historically it started out as a very crude comparison."[39] Muldoon's comparative thinking, then, does not hold cultures in isolation from one another but rather portrays an intermingled and violent history of the North Atlantic that is fundamentally enmeshed with the forces of British imperialism across the globe. The poet articulates a complicated notion of comparison, which has not only mobilized an ethics of postcolonial solidarity but also undergirded colonial rationale from the outset. Comparative thinking can propel the violent power dynamics that have constituted colonial rationale: the "crude comparison" of British imperialism created transnational affiliations among different cultures but did so in order to arrange them along a hierarchical scale and incorporate them into developmental narratives of modernity. Franz Fanon underscores the underbelly of comparison when he suggests that postcolonial Antillean subjectivity, pillaged of its history and culture, can only articulate itself in comparison: "Negroes are comparison . . . Antilleans have no proper value; they are always contingent on the presence of the Other."[40] Comparison is a double-edged sword that can either open up new possibilities of transnational histories and cultures or become the only means of subjectivity for the postcolonial subject.[41]

We can tease out the complexities of Muldoon's comparative poetics by focusing on one of his later treatments of Native Americans in the poem "Perdu" from the collection *Horse Latitudes*. The poem's speaker is a "Salish man" (referring to the Salish peoples, the Indigenous peoples of British Columbia and the US Northwest) who stands watch over his community only to be taken prisoner and tortured by his captors.[42] Whereas the Troubles served as the backdrop for Muldoon's earlier depictions of

Native Americans, the War on Terror instead shadows *Horse Latitudes*, which Muldoon published in 2006 and wrote amid the 2003 US invasion of Iraq. The collection opens with a crown of sonnets, all titled after battles beginning with "B" (such as "Battle of Bunker") with the notable exception of "Baghdad," so as to emphasize the war's centrality through its absence. Like many of Muldoon's works, "Perdu" follows a strict form with eleven rhyming couplets, in which a couplet's second line is repeated in the next couplet's first line: "I've stood sentinel here for a long time. / A long time since I dropped down . . ." The poem's formal constraint parallels the gruesome torturing of the speaker, whose bones are broken so that his body can be contorted to fit a grave: "They were breaking my legs so I would fit / when I came to and called for an end to it." Indeed, the "fitting" of the speaker's body into a confined space alludes to the "enhanced interrogation techniques" (particularly the use of cold cells) that occurred at Guantanamo Bay. (The title "Perdu" also is a nod to the concealment of human rights abuses there and at Abu Ghraib.) Kenneth Keating reads the poem as Muldoon's metapoetic commentary on the violence of interpretation, or "reduc[ing] the poet and the poem by those who attempt to confine both to one singular identity and meaning . . . 'Perdu' foregrounds the critical attempt to visit violence and even a death of sorts upon the body of the poet to make it 'fit' . . ."[43] For Ruben Moi, the poem's repetitions and structure ("Perdu" opens and closes with the exact same couplet) mirrors the cyclicality of genocidal violence, "the binary deadlock of one culture being brutally extinguished by another. Sameness in the first and final couplet creates a double sense of adamant resolve and repetitive inevitability."[44] But we might also read the poem's violence in another direction: Muldoon intimates the violence of poetic form itself, of bending and breaking a poem's content to "fit" a certain pattern and rhyme scheme. Muldoon has often spoken about how the constraints of traditional verse forms, particularly those that employ repetition, can be productive. He remarks with trademark wit that "form is a straitjacket in the way that a straitjacket was a straitjacket for Houdini."[45] But in "Perdu," poetic form does not offer the pleasurable challenge of escape so much as confine and entrap its subject.

Muldoon therefore seems to evince an awareness of the dangers of cross-cultural comparison in his own work, of taking the Salish peoples as the object of comparison in his poetic reflection on the brutalities of a post-9/11 world. In an interview, Muldoon outright acknowledges that "working with this [Native American] material one still runs the risk of reducing an artwork to an analogy, which then is basically empty but for values to insert from history." Yet moments later in the same interview, Muldoon undoes this self-awareness when he confesses: "I've always wanted to be an Indian. When I was a child I had a tent, a bow, and arrow. I still have a bow and arrow."[46] Like much of Muldoon's poetry, "Perdu" crafts a complex global matrix that threads together several sites and histories: the US and the War on Terror in Iraq and surrounding regions in the Middle East; the genocide carried out against the Salish peoples and other Indigenous groups in North America; even Northern Ireland and the Troubles, as the poem hearkens back to the poet's earlier works in *Madoc* and *Meeting the British*. But "Perdu" also risks the very pitfalls that Muldoon had cautioned against; the poem works as an "analogy" in which the barbarism of the US invasion of Iraq is brought into relief by the genocide of Native Americans. As Fanon puts it, the Salish are comparison, existing only to accentuate the cruelties of US imperialism. Or to borrow from Chen and Kreiner's critique of conceptual poetry cited earlier in this chapter, Native Americans are reduced to "raw material" (incidentally the same word that Muldoon uses in his interview) that is appropriated and recontextualized by "formal strategies conceived elsewhere, in race-neutral terms."[47] Sarah Dowling expresses a dissatisfaction with critics of conceptual poetry and other appropriation-based poetries, who see the circulation of texts as "frictionless" and "neutral": "These accounts of textual mobility . . . sugges[t] that the ease with which texts can be transferred from one place to another speaks to the connectedness of our globalized world . . . [T]heir failure to consider how movement is forced and directed by global capitalism leads them to misconstrue or neglect the most obvious questions appropriation raises—namely, property and priority (or inversely, dispossession and displacement)."[48] Moreover, as Dowling points out, the very definition of appropriation is bound up with legal processes of property and possession and thus settler colonialism itself. Such critiques therefore should have bearing on a poem like "Perdu," which traffics Native American history from North America to the Middle East and Northern Ireland.

There is a temptation to disregard critiques of Muldoon's poetry as the "policing of literary identities," what Ramazani describes as the misguided forbiddance of any kind of "cross-cultural contamination and leakage" and insistence that poets stay in their own cultural lanes.[49]

But the purpose of this chapter is neither to vilify Muldoon's work nor to rescue it. Rather, I approach Muldoon's poetry as an opportunity to think seriously about the forms and figures of poetry that can accommodate and also obstruct cross-cultural comparison. In their influential essay "Decolonization Is Not a Metaphor," Eve Tuck and K. Wayne Yang critique the co-optation of "decolonization" within recent education advocacy work, such as in calls to "decolonize schools" or "decolonize student thinking." Tuck and Yang's cogent analysis has been widely lauded as a necessary corrective to social justice projects that superficially adopt the rhetoric of decolonization while sidelining its specific mission of repatriating Indigenous lands. But for the purposes of this chapter, I approach Tuck and Yang's work as a treatise on the limitations of figurative language—that is, on how decolonization works, and does not work, as metaphor: "When metaphor invades decolonization, it kills the very possibility of decolonization; it recenters whiteness, it resettles theory, it extends innocence to the settler, it entertains a settler future . . . When we write about decolonization, we are not offering it as a metaphor; it is not an *approximation* of other experiences of oppression. Decolonization is not a *swappable term* for other things we want to do to improve our societies and schools. Decolonization doesn't have a *synonym*."[50] For Tuck and Yang, the perniciousness of "decolonization" stems not from its empty virtue signaling but from its use as a metaphor that attempts to compare—in their words, to approximate, to swap and find a synonym for—the violent structures of settler colonialism. At its core, metaphor is a figure built on comparison, highlighting the similarities between tenor and vehicle.[51] To cite a famous example: love (tenor) is a red, red rose (vehicle). But the components of metaphor do not meet on equal ground: the vehicle is indentured to the tenor, the rose to love, the object to subject.[52] The hierarchical structure of metaphor is exacerbated when tenor and vehicle are already vexed by uneven power relations, as is the case with the rhetoric of decolonization critiqued by Tuck and Yang.[53]

But the recent domestication of decolonization in contemporary social justice circles is far from the only instance when metaphor has abetted the erasure of Indigenous peoples. There has been a long history of Irish identification with Native Americans, which was first spurred by British colonial rhetoric that racialized both groups as "savage" and which eventually evolved into a strain of Irish anticolonial thought that mythologized their shared anticolonial struggles.[54] For scholars like Cullingford, this comparative approach in Irish studies allowed for a politics of imaginative solidarity and forged a pathway toward real political action: "If the effective use of metaphor is commonly privileged as the gold standard of good poetry, the ability to see one's own political predicament mirrored in that of others might be called the gold standard of the politics of empathy."[55] But what looks like "good poetry" and a politics of empathy from one angle can, from another, appear like comparisons that absorb and thereby erase Native lives. As Mary Mullen incisively argues, such analogies not only mistake affective connections for material realities but also erase the violent history of Irish participation in white settler colonialism in the Americas and Antipodes: "The truth is that the empathy and affinity that Irish Studies scholars frequently claim Irish people have for Indigenous peoples often functions . . . as metaphors detached from material practices and acts. Claims of shared histories of colonialism that evacuate Indigenous histories only participate in settler colonial formations."[56] Furthermore, Andrew Fox observes that such analogies perpetually place Native culture and history at the service of articulating a globalized sense of Irish identity: "The metaphorical declaration 'I am Indian' might well free the Irish subject from the historical burden of 'I am Irish'; but . . . the easy movement from the former to the latter also . . . reduces Native identity to a tool with which to explore issues of Irishness."[57] In an early appraisal of Irish studies, David Lloyd pushes against what he sees as the "universalizing drive of 'comparative studies'" that motivates much scholarship in the field: "Suspicion of much contemporary 'post-colonial theory' has been justly grounded in the criticism of its easy transferability which, like metaphor itself, risks discovering identity at the expense of significant difference."[58] That Mullen, Fox, and Lloyd all link the too easy "transferability" of Irish studies with the figure of metaphor is no accident. In this book's previous chapters, I have traced contemporary poets' engagements with the long memories of poetic genres and forms, which are used to articulate new senses of locality and place in an increasingly globalized Ireland. But just as poetry contains these generative literary genealogies, figures like metaphor have also been conscripted to violent purposes of erasure and displacement. This is not to argue that metaphor is inherently violent but to highlight how the comparisons structured within metaphor can operate on uneven footing, especially in the context of Irish literature and criticism.

IV.

What poetic forms, if any, can recuperate cross-cultural comparison and relationality? While Muldoon's metaphors can produce "crude comparisons," he also turns to the comparative possibilities enabled by another poetic figure: conceit. An extended metaphor that compares two dissimilar concepts and continues the comparison through an entire passage or poem, conceit was the central literary device for the seventeenth-century Metaphysical poets. In his famous critique of the Metaphysical poets, Samuel Johnson denounces their use of conceit that takes heterogeneous ideas and "yok[es] them by violence together": "Nature and art are ransacked for illustrations, comparisons, and allusions; their learning instructs, and their subtlety surprises; but the reader commonly thinks his improvement dearly bought, and though he sometimes admires, is seldom pleased."[59] But since Johnson's condemnation, scholars have recuperated the potentials of conceit, especially in contrast to the limitations of metaphor. Helen Gardner argues that conceit "forces fresh points of likeness upon us" and works by means of a " 'hammering out' by which a difficult join is made."[60] Quoting from Gardner's study, Muldoon emphasizes the ephemerality of the connections borne by conceit:

> The aspect of Metaphysical poetry that continues to exercise me most is that of the conceit, a "comparison whose ingenuity is more striking than its justness" . . . All comparisons discover likeness in things unlike. A comparison becomes a conceit "when we are made to concede likeness while being strongly conscious of unlikeness." Here a conceit is like a spark made by striking two stones together. After the flash the stones are just two stones . . . Helen Gardner's insistence on the autonomous or discrete nature of the two unlike things brings me back to two of those images . . . I immediately see a connection. Put more graphically, a connection sees me.[61]

According to Muldoon, conceit differs from metaphor because it is only partially successful, creating only momentary sparks of connection. Conceit draws its power not from the "justness" of comparison but from strange or "striking" likenesses, and the reader always remains aware of the autonomy and "unlikeness" of the objects being compared. In the previous section, I discussed how scholars like Mullen, Fox, and Lloyd have critiqued the "easy transferability" of metaphor; but conceit, Muldoon suggests, instead highlights the uneasiness of comparison, the difficulty by which a join is made.

Muldoon repeatedly emphasizes the coerciveness of conceit. In another interview, Muldoon further details how conceit compels the reader to "concede" the likeness in things unlike: "I read John Donne again and again. What's one admiring when one reads that the lovers, the marriage bed, and marriage temple equal the flea? We know that's not the case . . . And we come away from it again and again saying, OK, I believe you. The marriage bed is indeed embodied in the flea."[62] The reader hesitates over the "unlikeness" of the marriage bed to the flea but nonetheless is browbeaten into conceding the comparison.[63] Whereas Coleridge's suspension of disbelief relies on an act of poetic faith on the part of the reader, Muldoon depicts conceit as a gradual wearing down of the reader, who seems bullied to concede likeness and acquiesce reluctantly, "OK, I believe you." (Perhaps Johnson's rebuke of the violence of conceit has some merit here.)

By strong-arming connections between the most unlike of things, conceit may seem to perpetuate the violence of metaphor. As discussed earlier, Muldoon's cross-cultural comparisons can dehistoricize the specific material conditions of white settler colonialism and subordinate Native history to Irish history. Would conceit not also run roughshod over their cultural and historical differences? But in his turn to conceit, Muldoon points to an alternative form of relationality not based on the matching of cultural experiences but on what he calls the "reconciliation" of disparate cultures and histories: "Art, if I may be grandiose for a moment, is about the *reconciliation* of opposites. I don't mean in the sense of bringing people together under false pretences, because one of the things I'm definitely not interested in is art as a reconciling force in societal terms. But there is that momentary coming together, which is where the poem resides."[64] The precise meaning of "reconciliation" is vital here: Muldoon does not posit art as a political arbiter or peacemaker but instead speaks of the reconciling power of poetry as a "momentary coming together," denoting "reconciliation" in its other sense of making compatible or comparable.[65] The poet's emphasis on the transience of reconciliation closely echoes his definition of conceit as the fleeting "flash" of connection. As he points out, the effects of conceit are short-lived: after the "spark" of comparison, Muldoon argues, "the stones are just two stones." The poet's concept of reconciliation involves a delicate balance of comparing without eliding difference, allowing connection to occur without losing sight of alterity.

We can see such reconciliation at work in Muldoon's "Cauliflowers," a sestina from *Madoc*. While not strictly an example of conceit, the rigid and repetitive pattern of the sestina serves as a vehicle for comparison for Muldoon: "To reconcile the two is the trick, the ready-made and the random . . . It's a feature of any form that uses repetition, whether a ballad or a sestina, anything where repetition is part of the deal, where little things change."[66] In the case of "Cauliflowers," Muldoon exploits the sestina's repetition of end-words to contrast the various mutations of meaning undergone by the words "pipe," "light," and "go down" over the course of the poem. Highlighted by enjambment, the repeated phrases in the poem provide a linguistic link between the two very different settings of the poem: the family farm in rural Northern Ireland and the speaker's Oregon motel room. The poem opens with the speaker's father lighting his tobacco pipe, concerned about the drop in the price of cauliflower (which has "gone down / two weeks in a row on the Belfast market").[67] Later his attention is drawn to a "platoon of *Light* / Infantry *going down* / the road to the accompaniment of a *pipe-* / band." By the poem's midpoint, we learn that "All this" occurs thousands of miles away as the speaker eavesdrops on his neighbors' sexual activity:

> All this as I listened to two lovers
> repeatedly *going down*
> on each other in the next room . . . 'light
> of my life . . .' in a motel in Oregon.

The meanings of the repeated words transform from the everyday (a smoking pipe) to the military (a pipe-band), the economic ("price of cauliflowers / has gone down") to the sexual ("lovers / repeatedly going down / on each other"). Even more jarring is the series of line and stanza breaks that follows: "Magritte's / pipe / and the pipe- / bomb." The abrupt contrast between the surreal painting (no less by an artist often accused of vacuity and political evasiveness) and the weapon that has come to symbolize the Troubles' violence invites a meditation on Muldoon's role as a Northern Irish poet and the ability of playful postmodern art to grapple with the reality of political violence. (The title of Magritte's painting, *The Treachery of Images*, suggests that Muldoon is well aware of how his playfulness may be vilified.)

"Cauliflowers" is a prime example of conceit's "yoking together" of heterogeneous ideas, facilitating comparisons among the most incomparable of people, places, and ideas. The farfetchedness of such comparison is allegorized in the poem's prefacing quotation from the *National Enquirer*, which reports a gene-splicing experiment that created glow-in-the-dark plants by introducing the light-producing bacteria found in fish to vegetables. Muldoon purposefully chooses a tabloid famous for its dubiousness, questioning the plausibility of such comparisons at the start of the collection. There are no guarantees in Muldoon's poetry: many comparisons are forced and as many are made as missed. We are left to wonder whether the poem's linguistic play can traverse the distance between Belfast and "All this" and how precisely such connections can be forged. In other words, Muldoon suggestively juxtaposes the images of Magritte's pipe and the pipe bomb but stops shorts of providing a conclusive interpretation for the reader. As Prynne observes, the semantic links in poetry are often absent and left for the reader to rebuild: "A reader can move slowly through dense compositions of this kind, and pauses at moments of choice can enrich the activity of reading; it's not necessary all the time to make precise decisions, because uncertainty may be intrinsic to the text and its internal connections to its method of thought."[68]

In addition to exacting verse forms like the sestina, Muldoon turns to the list as an organizational framework in many of his poetry collections and essays. For instance, the chapter headings in *Madoc* are organized as a chronological list of canonical Western philosophers that Muldoon borrowed from an anthology's table of contents.[69] Likewise structured chronologically, *The Prince of the Quotidian* is a collection of "diary poems," each depicting a day in the life of the poet during his move from Ireland to America. Muldoon also strays from chronology and alphabetically systematizes much of his work, including *To Ireland, I*, a compilation of lectures delivered at Oxford that presents a survey of Irish literature in an alphabetized list. Within the long poem "Yarrow" appear a number of similar fictional abecedariums, such as "*Bridge from A to Z* by George S. Coffin," "from *Alamein to mon Zem-Zemblable*," and the humorously brief "*Ulster: From C.S. Lewis to C.S. Gas*." The poems in *Hay* are overwhelmed with alphabetized lists of record collections ("from Abba to Ultravox") and dictionaries (such as Alfred Newton's *Dictionary of Birds*) cluttering the speaker's home.

While Muldoon's plentiful lists are organized by the alphabet and calendar, they at the same time reveal and ridicule the arbitrariness of these forms of order. In fact, the list encapsulates a tension that looms large in all of Muldoon's writing: the polarity between the rigidity of his poetic formalism and the seeming randomness of his cultural and historical allusions. (This tension is often implicit in reviews of Muldoon's work that try to decide whether the poet actually articulates a coherent politics or simply delights in his poetic virtuosity.) As Eric Falci astutely observes, Muldoon's poetry is shaped by both its disciplined formalism and its freewheeling unpredictability: "Such hyperformalisms, cut across by an insistent—and winningly maniacal—associative motor, result in shapes that are both rigidly cohesive and rigorously unmoored."[70] The tension between hyperformalism and utter randomness is at the center of "Birth," which expresses the poet's anxieties as he witnesses his daughter's entry into a chaotic world. The "inestimable realm" of the world is transfigured into an alphabetized list of random objects: foods ("apple-blossoms and chanterelles and damsons") are found alongside animals ("foxes," "jennets," "Russian sable," and "widgeon") in a list that also includes the Kickapoo tribe (a continuation of Muldoon's interest in Native American culture) and nonsensical words ("the peekaboo-quiffs").[71] Muldoon's reference to "lemniscs," a part of the brain stem that links sound with meaning, self-consciously alludes to the poem's own wordplay of alliteration ("windlass-women," "gralloch-grub," "footling foot") and clever half-rhymes ("Kickapoos" with "peekaboo," "hubbub" with "rub-a-dub"). Nonetheless, the tumult of objects is organized by the strict order of the alphabet and is brought to a halt with the enunciation of the daughter's full name, itself an amalgamation of Irish and Jewish names and the product of a multicultural marriage:

> Dorothy Aoife Korelitz Muldoon: I watch through floods of
>   tears
> as they give her a quick rub-a-dub
> and whisk
> her off to the nursery, then check their staple-guns for
>   staples.

Two opposing forces are at work in "Birth" and Muldoon's other list poems, in which disarrayed lists of unrelated objects threaten to collapse into nonsense and yet are yoked together at moments by chronological, calendrical, and alphabetical orders. As with conceit, Muldoon mobilizes the list to create relations between the seemingly unrelatable. A question arises over which force ultimately triumphs in Muldoon's poetry: Is the "inestimable realm" momentarily pulled into alphabetical order, or does it ultimately resist such attempts at order? To phrase the question another way, does the list intimate the possibility of interconnection among these items, or does it simply highlight their incongruencies? Such questions are left open-ended with the closing image of the doctors checking their staple guns for staples. As usual, Muldoon makes no guarantees as to whether the poem is successful in bringing together the many disparate elements and the reader is left to ponder the exact nature of relationality.

The overabundant lists in Muldoon's poetry confront the reader and form an impenetrable wall of references that she can never hope to fully grasp. As the aforementioned reviewers make clear, reading Muldoon's poetry and wading through its many elusive allusions is never a passive experience but instead alienating and unsettling. This becomes nowhere clearer than with the lists in the long poem "Incantata," an elegy from *Annals of Chile* that mourns the death of the artist Mary Farl Powers, Muldoon's former partner. "Incantata" opens with an invocation of Powers, which is made up of repeated second-person refrains ("I saw you again tonight"; "I remember your"; "I thought of you again") as the speaker attempts to summon her spirit by recounting memories of their shared life. Enraged by his fruitless efforts to revive Powers, the speaker explodes into an exclamation of "self-opprobrium" that spurs a list of "all that's left" of the relationship that continues to the end of the poem:

> . . . that potato-mouth; that mouth as prim
> and proper as it's full of self-opprobrium,
> with its '*quaquaqua*,' with its 'Quoiquoiquoiqoiquoiqoiquoiq.'
> That's all that's left of the voice of Enrico Caruso
> from all that's left of an opera-house somewhere in Matto
>   Grosso,
> all that's left of the hogweed and horehound and cuckoo-pint,
> of the eighteen soldiers dead at Warrenpoint . . .[72]

Like Muldoon's other poetry, "Incantata" crams within a tight space an overwhelming assortment of references, ranging from the cultural (early-twentieth-century Italian opera) to the historical (the Warrenpoint ambush was the British army's greatest number of casualties in a single incident during the Troubles). The recurring image of the "potato-mouth," Muldoon's figure for the poet's voice, facilitates the transhemispheric movement between Ireland and South America that the poet earlier describes: "I wanted the mouth in this potato-cut / to be heard far beyond the leaden, rain-glazed roofs of Quito, / to be heard all the way from the southern hemisphere to Clontarf or Clondalkin, / to wherever your sweet-severe spirit might still find a toe-hold in this world."[73] Nonetheless, a sense of futility plagues the poem as Muldoon recognizes that the elegy is ultimately a failed desire to conjure the spirit of Powers, who herself would be "aghast at the thought of my thinking you were some kind of ghost who might still roam the earth." (The "*quaquaqua*," an allusion to Beckett's *How It Is*, further underscores the feelings of futility.) While the list builds with Muldoon's poetic virtuosity and amasses a procession of shared memories, it nonetheless centers around an absence: the abundance of detailed memories documents the rich "plentitude" of their relationship but is ultimately a catalog of all that is now lost. Indeed, Muldoon's image of the potato-mouth recalls the Whitmanian "I" that congeals its multitudinous lists, but with a twist: in "Incantata," the poetic voice is not a container of multitudes but rather marks a void of "all that's left."

In fact, the sheer volume of memories better registers the speaker's grief than the individual memories do themselves. The elegy's poignancy is achieved more so by the list's anaphoric structure (which stretches over twenty stanzas and 160 lines) than by any of the particular references within it. Sianne Ngai argues that the rhythmic pattern in anaphora creates a feeling of senseless repetition and atonal "noise," which produces a "hum" that escapes language: "The anaphorization of speech foreground[s] repetition *over* substitution and sonority *over* semantics, culminating in a 'hum' reconfiguring feeling in excess of the terms in which it has initially been transacted."[74] In other words, anaphora foregrounds the phonic over the semantic, sound over content, and in so doing produces that "hum" that encodes inarticulable feelings. In "Incantata," Muldoon welds together both the form of the list and anaphora, coalescing the assorted items ("hogweed and horehound and cuckoo-pint" and "oxslips and cowslips") into an incomprehensible tidal wave of references that threatens to drown the reader. At moments, the poem's hum is even rendered as incoherent babble—"*quaquaqua*" and "Quoiquoiquoiqoiquoiqoiquoiq"—that signifies the inarticulable sounds of grief stammered by the potato-mouth.

In keeping with Muldoon's other poems, "Incantata" compresses a variety of locales and cultures in lists that span only a stanza or even just a single line. With no geographic or historical continuity, the list's rapid succession of different locations never allows the reader to comfortably inhabit a single space as one could in other genres of writing like travel writing or ethnography. Ramazani categorizes such literature as "traveling poetry," which is distinguished from other forms of transnational poetry by its condensed style that "eschews density of social detail, resists translation, interrupts mimesis, meditates on its linguistic surface, and fractures the spatiotemporal passage from one 'zone' to another."[75] The traveling poem "interrupts mimesis" or, in other words, prevents the fulfillment of representation. Even the most dutiful reader can never fully absorb the cultural or historical references in a poem like "Incantata" but instead remains suspended on the poem's "linguistic surface." Muldoon's purposeful superficiality ensures that "Incantata" does not act as native informant for the reader, initiating her into a new culture or space, but instead repels her and compels her to float only on its surface. The purpose of such "noise" and "superficiality" is not to flatten the differences among the items in the lists in "Incantata"—to somehow equate Quito with Clontarf, or the massacre at Warrenpoint with Italian opera. While the list's paratactic structure certainly invites comparisons among its varied objects, it is predicated on a relationship of proximity and not equivalence. Parataxis omits an explicit organizational principle and can facilitate multiple venues of connection and meaning, leaving the reader to deduce their relationships. The lists in Muldoon's poetry dance between conjunction and disjunction. On the one hand, they follow the procedural forms of the alphabet, calendar, and sestina; on the other, they confound any attempts at order, and the speaker of "Incantata" even warns against the "daft urge to . . . make sense of the clutter / of false trails."[76]

Muldoon's strategies compel relations among the most unrelatable of things and, in doing so, test the possibilities and limitations of poetic comparison. As his purported difficulty makes clear, Muldoon refuses to act as a cultural broker to the reader, but he stops short of a flat-out refusal of comparison. While he discourages any attempts to make sense of the "clutter" in "Incantata," the poem's many "false trails" nonetheless return to a single origin: the "potato-mouth," or poet's voice, which is all that remains of the life shared between Powers and the speaker and which grounds the disjointed items in the poem's lists. Muldoon treads a delicate line in his poetry, which resists the reader's comprehension with its impenetrable references and yet also offers the possibility of comparison.

V.

As stated previously, this chapter seeks neither to condemn the poet's work nor to brush aside his troubling instances of cultural and racial appropriation. Muldoon is well aware of the murky lines between love and thievery; he recognizes that "these analogies are true only for a moment, for an instant. And if one tries to extend them one runs into trouble."[77] As I have tried to demonstrate, there are moments when Muldoon's traveling poems offer formal strategies for representing an increasingly globalized and interconnected world; there are also times when, despite his moments of clarity and self-awareness, the poet runs into trouble with his engagement with Native American "material."

I conclude by viewing Muldoon's comparative poetics from the vantage point of the present and highlighting how his poetry registers a particular historical moment of Irish political and cultural identity. As discussed earlier, the poet's work can be placed within a wider critical tendency in Irish studies to emphasize the shared experiences of imperial oppression and anticolonial resistance between Ireland and other nations in the Global South, particularly in Africa and Asia. In fact, John Brannigan argues that these kinds of cross-cultural and cross-racial comparisons were at the foundation of Irish studies when it was being cemented as an institutional discipline in the 1980s and 1990s, particularly in germinal scholarly works like C. L Innes's *The Devil's Own Mirror*, the Centre for Research and Documentation's *Is Ireland a Third World Country?*, and Seamus Deane's *The Field Day Anthology of Irish Writing*.[78] But as Ireland proves to be more and more comfortably absorbed within (and perhaps even a leading nation of) a twenty-first-century neoliberal world order, there is increasing unease in studying contemporary Irish society and culture under the comparative frameworks of postcolonial theory that were foundational to Irish studies in its nascent years. Such analytical lenses seemed more appropriate then, when Ireland was still a struggling economy on the fringes of Western Europe and mired in a seemingly unceasing sectarian conflict. But as Renée Fox, Mike Cronin, and Brian Ó Conchubhair write in their editorial introduction to *The Routledge International Handbook of Irish Studies*, these kinds of comparative approaches now seem mismatched with the present realities of the Republic: "For Irish Studies, a fairly parochial discipline whose primary theoretical foundation rested on the insistence that Ireland be numbered among the immiserated victims of European colonialism despite its outsized cultural influence, an Ireland at the forefront of globalized capital would clearly require a new set of critical frameworks."[79] In short, the continued comparisons between Ireland and nations of the Global South are at best embarrassing and at worst a willful oversight of Ireland's own privileges as an Anglophone and relatively affluent country in the EU. The field's need for different critical frameworks has simultaneously been exacerbated by recent economic and political pressures within academia, leading to the closure of Irish studies programs and the rightful prioritization of resources to critical race and ethnic studies programs. As the editors put the question, "how might Irish Studies learn to accommodate the demands of an academy in which shrinking humanities enrollments and increasing attentiveness to the cultural productions and needs of underrepresented populations made conventional approaches to teaching Irish literature and history seem out of touch?"

Again, the purpose of this chapter is not to blow the whistle on the outdatedness of Muldoon's poetry, which would be not only ungenerous but also foolishly presentist. Rather, an analysis of Muldoon's work helps illuminate a tension animating Irish studies today—one seen in the aforementioned editorial introduction and in the many other calls for a "new Irish studies" that can take into account the geopolitics and lived experiences of a post–Celtic Tiger Ireland.[80] On the one hand, the previous modes of comparison are no longer viable (if they ever were in the first place). And yet this is precisely a moment when Irish studies is poised to rethink Ireland's position on the global stage today and its relationships with other parts of the world, whether in its new role within the EU after Brexit or in its treatment of asylum seekers through the direct provision system. How does one move beyond the previous modes of cross-cultural comparison without retreating into insularity?

Muldoon's comparative poetics offer one model of thinking through and living with, rather than resolving, this tension. Rather than proffering seamless analogies between different cultures, Muldoon uses conceit to forefront the difficulty of forging comparisons, especially across different peoples and places around the world. Conceit does not facilitate an easy transferability but instead highlights the seams and cracks at which a join is made. It claims to produce not parallels or correspondences but rather "striking" and provisional juxtapositions. In this way, Muldoon's poetry makes things comparable without making them commensurable, and invites us to imagine forms of solidarity that do not rely only on shared experiences.

Coda

Race, Place, and the Grounds of Irish Geopolitics

I.

In 2019, Donald Trump visited Ireland for the first time during his presidency. The brief stopover was little more than an opportunity for Trump to stay at his hotel and golf resort in County Clare at the start of his European tour, but it nonetheless sparked a frenzy of media attention and protests across Ireland. At Shannon Airport, Trump held a press conference with a visibly tense Taoiseach Leo Varadkar and quickly stumbled into a major gaffe when the conversation drifted to Ireland and Brexit. "I think [Brexit] will all work out very well, and also for your wall, your border. I mean, we have a border situation in the United States, and you have one over here," Trump said, "but I hear it's going to work out very well here." A journalist reported that there was a collective gasp in the room at the mention of "your wall, your border," and Varadkar took a steadying pause before gently qualifying the president's comparison of the US-Mexico border and the border between Northern Ireland and the Republic. With a taut smile, the Taoiseach politely interjected, "The main thing we want to avoid, of course, is a border or a wall between both sides."

Trump's blunder was widely reported in both US and Irish media and seen as yet further evidence of his extraordinary cluelessness in foreign affairs. After all, one of the great threats of Brexit is the possible return of a "hard border" between Northern Ireland and the Republic, which is now the only land border between the UK and the EU. New customs checkpoints and other border infrastructure could become potential targets for sectarian violence and threaten the hard-earned peace of the Belfast Agreement. (The alternative to a land border, the establishment of a trade border in the Irish Sea, has still fueled outrage among Unionists.) Although Trump scratched at old and deep political wounds, his misstep was seen as an unfortunate faux pas that just happened to occur on Irish soil.

But a closer look at the slipup reveals the more complicated story of contemporary Irish geopolitics. Trump's acquisition of the County Clare golf resort was an aftereffect of the Celtic Tiger's collapse: the original golf course closed as a result of the economic downturn, and Trump purchased the property at a steep discount in 2012. Two years later, Trump's company filed a petition to build seawalls to protect the resort from coastal erosion, but environmentalists successfully blocked their construction, which would have destroyed local ecosystems. (The media quickly pointed out the irony that the resort's petition cited rising sea levels and extreme storms as potential environmental threats as meanwhile Trump dismissed climate change as a hoax and withdrew the US from the Paris Agreement.) During his tour through Europe, Trump brought up the Irish resort dispute several times, calling it a "classic example of EU bureaucracy," nothing more than "environmental tricks," and an altogether "very bad experience."[1] (Some journalists even credit the dispute for sparking Trump's aversion to the EU and pro-Brexit stance.)[2] Because the controversy unfolded as Trump was campaigning on the promise of constructing a wall along the US-Mexico border, the proposed seawalls were jokingly referenced in the media and by protestors as "Trump's Irish wall."[3] What's more, Varadkar's restraint during the press conference was not simply an example of international diplomacy but a calculated decision: at the time, the Irish government had been lobbying for access to the E3 visa program, which is seen as a potential pathway toward legal status for the estimated fifty thousand undocumented Irish immigrants living in the US. If there had been any doubt before about the racism driving the Trump administration's anti-immigrant policies, it should be extinguished by the president's open support of a bill granting work visas to undocumented Irish immigrants.

This seemingly accidental gaffe reveals the global web of political, environmental, and race relations that underwrites Irish geopolitics today: the ethnonationalism that deems some people "undocumented" but worthy of citizenship and others "illegal" and always "alien"; the battle between environmentalists and multinational corporations over a small stretch of coastal landscape; a world seemingly linked together by a matrix of borders and walls. What's also revealed, as my book has argued, is the enduring centrality of place in the imagining of Irish political identity, whether in the language of "hard borders" and "Irish walls" or the territorial contentions of who does and does not count as a citizen. The previous chapters of this book have contended that the processes of globalization are integral to the story of contemporary Ireland. For my coda, I veer my attention in a different, albeit related, direction, tracing how the relationships between race and place have been and will continue to be crucial to Ireland's geopolitical identity.

In so doing, this conclusion eschews the usual protocols of codas by acting not as the closing words of an argument but as a missive to the future, working in concert with emergent conversations in Irish studies scholarship and opening up questions about Irish poetry, race, and place for current and new generations of scholars to explore. Ireland is far from impervious to the resurgent waves of ethnonationalism and white supremacy sweeping across the globe but instead is often located in the eye of this maelstrom. In the US, white supremacist groups have frequently weaponized Irish history and culture to attack the legitimacy of institutional racism. As a response to the Movement for Black Lives, memes about the myth of "Irish slavery" (a gross equivalence made between Irish indentured servitude and chattel slavery) circulated widely on the internet as a way of undermining calls for reparations.[4] At the same time, J. D. Vance's memoir *Hillbilly Elegy* topped bestseller lists and was touted as an insider's guidebook to understanding the white underclass that fueled Trump's presidential campaign. The book rests on a thinly veiled theory of racial determinism about the Appalachian "Scots-Irish," whose racial temperament (and not racism) supposedly drove them to vote for Trump.[5] These recent mythologizations of Irish history are preceded by older co-optations of Irish ethnicity, such as the Stormfront website's adoption of the Celtic cross as its logo (now a popular and more covert insignia of white supremacy). As such examples show, Irishness has become a code for whiteness in a more "politically correct" US; by serving such a function, Diane Negra argues, "concepts of Irish whiteness play a particular part in what Ghassan Hage has termed 'the psychopathology of white decline,' the terror that whiteness in America is losing its social purchase."[6] Much has been said about how the consumers of what we call Irish culture and literature come from outside the island of Ireland. It is perhaps time to also think about how they have been weaponized.

Nor has the Republic been immune to the resurgence of ethnonationalism in the new millennium. The 2004 and 2018 Irish referendums—arguably the most significant constitutional amendments in the twenty-first century so far—have centered around the control of racialized and gendered bodies. Man Levette Chen was a Chinese migrant who gave birth to a daughter in Belfast and petitioned to apply for Irish and EU citizenship. Amid a swell of xenophobic panic, her case was tried in the EU Court of Justice and pivotal to the campaign for the 2004 Citizenship Referendum, which changed the very basis of Irish citizenship laws. (Later in this coda, I will delve further into the history and long-term consequences of the Citizenship Referendum.) More than a decade later in 2012, Savita Halappanavar, an Indian dentist living in Galway, died from a septic miscarriage after being refused an abortion; her death spurred the Repeal the 8th movement, which successfully legalized abortion in the Republic. Such events painfully underscore both the precarity and centrality of women of color in contemporary Irish history, even while they are often erased from these narratives.

While many scholars have paved the way in bringing together critical race studies and Irish studies, there remains much more work to be done in examining race in modern and contemporary Irish literature.[7] As I argued in the preceding chapter, in the past Irish studies scholars have often brushed off racism in Irish history and culture as the unfortunate by-products of imperial ideologies, and their critical attention focused on the racialization of the Irish as nonwhite others within British imperial rhetoric. Such scholarship has promulgated problematic comparisons between the experiences of the Irish and oppressed communities of color, allowing Irish subjects to claim victimhood while ignoring the history of Irish participation in settler colonialism and racist violence, particularly in North America. This coda therefore revisits the stakes and relevance of Irish studies at a specific historical moment. As a discipline, Irish studies has long meditated on ethnoreligious sectarianism, emigration, and diaspora—questions that find themselves rekindled with pressing urgency in the current moment, as demonstrated by the proliferation of recent calls for a "new Irish studies." How might the field offer a unique and valuable perspective to these pressing conversations around xenophobia and anti-immigrant rhetoric and policies? How can we rethink how Irish studies understands race, participates in whiteness, and intervenes in contemporary politics?

Such questions warrant more than a brief coda, of course, and point to my own book's blind spots. But in acknowledging my project's limitations, I hope to point toward new avenues of investigation that might shape scholarship in the field yet to come. In what follows, I first track the spatial motifs—particularly the rhetoric of "soil"—that have underlain discussions around race, nation, and citizenship in Irish history, from the nineteenth century to the present. Then, as a way of suggesting the new insights afforded by this perspective, I take up as a literary case study Seamus Heaney's famed bog poems, which were inspired by the archaeological excavations of bogs across North Atlantic Europe. Despite the centrality of soil and kinship in these poems' archaeological and genealogical allusions, Heaney's work is rarely studied in relation to race.[8] I show how an interpretive account that considers the racial discourse around place draws attention to details of Heaney's poetry that critics have tended to ignore. As Dorothy Wang argues, in studies of poetry, questions of race are often subsumed under the umbrellas of the "cultural" and "political" and thereby are sidelined and remain uninterrogated: "Race seems to me the most salient, contested, and painfully charged social difference in the American context, and one that imbues—and must be disguised by—the more generic terms 'cultural' and 'political' when they are raised in opposition to the 'literary.'"[9] While Wang makes her incisive critique in the context of US poetry, her arguments help us see what is overlooked in criticism on contemporary Irish poetry (particularly Heaney's work), which has often been read against the backdrop of colonialism, decolonization, and partition but rarely race. What new insights might be revealed by situating Irish poetry within a framework that forefronts race?

Such a perspective helps us recognize the pervasive racist ideologies that have long percolated Irish cultural and political identity. Racism in Ireland is often seen as a solely contemporary phenomenon born during the Celtic Tiger. Certainly, during the boom period, there was a visible rise in violence against immigrants from Africa, China, and Eastern Europe. But it is dangerously misleading to understand racism in Ireland as the exclusive product of the Celtic Tiger—to see it, as John Brannigan wryly puts it, as having "arrived in the 1990s, as if on a flight from Lagos or Vilnius."[10] Instead, the recent attention on racism and xenophobia in the "new Ireland" must be situated within a longer genealogy of racial discourse in Irish political and cultural life. It is tempting to see racism in Ireland today as a mere hiccup in the growing pains of a hastily globalizing society, or to write it off as the regrettable but otherwise unrepresentative behavior of a reactionary minority. But instead we should understand how the contemporary moment emerges from a long lineage of racial ideologies that have underwritten the formation of the Irish state over the course of the nineteenth and twentieth centuries and that continue to endure in and shape the present. It would be an obvious distortion to draw a straight line between the racial ideologies of nineteenth-century Ireland to those of today; instead, I highlight pivotal moments when the constructions of Irish racial identity have been entangled with place, that most Irish of obsessions.

II.

The intimacies between race and place in Irish political discourse have a long history, stretching back to the plantation of Ireland in the sixteenth and seventeenth centuries. During the plantation era, the English distinguished the Irish as racially other on the basis of their supposedly innate inability to develop a productive and profitable agricultural economy. Of course, this conveniently rationalized the British conquest of Ireland, and as Steve Garner argues, "the drive to make Irish soil more productive lies at the heart of the English initiatives from the mid-sixteenth century."[11] Later, this idea of Irish unproductivity would also be used to link the Irish with other colonial subjects. David Lloyd argues that in the nineteenth century both Irish cottiers and the recently emancipated enslaved peoples in the West Indies were regarded as "surplus populations of the Empire" who lacked the capacity to cultivate the land. The "solution," proposed by nineteenth-century thinkers like John Stuart Mill, was to forcibly transform these populations into productive wage-laborers: "Security of tenure (a 'permanent interest in the soil') would . . . provide an inducement to labor discipline among the dispossessed. Thus the possessive individual was to be produced out of the former savage."[12] Central to the early racializations of the Irish was the perception of their unproductive relationship with the land, which in turn justified their dispossession.

But the Young Ireland movement subverted this colonial rhetoric of Irish unproductivity and dispossession and used it as an engine to campaign for Irish nationalism. The Young Irelanders capitalized on the practices of absentee landlordism (such as rack-renting and inefficient land management) to argue that Irish tenants had stronger claims to the land than did their negligent Anglo-Irish landlords. Dispossession—what had marked the Irish as racially inferior to the English—was mobilized by the Young Irelanders as the basis for their nationalist cause. As Sara Maurer argues, the Young Irelanders transformed the stain of Irish dispossession into a point of nationalist pride and even the basis of national identity itself. "[The Young Irelanders] imply that what the Irish do not have is what they are," Maurer explains, and in so doing, they have "fused Irish identity, Irish possession of the land, and even Irish dispossession from it into one irreducible bond."[13]

Of course, historians have long traced the import of "the land question" to Irish nationalism. But what is less emphasized is how relationship to land was also integral to the formation of Irish racial identity. There is a common perception that culture and not race forms the basis of Irish national identity in the nineteenth century. There is some truth to this claim, as the Young Irelanders did promulgate a cross-sectarian sense of nation that could supersede ethnic, religious, and class differences and include both Catholics and Protestants, Anglo-Irish landlords and tenant farmers. For the Young Irelanders, Irish national character is not inherited but rather forged through a shared culture, be it the Irish language, literature, or nationalist politics. This is readily apparent in the famed motto of the *Nation*, the weekly newspaper and political organ of the Young Ireland movement, which aimed "to create and foster public opinion in Ireland, and make it racy of the soil." The grammatical order is crucial to this formula of nationalism: one must first cultivate the proper "public opinion," which in turn is made "racy of the soil." In other words, culture precedes race. For the Young Irelanders, the nation is based on a reverse form of autochthony, in which a nationalist culture precedes and forges a connection between a people and the soil. This is readily apparent in the use of "foster," which suggests that a people severed from their ancestral forefathers could be "restored" to a new line of parentage.

But the language of fostering also brings up notions of biological kinship by implicitly suggesting that there once existed a coherent Irish racial lineage before it had been ruptured by British imperialism. And while the Young Irelanders were propagating an inclusive form of Irish national identity, they also exploited the Celtic-Saxon racial dichotomy that had been wielded against them, often relying on a narrative of the subjugated Celt struggling for liberation from oppressive Saxon reign.[14] Moreover, the Young Irelanders' utopian project of creating a national identity outside all ethnoreligious difference is part of a larger racial and imperial regime that idealizes a universal and "unmarked" subject, what Lloyd calls the "Subject without properties," which is "constitutively unavailable or barred to the racialized subject" and also "the philosophical figure for what becomes, with increasing literalness through the nineteenth century, the global ubiquity of the white European."[15]

To be made "racy of the soil," then, is no clear task. The *Nation*'s motto suggests how racial and cultural constructions of Irish identity cannot be easily separated, as well as how the rhetoric of soil has been central to the racial discourses underpinning Irish nationalism. Seamus Deane explains that the term "soil" carried specific political valences in nineteenth-century Ireland: whereas "land" connoted the legal realm of property rights and tenancy laws, "soil" implied more romantic notions of place-attachment and an even umbilical connection between the Irish and Ireland. James Fintan Lalor makes clear this distinction when he dismisses the abstraction of land in favor of soil in his celebrated clarion call for "Ireland her own—Ireland her own, and all therein, from the sod to the sky. The soil of Ireland for the people of Ireland, to have and to hold from God alone who gave it—to have and to hold to them and their heirs forever." For Lalor, who was arguing against what he saw as the shortsightedness of the Repeal movement, such inalienable rights to the soil are not to be confused with the "mock freedom" of land rights promised by "constitutions, and charters" whose substance is mere "paper and parchment."[16] While previous systems of communal land ownership had been irrevocably corrupted by British proprietary laws, the connection with soil remained unspoiled and therefore could form a viable basis of Irish national identity. As Deane argues, "[Lalor] appeals to the power of the distinction between soil as a material-metaphysical possession and land as a political-legal entity. The nation is of the soil; the state of the land."[17] In this way, the rhetoric of soil acts as a shorthand for the fusion of national identity and land.

Lalor's vision of "the soil of Ireland for the people of Ireland" would reemerge, albeit in transformed form, in Eamon de Valera's St. Patrick's Day radio speech in 1932. Taking office just weeks after a close general election and in a country still healing from the wounds of civil war and partition, de Valera sought to regain some semblance of stability and unity in his speech. Adding to the challenge was the far-reaching audience of de Valera's radio speech, which was simultaneously broadcasted in the Irish Free State and the US. De Valera acknowledges the geographic breadth of the Irish diaspora, the "vastness of the country in which so many of the children of our race have found a home and the magnitude of the dispersion of our people."[18] Addressing his far-flung audience, de Valera repeats Lalor's aforementioned words as the governing precept of the newly elected Fianna Fáil party, explaining that "I know no words in which I can express [the aims of government] better than those of Fintan Lalor." In Lalor's original formulation, the language of sod, sky, and soil belonging to the Irish and "their heirs" was used to challenge systems of British property laws and to articulate more radical forms of land reform. But in a radio speech directed toward the Irish diasporic community, or the "children of our race," de Valera projects the image of Ireland as a racially homogenous, if geographically scattered, people held together by their divine right to the soil of Ireland. In so doing, de Valera affirms the Irish as a racially cohesive community that can sustain the recent blows to Irish national sovereignty and also bridge the geographic expanse of diaspora. As Brannigan argues, "the touchstones of de Valera's nationalism are in these key words, 'soil,' 'people,' and 'God,' and in the relationship between them in which the convergent soil and people hold their sovereignty forever as the gift of God."[19] While Lalor and the Young Irelanders may have articulated conflicting conceptualizations of Irish national identity, under de Valera's vision the rhetoric of soil became resolutely synonymous with a racialized Irish identity.

The rhetoric of soil has more recently resurfaced with the 2004 Citizenship Referendum, which rescinded *jus soli* ("rights of the soil") nationality laws that granted automatic citizenship to any person born in Ireland. Replacing birthright citizenship laws was the policy of *jus sanguinis* ("rights of the blood"), which dictates that citizenship is determined by the nationality of one's parents. At first glance, the Citizenship Referendum seems incongruent with conceptions of Irish identity that strongly tie people and territory together; as Bernard Ryan argues, the "emphasis on *jus soli* in Irish law, and its application to both the Irish state and Northern Ireland, reflects an underlying territorial understanding of who the Irish are in the first place."[20] Birthright citizenship had existed in Ireland since the establishment of the Free State in 1922, was codified in the Irish Nationality and Citizenship Act in 1935, and was later enshrined in the constitution in 1937 and again in the Belfast Agreement in 1998. (In fact, up until the referendum, Ireland was the last remaining country in Europe with nationality laws based on *jus soli*.)[21] The campaign for the Citizenship Referendum was fueled by racist and xenophobic panics over so-called "birth tourism" and the arrival of refugees and asylum seekers during the Celtic Tiger. (The perceived exploitation of Ireland's citizenship laws was hugely overblown. According to a study, births to non-EU national mothers constituted less than 2.4 percent of total births at Dublin's three major maternity hospitals in 2003.)[22] Passed with a landslide by nearly 80 percent of the electorate, the Citizenship Referendum reflected a startling change in the conception of Irish nationality. In the Dáil Éireann debate on the referendum, the then minister of justice Michael McDowell argued that Ireland's birthright citizenship laws were being exploited by "persons with no tangible link to the nation or the state whether of parentage, upbringing or of long-term residence in the state."[23] In other words, the "tangible link" between the Irish citizen and the nation is no longer the shared soil of Ireland but instead race.[24] (The racialization of Irish citizenship is further underscored by current nationality laws, which allow up to third-generation emigrants to claim citizenship.)

On the surface, the Citizenship Referendum seems to contradict the historically territorial conceptions of Irish national identity. But the referendum is less surprising and more a logical outcome when examined as part of the shifting relationship between race and place in modern and contemporary Ireland. As de Valera's speech makes clear, the rhetoric of soil has also been used as a means to connect the globally dispersed Irish diaspora. Over the 1990s, the concept of the Irish diaspora gained currency in political spheres, popularized first by Mary Robinson during her presidency. In her oft-quoted 1995 Oireachtas address, Robinson championed the diaspora as the cornerstone of Irish identity, asserting that "Irishness is not simply territorial. In fact Irishness as a concept . . . can be strengthened again if we turn with open minds and hearts to the array of people outside Ireland for whom this island is a place of origin."[25] But while Robinson and her successors may have stressed the diversity of the Irish diaspora, they also unwittingly helped lay the groundwork for the Citizenship Referendum in the following decade. As Ronit Lentin argues, by redefining Irish identity in terms of bloodline rather than territory, the redefinition of Ireland as a "diaspora nation" facilitated the erosion of *jus soli* in favor of that of *jus sanguinis*.[26] That is to say, the propagation of the Irish diaspora simultaneously fostered a globalized sense of Irish identity and helped solidify Ireland as a racial state. Such deterritorialized notions of the "global Irish family" (President Mary McAleese's favorite term for the diaspora) may seem to encourage liberal viewpoints that would negate nativism and xenophobia. But far from an antidote to ethnonationalism, the globalizing of Irish identity instead often came hand in hand with its racialization.[27]

III.

As this complicated history shows, the rhetoric of soil has provided not so much a stable ground for Irish identity as a fungible trope yoked to different ends. Given, then, the looming presence of landscape in the Irish literary and political imagination, how do the complex relations between race and place manifest in Irish poetry? I make modest steps toward a response by turning to an unlikely archive: the bog poems of Seamus Heaney, which take as their central figure the excavated bodies of Iron Age Vikings discovered across Northern Europe. Even though there is ample scholarship on these poems, few critics have mined their racial underpinnings despite the abundant allusions to archaeology and prehistoric geography, fields of study that have been pivotal to contemporary conceptions of Irish racial identity.[28] Such an oversight stems from several things. First, Heaney frequently turns to Viking histories and mythologies, which are often coded as white and seen as "pre-racial."[29] But more importantly, there is a presiding presumption that race in Ireland is a recent product, born during the Tiger and "imported" from outside. Such assumptions obscure how a major writer like Heaney, considered the poetic spokesperson of Ireland and writing at an earlier moment of history, was deeply interested in questions of race. If my coda so far has outlined how tropes of place are entrenched in Irish racial formation, I conclude by highlighting how that relation has often been obfuscated in Irish cultural criticism, even when it is explicit. That Heaney's work is not thought of in relation to race—even while he so clearly mobilizes tropes of soil, tribalism, ancestry, and kinship—shows how whiteness remains invisible in (and therefore reproduced by) Irish studies scholarship today. It is nothing new to say that Heaney understands Irish identity as rooted in place. But how might we analyze the discourses of indigeneity and nativism underlying Heaney's infamous bog poems as specifically racial discourses?

While the bog poems crop up throughout the poet's early and midcareer collections, they are most closely associated with *North*, in which the landscape is figured as a natal source of life. Heaney flanks the collection's central section with two poems about Antaeus, the Greek deity who was the son of Gaia and who gathered his strength through contact with the earth. In the opening poem, Antaeus declares, "I cannot be weaned / Off the earth's long contour, her river-veins . . . / I am cradled in the dark that wombed me / And nurtured in every artery / Like a small hillock."[30] But in the closing poem, the autochthonous Antaeus is "weaned at last" and defeated by Hercules, who lifts the god off the ground and rips him from the earth's "cradling dark" and "hatching grounds / of cave and souterrain."[31] Antaeus is mourned by "elegists" alongside other defeated heroes like Balor (the Irish god-king killed by the Tuatha Dé Danann), Byrthnoth (the Anglo-Saxon earl who died at the hands of Viking raiders), and Sitting Bull (the Hunkpapa Lakota chief murdered by Indian agency police). By evoking these mythic and historic figures, Heaney imagines a tradition of indigenous heroes who were defeated by and lost their lands to "invading forces," and in so doing portrays the Troubles as part of a similar history of dispossession. Like the Young Irelanders, Heaney implies that Irish identity is defined by both an intimate relationship to the land and dispossession from it.

While many scholars have explored the transhistorical dimensions of these poems' archaeological motifs, few have explored their racial implications despite the frequent references to ancient "origins" and indigeneity. (We should note the previous poem's reference to "souterrain," or the Iron Age underground structure thought to have been brought to Ireland and Scotland by the Gauls. Such an archaeological allusion further demonstrates how Heaney intentionally looks to the prehistoric European Atlantic as a source of Irish indigeneity, even in his poems of Classical mythology.) Such an oversight is conspicuous given the prominent role that archaeological and genealogical projects have played in cultivating a racialized sense of Irish identity. As Catherine Nash argues, the racialization of Irish identity was heavily influenced by the country's subsidization of anthropological and population genetics studies, such as the Harvard Irish Survey. Although conversations around "natives" and "non-natives," "settlements" and "invasions," have roots stretching back to eighteenth-century antiquarianism, interpretations of prehistoric geography have continued to inform theoretical perspectives in contemporary Irish historiography. As Nash argues, such geographic imaginations of prehistoric origins have not only lingered in the academy but also "disseminate[d] into the public culture of ethnic identification and the making of ethnic distinction."³² Heaney himself was not immune to the popularity of anthropological archaeology, and in various interviews the poet recounts his frequent visits to the Viking exhibitions at the National Museum in Dublin and to excavation sites in Denmark in the 1960s and 1970s.³³

How, then, might we read the archaeological imagery in Heaney's poems as more than just figurative? We can begin with "Kinship," which opens:

> Kinned by hieroglyphic
> peat on a spreadfield
> to the strangled victim,
> the love-nest in the bracken,
> I step through origins
> like dog turning its memories of wilderness
> on the kitchen mat . . . .³⁴

The poem animates a motif that recurs throughout the work of Heaney, who depicts the Irish landscape as an infinite repository of history that yields to the archaeologist's (or poet's) touch. The bog is "hieroglyphic peat" that is readily deciphered and acts as a storehouse of Ireland's ancient past ("Earth-pantry / bone-vault, /sun-bank, embalmer / of votive goods / and sabred fugitives"). Moreover, its unique preserving qualities work like a topographic time machine through which the speaker can "step through origins" and retrieve "memories of wilderness." Scholars have usually understood "kinship" in the looser senses of the word, reading the poem as a reflection on the paralleled histories of violence in the Iron Age and the Troubles. For instance, Heather O'Donoghue explains that the poem "recognize[s] our kinship with an otherwise strange and distant past" and "makes explicit the link between Ireland and . . . Scandinavia."³⁵ But we might also read "kinship" as denoting blood relation; seen from this more literal reading, the poem emphasizes instead a "kinned" or racial relation between the speaker and the ancestral "strangled victim" that is forged through a common bond to the "hieroglyphic peat." In other words, the bog operates not so much as the grounds of comparison as the grounds of racial ancestry.

Such a rereading brings to light the themes of descent and heritage depicted in Heaney's other bog poems, such as "Belderg," which is set in the Céide Fields, the largest Neolithic site in Ireland and one of the oldest field systems in the world. The poem comprises a conversation with a local turf cutter–turned–archaeologist, who unearthed the ancient farmlands when he "stripped off blanket bog" to reveal a "landscape fossilized." (The poem's interlocutor is modeled after Patrick Caulfield, a schoolteacher who originally discovered the site when cutting turf in the 1930s. Inspired by his visit with Caulfield, Heaney wrote "Belderg" and enclosed the poem along with a thank-you note to him.) The poem opens with the initial misidentification of the quernstones and other artifacts at Céide: " 'They just kept turning up / And were thought of as foreign.' "[36] While the archaeologist does correct the misclassification of the quernstones, the confusion over their perceived "foreignness" is telling, raising questions about who counts as "native" or "non-native" in Ireland's early history. The speaker (a stand-in for Heaney) and archaeologist articulate two competing interpretations of Ireland's prehistoric geography. On the one hand, the speaker underscores the dual, "mutable" etymologies that make up Mossbawn (the name of Heaney's childhood farm), describing his heritage as a "forked root" made up of different lineages, whether that of the "English fort" or of the Irish "sanctuary." For him, it is up to the poet to decide which to emphasize: "I could derive / A forked root from that ground, / Make *bawn* an English fort, / A planter's walled-in mound, / Or else find sanctuary / And think of it as Irish." But the archaeologist pushes against this "mutable" interpretation and asks about the "older strains of Norse" that also make up Mossbawn's etymology. He questions, " 'But *moss*?' " and later again, " 'But the Norse ring on your tree?' " (The word "mose" comes from the Danish and Icelandic words for "bog.")[37] More than simply insisting on the speaker's Norse heritage ("the Norse ring on your tree"), the archaeologist conceives of a different vision of history as tree rings, as a "congruence of lives" and shared timeline of the "iron, flint, and bronze" ages. In other words, the poem proposes the possibility of not an analogous but a genealogical relationship between the Norse and the Irish.

If this analysis seems unfair to Heaney, to read "too much" into his poetry, I should make clear that this reading is not designed to condemn his work as somehow covertly racist. In fact, Heaney's "Belderg" poem ends in a pluralistic if macabre vision of Ireland's racial past: the "world-tree" or Yggdrasil (the mythical tree in Norse cosmology), which gruesomely grinds and mixes together the vertebrae of Norse, English, and Irish cultures: "A world-tree of balanced stones, / Querns piled like vertebrae, / The marrow crushed to ground." As Henry Hart argues, the poem concludes with "the painful, cosmic revelation . . . in which Heaney envisions himself as no longer possessing an identity, but ground and mixed up in the warring factions of all history."[38] Rather than positing a racially "pure" conception of Irish identity, the poem concludes with an epiphany about its transnational pluralism. (Indeed, in her aforementioned presidential address, Mary Robinson specifically mentions the Céide Fields when she commends archaeologists and genealogists for bringing public awareness to the long history of migration in Ireland.) But at the same time, Heaney's poems of the soil nonetheless rely on a racially and territorially bound form of Irish identity. By depicting the bog as soft, yielding, and supple, Heaney not only casts the landscape as an archive of Irish history; he also suggests how it literally swallows all those who step foot on Ireland. (In one poem, Heaney describes the bog as an "Insatiable bride.")[39] Heaney seems to conceptualize another version of *jus soli*: to step foot on Ireland—and, more importantly, to be buried there—is to be Irish.

If the primary purpose of my reading of Heaney's bog poems has been to show how Irish cultural nationalism has been deeply tied together with place and race, then its secondary ambition is to show how that racial formation has been erased within Irish studies—and how that erasure itself conflates Irish culture with whiteness. Again, the purpose of this rereading is not to "reveal" an underlying racism in Heaney's poetry but rather to show how racial ideologies are naturalized and therefore go unexamined in the most canonical works of Irish literature. In part, my coda wishes to challenge some of the predominating narratives about Irish and race—namely that the Irish became white after waves of migrants arrived to the US beginning in the eighteenth century and assimilated by adopting brutal practices of racism and oppression against African Americans. While Noel Ignatiev's radical scholarship and activism continue to reverberate in meaningful and unfinished ways, I want to emphasize that Irish nationalist formations were never separated from race—not only because of British imperial ideologies that racialize the Irish but because the very idea of Irish cultural nationalism has always been intimately connected to race and place. In *Playing in the Dark*, Toni Morrison argues that "the readers of virtually all of American fiction have been positioned as white," and the consequence of this assumption is that instances of Black presence are marked as racial while figures of whiteness are "race-free" and therefore remain invisible.[40] I see an analogous situation at work in Irish studies today, where because race is associated exclusively with the "new Irish," something that has emerged only within the twenty-first century, we remain blind to how major works of Irish literature were already deeply invested in race. As I hope to have shown in this reading, it is not enough to tease out the submerged presences of race (which, as I argue, were never that hidden to begin with). Instead, in order to understand race in Irish culture and history, we must examine the instances where it is made explicit and where it is rendered invisible.

There is often an assumption that a turn to the global can remedy the foundations of nativism and xenophobia that are often at the root of racism. But as shown by my analyses of Heaney's poetry and the history of the Citizenship Referendum, a politics of global pluralism is by no means a guaranteed antidote. While Heaney may advance a more transnational understanding of Irish identity, his poetry nonetheless consolidates an understanding of Irish identity as white. And far from an antidote to ethnonationalism, the globalizing of Irish identity instead came hand in hand with its racialization as white. If the story of contemporary Ireland is incomplete without recognizing globalization, as *Poetics of the Local* argues, then it is also important to acknowledge that any study of global capitalism would be incomplete without reckoning race.

IV.

How then do we understand the place of Ireland in the world, particularly at a time when its global future seems so uncertain? Throughout this book, I have traced the ways that contemporary Irish poets have posed this question in varying forms and with varying responses. While none offer any straightforward answers or clear-cut solutions to globalization's displacements and other violences, they do provide a complex vocabulary of poetic genres, figures, and forms for understanding the turbulently changing landscape of Ireland in the late twentieth and twenty-first centuries. With *Poetics of the Local*, I hope to offer critical frameworks that demonstrate how Irish poetry has been and will continue to be shaped by the forces of globalization, which have dominated contemporary Irish geopolitics over the past four decades. And yet, while this book aims to show the deep entanglements between Irish poetry and global capitalism, I also hope to do more than chart a new periodization of Irish literary and cultural production. As scholars have long noted, Ireland's politico-economic networks have never been limited to its relationship with the UK, nor have Irish literature and culture ever been confined to the parameters of its national borders, despite the disproportionate attention given to the "nation question." As Irish literature becomes ever more entrenched in global capitalism over the post-Fordist era, it behooves Irish studies scholars to ask new questions—sociohistorical, formal, and ethical—of both its objects of study and their own critical frameworks.

One of the central questions in *Poetics of the Local* has revolved around the role of poetry in a developed global economy like Ireland's. Take as one final example the Global Irish Economic Forum (GIEF), an international Davos-style conference that was founded in response to the 2008 financial crisis and first held in 2009. As the minister of foreign affairs explained in his presidential address at the forum's inaugural meeting, the explicit purpose of the GIEF is to recruit members of the Irish diaspora ("the most influential members of the global Irish community with a record of high achievement in business and culture")[41] to contribute to efforts at economic recovery. Throughout the conference, participants strategized ways to leverage Irish culture to make the country more appealing to investors in a competitive global market. (Such messaging was widely reported in and amplified by media coverage of the event.) One telecoms CEO noted that Irish culture gives the nation a globally recognized cachet that sets it apart from other countries: "The fact that we have such a strong culture as a country really gives us one of the big advantages of any nation in the world."[42] Another tech billionaire reiterated with more candor, "We are famous for our writers, our artists, our poets and we are not famous for much else."[43] In an oft-quoted session, film director Neil Jordan went so far as to claim that while Ireland had been betrayed by its banking and real estate financiers, it had not been failed by its cultural industries, which "are perhaps the only success story that remains after the last twenty years."[44] Although such commentary may exaggerate the stature of cultural industries in post-crash Ireland, it has become commonplace to see literature and culture as some of the remaining "homegrown" commodities in an economy that primarily operates as a hub of foreign direct investment.[45] How then do we understand poetry as not just representing these neoliberal developments but also constitutive of them? Breda Gray argues that diaspora engagement initiatives like the GIEF create a new kind of citizen (what she terms "netizens") who show their allegiance to the state by "commit[ting] to the agenda of embedding Ireland in the global economy"; such organizations appeal to diasporic communities by promoting cultural and heritage projects that "foster 'a greater sense of identity and belonging within Irish communities and strengthen their links with Ireland.'"[46] Given that culture has become essential to discussions of Ireland's economic recovery and its sense of a globalized identity, scholars must focus on literature as not only representing or resisting processes of globalization but also imbricated within them.

This coda offers questions for further contemplation rather than any last words. But I make moves toward a conclusion by turning to Ciaran Carson's final collection, *Still Life*, which was published just a few days after his death in 2019 and gives a departing reflection on the relationship between poetry and place in a hurriedly changing country. *Still Life* comprises seventeen ekphrastic poems on works by artists ranging from Paul Cézanne to Diego Velázquez to Basil Blackshaw. What's notable about the artworks in Carson's ekphrastic poems is that they are not cloistered inside galleries and museums but instead located inside artists' studios and people's homes. (A couple were even in the poet's own possession.) The consequence is that the boundaries between artwork and the outside world are much hazier; a painting by Claude Monet, for example, is infused with the "high pollen count of a high summer's day" as the Impressionist paints *en plein air*. Ekphrasis therefore allows Carson the opportunity to meditate jointly on two of his lifelong obsessions: the poems blend together detailed descriptions of artwork (the term "ekphrasis" comes from the Greek word for "description"), which in turn spark memories of his life in Belfast. For instance, one of Yves Klein's blue monochrome paintings triggers memories of the now-decommissioned White Mountain quarry ("a cloud of limestone elevated in the intervallic blue above the mountain") as well as of the poet "lying on my back in the back garden of Mooreland Drive, gazing mesmerized into the blue," only for his reverie to be interrupted by the sound of distant gunfire ("Out of the blue as it were")—what he later learned were shots fired during Bloody Friday in 1972.[47] In other words, the borders between the painting and the world outside the canvas are blurred; as the poet is quick to remind us, "everything gets into the painting."[48] The same, he suggests, is true of poetry.

The collection's final poem takes as its subject a James Allen print of a Victorian house where Carson rented his first flat in Belfast. The poem seems to take aim at the growing pains of a city that was once more famous for its security checkpoints and bombed hotels and now instead is built up with luxury apartment complexes that would resemble a "newly excavated Ancient Roman villa, were [they] not so pristine in appearance." He wonders perplexedly, "when Belfast people started to dwell in 'apartments.' / What happened to 'flat'?"[49] Carson's poem seems to return us to the predicament that opened *Poetics of the Local*: the persistent centrality of place in contemporary Irish poetry can easily lapse into conservative forms of nostalgia that are even more dangerously charged in a city like Belfast, which purports to be "post-conflict" but has yet to remedy its still-seething problems of segregation, class inequity, and tensions between ethnoreligious groups. But Carson does not so much bitterly grumble about the development of Belfast into a global city robbed of its local linguistic and architectural textures as adopt a tongue-in-cheek attitude about the ironies of the urban revitalization plans dominating the present "Peace Era": "But no matter. The day has been showery, with windows / Of sunshine, one of which has just appeared, so off we go to view the progress / Of the new whatever you might call them. Significant development!"

Instead, Carson focuses on the disjuncture between the world contained within a work of art and the world that it purports to represent—the "real world as it was" versus "this print of it," as he puts it. While he emphasizes the historical links between place and poetry (he notes that the words "estate" and "stanza" share the same Latin root as *status*), Carson also acknowledges that it is neither possible nor desirable for poetry to perfectly document the world. Quoting Wittgenstein, he questions, "'Is it even always an advantage / To replace an indistinct picture by a sharp one? Isn't the / indistinct one often exactly what we need?'"[50] In a strange twist of events, Carson recounts how the house in Allen's painting has been demolished since he resided there but a replica of the original building now stands uncannily in its place: "A reproduction . . . now accommodates a First Trust Bank. 33 University Road, Belfast. / You can look it up on Google Street View, as I did just now. I'm comparing like with not quite like." The poem closes with one last parting vision from the poet:

> How I loved that old dilapidated flat! . . .
> And I loved the buzz of the one-bar electric heater as a
>   bus or a truck passed by,

> And I loved the big windows and whatever I could see
>   through them, be it cloudy or clear,
> And the way they trembled and thrilled to the sound of
>   the world beyond.⁵¹

The windows do not necessarily allow clear views onto the outside; contingent on the weather and clarity of the sky, they show "whatever I could see through them." As Carson suggests, poetry works not as a map but as an imperfect window quivering and reverberating with the tremors of the city outside. The same may be said of the works of poetry in this book, which act like tuning forks keyed to the vibrations of the world beyond their pages.

Notes

Introduction

1. Seamus Heaney, *Preoccupations* (New York: Farrar, Straus and Giroux, 1980), 207.

2. Doreen Massey, *Space, Place and Gender* (Minneapolis: University of Minnesota Press, 1994), 146.

3. For an overview of the many contestations over the definition of globalization, see: Paul Jay, *Global Matters: The Transnational Turn in Literary Studies* (Ithaca: Cornell University Press, 2010).

4. This book is indebted to the work of Irish studies scholars who have remedied the prior scholarly tendency to frame twentieth-century Irish history and culture exclusively within the parameters of Irish independence and subsequent Troubles. For scholarship centered in a primarily postcolonial studies framework, see: Joe Cleary, *Outrageous Fortune: Capital and Culture in Modern Ireland* (Dublin: Field Day, 2006); Eóin Flannery, *Ireland and Postcolonial Studies: Theory, Discourse, Utopia* (Basingstoke: Palgrave Macmillan, 2009); Kevin Kenny, ed., *Ireland and the British Empire* (Oxford: Oxford University Press, 2004). Since its publication and translation into English, Pascale Casanova's pioneering work remains a vital perspective on the status and position of Irish modernism within world literature; see: Casanova, "The Irish Paradigm," in *The World Republic of Letters*, trans. Malcolm DeBevoise (Cambridge: Harvard University Press, 2007). For more recent scholarship that takes a transnational approach to contemporary Irish history and culture, see: Joe Cleary, *The Irish Expatriate Novel in Late Capitalist Globalization* (Cambridge: Cambridge University Press, 2021); Seán Ó Riain, *The Rise and Fall of Ireland's Celtic Tiger: Liberalism, Boom and Bust* (Cambridge: Cambridge University Press, 2014); Amanda Tucker and Moira E. Casey, eds., *Where Motley Is Worn: Transnational Irish Literatures* (Cork: Cork University Press, 2014).

5. While the claim is debatable, since the late 1990s Ireland has often been touted as the most globalized country in the world by many economists,

who cite metrics such as the KOF's Globalisation Index. For a more detailed analysis of these metrics, see: Alex Dreher, Noel Gaston, Pim Martens, and Willem Jozef Meine Martens, *Measuring Globalisation: Gauging Its Consequences* (New York: Springer, 2008).

    6. David Harvey, "Globalization and the 'Spatial Fix,'" *geographische revue* 2 (2001): 24.

    7. Anthony Giddens, *The Consequences of Modernity* (Palo Alto: Stanford University Press, 1990), 64.

    8. Ursula Heise, *Sense of Place and Sense of Planet: The Environmental Imagination of the Global* (Oxford: Oxford University Press, 2008), 39.

    9. Modernist scholars' preoccupation with scale is an aftereffect of the (not so) new modernist studies, which Douglas Mao and Rebecca Walkowitz have framed as an attempt to broaden the field's narrow geographic and period boundaries. In a cluster of essays, Walkowitz offers a reappraisal of the "scale-attentive" scholarship generated since her and Mao's initial call for the new modernist studies. See: Mao and Walkowitz, "The New Modernist Studies," *PMLA* 123, no. 3 (2008): 737–48; Walkowitz, "After Close and Distant: Modernist Studies and the New Turn to Scale," *Modernism/modernity* Print Plus 3, no. 4 (2019), https://modernismmodernity.org/forums/what-scale-literary-object.

    10. Anna Tsing, *The Mushroom at the End of the World: On the Possibility of Life in Capitalist Ruins* (Princeton: Princeton University Press, 2015), 38.

    11. Thomas S. Davis and Nathan Hensley, "Scale and Form; or, What Was Global Modernism?" *Modernism/modernity* Print Plus 2, no. 4 (2018), https://modernismmodernity.org/forums/scale-and-form.

    12. Susan Stanford Friedman, *Planetary Modernisms: Provocations of Modernity across Time* (New York: Columbia University Press, 2015), 93.

    13. Elizabeth Butler Cullingford, "'Thinking of Her . . . as . . . Ireland': Yeats, Pearse, and Heaney," *Textual Practice* 4, no. 1 (1990): 1.

    14. Geraldine Pratt and Victoria Rosner, "Introduction: The Global and the Intimate," *Women's Studies Quarterly* 34, nos. 1 and 2 (2006): 16.

    15. Jahan Ramazani, *Poetry in a Global Age* (Chicago: University of Chicago Press, 2020), 53.

    16. Ramazani, *Poetry in a Global Age*, 58.

    17. Ramazani, *Poetry in a Global Age*, 74–5.

    18. Sinéad Morrissey, *Between Here and There* (Manchester: Carcanet Press, 2002), 13, emphasis mine.

    19. Andrew Weaver, "It is I: Robert Creely's Deictic Subjectivity and the Sublime Self," *Journal of Modern Literature* 41, no. 3 (2018): 80.

    20. For more analysis on this new generation of Northern Irish poets, see: Neal Alexander, "Remembering the Future: Poetry, Peace, and the Politics of Memory in Northern Ireland," *Textual Practice* 32, no. 1 (2018): 59–79; Gail McConnell, "No 'Replicas / Atone': Northern Irish Poetry after the Peace Process," *boundary 2* 45, no. 1 (2018): 201–29.

21. Aaron Kelly damningly criticizes what he sees as the empty rhetoric of "bourgeois reconciliation," which disguises the still unresolved class inequities left over from the Troubles: "The state-sponsored aspects of the Peace Process—extending British 'Third Way' capitalism westwards and the Celtic Tiger northwards through the promotion of private finance and the exclusion of the poor from public life—aim at establishing a wishy-washy and market-driven postmodern pluralism that actually serves to mask the real socioeconomic divides in our city that threaten ultimately to remove power from people completely." See: Kelly, "Geopolitical Eclipse: Culture and the Peace Process in Northern Ireland," *Third Text* 19, no. 5 (2005): 548.

22. Morrissey, *Between Here and There*, 14, emphases mine.

23. In an interview, Morrissey emphasizes that her poem "Tourism" gives an optimistic vision of the multiculturalism that tourists could bring to Northern Ireland: "I suppose the poem articulates a view of tourism as the great white hope of the future for Northern Ireland in a way. Not so much in the inherent superficiality of much tourism, but in the more basic fact of other people coming here. Northern Ireland is so narrow and parochial—the gene pool is small, nearly everyone is white. I want Northern Ireland to be far more multicultural than it is—to open itself to the broader world and the broader human community. It might put some of our tribal conflict in perspective." Quoted in: Elmer Kennedy-Andrews, *Writing Home: Poetry and Place in Northern Ireland, 1968–2008* (Cambridge: D. S. Brewer, 2008), 264.

24. This is not to paint a rosy portrait of race relations in Northern Ireland, which has been a hotbed of xenophobia and anti-immigrant sentiment in recent decades. Belfast has been labeled by various media outlets as the "hate capital of Europe" after a steady rise of racist attacks in the 2000s. For many scholars, the rise in racist violence is linked with the ethnoreligious sectarianism that had not been resolved by the Peace Process. For more, see: Michel Savaric, "Racism and Sectarianism in Northern Ireland," in *The Politics of Ethnic Diversity in the British Isles*, ed. Romain Garbaye and Pauline Schnapper (London: Palgrave Macmillan, 2014), 174–88; Chris Gilligan, *Northern Ireland and the Crisis of Anti-racism* (Manchester: Manchester University Press, 2018).

25. Ramazani, *Poetry in a Global Age*, 13–14.

26. In the wake of the Celtic Tiger's collapse, Irish studies scholars have analyzed Ireland's current economic crisis in the context of global neoliberalism. For a more expansive overlook of the state of Irish literature in the aftermath of the recession, see: Joe Cleary, "'Horseman, Pass By!': The Neoliberal World System and the Crisis in Irish Literature," special issue of *boundary 2* 45, no. 2 (2018): 135–79. For scholarship that analyzes the response of Irish novelists (particularly Sebastian Barry, Colum McCann, and Colm Tóibín) to the developments of the Celtic Tiger and subsequent banking crisis, see: Elizabeth Butler Cullingford, "American Dreams: Emigration or Exile in Contemporary Irish Fiction?" *Éire-Ireland* 49, nos. 3 and 4 (2014): 60–94; Mary McGlynn,

"Things Unexploded: The Calculus and Aesthetics of Risk in Two Post-Boom Irish Novels," *boundary 2* 45, no. 1 (2018): 181–200. However, these analyses all focus on the contemporary Irish novel, and there has yet to be a sustained analysis on Irish poetry and globalization.

27. Saskia Sassen, *Expulsions: Brutality and Complexity in the Global Economy* (Cambridge: Harvard University Press, 2014), 1–2.

28. Annie McClanahan, "Financialization," in *American Literature in Transition, 2000–2010*, ed. Rachel Greenwald Smith (Cambridge: Cambridge University Press, 2017), 252.

29. Jason Moore, *Capitalism in the Web of Life: Ecology and the Accumulation of Capital* (New York: Verso, 2015), 10–11.

30. Sharae Deckard, "World-Ecology and Ireland: The Neoliberal Ecological Regime," *Journal of World-Systems Research* 22, no. 1 (2016): 150. Deckard also argues that the environmental exploitation of Ireland continued well into the twentieth and twenty-first centuries as it transformed into a tax and pollution haven for US and European multinational corporations looking to take advantage of both its low corporate tax rates and its relatively lenient environmental regulations, especially after the Clean Air and Water Acts were passed in the US in the 1970s. See Deckard, "World-Ecology and Ireland," 155–8.

31. Kennedy-Andrews, *Writing Home*, 5.

32. David Lloyd, *Anomalous States: Irish Writing and the Post-colonial Moment* (Durham: Duke University Press, 1993), 20–21.

33. Declan Kiberd, "After Ireland?," *The Irish Times*, August 29, 2009, https://www.irishtimes.com/news/after-ireland-1.728344. Kiberd has since tempered his critiques and extended them in his most recent monograph. See: Kiberd, *After Ireland: Writing the Nation from Beckett to the Present* (Cambridge: Harvard University Press, 2017).

34. Justin Quinn, "The Disappearance of Ireland," in *The Cambridge Introduction to Modern Irish Poetry, 1800–2000* (Cambridge: Cambridge University Press, 2008), 210.

35. Jefferson Holdridge and Brian Ó Conchubhair, *Post-Ireland? Essays on Contemporary Irish Poetry* (Winston-Salem: Wake Forest University Press, 2017), 10.

36. For an overview of the complex origins and developments of Irish studies as a discipline, see: Richard Kirkland, "Towards a Disciplinary History of Irish Studies," *The Irish Review* 48 (2014): 65–80.

37. In recent years, scholars have upended such reductive bifurcations of Irish modernism. Cóilín Parsons stresses modernism's indebtedness to Revivalism and argues that any account of modern Irish literature must take into account both the nineteenth and twentieth centuries: "There is no Yeats without Ferguson, no Joyce without Mangan, no Synge without Petrie." Joe Cleary argues that Revivalists and modernists were driven by a shared desire to create new art that would supplant what they saw as the failures of their

nineteenth-century predecessors, who produced only poor mimicries of English imperial culture; modernism, he says, should therefore be regarded as a "higher-order second-wave revivalism rather than something entirely contrary to the Irish Revival." See: Parsons, *The Ordnance Survey and Modern Irish Literature* (Oxford: Oxford University Press, 2016), 37; Cleary, "Introduction," in *The Cambridge Companion to Irish Modernism*, ed. Joe Cleary (Cambridge: Cambridge University Press, 2014), 12.

38. Such an askance view of Irish poetry's politics is not altogether undeserved. From an outsider's view, the landscape of contemporary Irish poetry is most notable for its enduring ties to the lyric poem and to traditional poetic forms. Aside from a few exceptions like Trevor Joyce, Billy Mills, Maurice Scully, and Catherine Walsh, the best-known and institutionally established Irish poets have eschewed altogether the questions of lyric subjectivity that were ignited by the Language poets in the 1970s and have since dominated poetry criticism. (Notably, these aforementioned experimental poets have neither achieved the same widespread popularity as many of their peers nor occupied the same kinds of high-status university positions.) For commentary that discusses formalism in contemporary Irish poetry, see: Fran Brearton, "'The Nothing-Could-Be-Simpler Line': Form in Contemporary Irish Poetry," in *The Oxford Handbook of Modern Irish Poetry*, ed. Fran Brearton and Alan Gillis (Oxford: Oxford University Press, 2012), 629–47; Eric Falci, "Rethinking Form (Yet Again) in Contemporary Irish Poetry," *Irish University Review* 50, no. 1 (2020): 164–74; Trevor Joyce, "Irish Terrain: Alternate Planes of Cleavage," in *Assembling Alternatives: Reading Postmodern Poetries Transnationally*, ed. Romana Huk (Middletown: Wesleyan University Press, 2003), 156–68; David Lloyd, "The Cultures of Poetry in Contemporary Ireland," in *Irish Literature in Transition: 1980–2020*, ed. Eric Falci and Paige Reynolds (Cambridge: Cambridge University Press, 2020), 44–64.

39. Shira Wolosky, "The Claims of Rhetoric: Toward a Historical Poetics (1820–1900)," *American Literary History* 15, no. 1 (2003): 14.

40. Walt Hunter, *Forms of a World: Contemporary Poetry and the Making of Globalization* (New York: Fordham University Press, 2019), 3.

41. Virginia Jackson and Yopie Prins, eds., *The Lyric Theory Reader: A Critical Anthology* (Baltimore: Johns Hopkins University Press, 2014); Dorothy Wang, *Thinking Its Presence: Form, Race, and Subjectivity in Contemporary Asian American Poetry* (Palo Alto: Stanford University Press, 2014); Harris Feinsod, *The Poetry of the Americas: From Good Neighbors to Countercultures* (Oxford: Oxford University Press, 2017); Hunter, *Forms of a World*; Sonya Posmentier, *Cultivation and Catastrophe: The Lyric Ecology of Modern Black Literature* (Baltimore: Johns Hopkins University Press, 2017); Ramazani, *Poetry in a Global Age*; Anthony Reed, *Freedom Time: The Poetics and Politics of Black Experimental Writing* (Baltimore: Johns Hopkins University Press, 2016).

42. Quoted in: Michael Parker, *Seamus Heaney: The Making of a Poet* (London: Macmillan, 2003), 120.

43. Margaret Greaves, "Punishing the Lyric: Seamus Heaney and the Poetics of a Communal Europe," *Éire-Ireland* 51, nos. 3 and 4 (2016): 219.

44. The journalist David McWilliams is widely credited for coining the term "ghost estate" in 2006. According to the National Institute for Regional and Spatial Analysis (NIRSA), a ghost estate is technically defined as a development lot (comprising ten or more houses) that has 50 percent or fewer of its residences occupied or fully constructed. See: Karen Keaveney, Rob Kitchin, Cian O'Callaghan, and Justin Gleeson, "A Haunted Landscape: Housing and Ghost Estates in Post–Celtic Tiger Ireland," National Institute for Regional and Spatial Analysis, Working Paper 59 (2010).

45. Alice Lyons, *The Breadbasket of Europe* (Surrey: Veer Books, 2015), 113.

46. Lyons, *Breadbasket of Europe*, 112.

47. Geographers Rob Kitchin, Cian O'Callaghan, and Justin Gleeson have analyzed the representations of the ghost estate in recent Irish news media. See: "Post-politics, Crisis, and Ireland's 'Ghost Estates,'" *Political Geography* 42 (2014): 121–33.

48. Terrence McDonough, "Economic Causes and Consequences of the Celtic Tiger Crash," *boundary 2* 45, no. 1 (2018): 25, emphasis in original. Of course, there are many parallels between the Irish and US real estate bubbles, which both played a significant role in the 2008 financial crisis. For an astute analysis on cultural representations of the US housing bubble, see: Annie McClanahan, "Photography and Foreclosure," in *Dead Pledges: Debt, Crisis, and Twenty-First-Century Culture* (Stanford: Stanford University Press, 2017), 99–142.

49. Barbara Johnson, "Apostrophe, Animation, and Abortion," *Diacritics* 16, no. 1 (1986): 30.

50. Margaret Ronda, *Remainders: American Poetry at Nature's End* (Stanford: Stanford University Press, 2018), 114.

51. As has become clear now since the outset of the financial crisis, property overdevelopment has also had significant environmental impact on Ireland. Unfinished and unoccupied ghost estates, derelict and standing in disrepair for over a decade now, have led to massive rat infestations. Moreover, many houses were discovered to be built on foundations laced with pyrite (also known by its apt nickname, fool's gold), which deteriorated and caused irreparable structural damage to the bedrock. (Lyons alludes to this earlier in "Developers": "Hard core might make it level.") The artist Anthony Haughey, who has photographed ghost estates across the country in his series *Settlement*, describes how the abandoned sites are "constant and painful reminder[s] of economic failure, indebtedness, and the environmental cost of rezoning and building in inappropriate areas, such as flood plains and remote rural regions with little or no access to transport, schools, and services." See: Haughey, "A Landscape of Crisis: Photographing Post–Celtic Tiger Ghost Estates," *The Canadian Journal of Irish Studies* 40 (2017): 61.

52. Fredric Jameson, "Culture and Finance Capital," *Critical Inquiry* 24, no. 1 (1997): 251.

53. Joseph Vogl, *The Spectre of Capital* (Palo Alto: Stanford University Press, 2014), 4, 8.

54. Ruth Jennison, "29 | 73 | 08: Poetry, Crisis, and a Hermeneutic of Limit," *Mediations* 28, no. 2 (2015): 40.

55. Lloyd, "Cultures of Poetry in Contemporary Ireland," 45–46.

56. That said, the field of Irish poetic criticism has weathered rightful criticism for its marginalization of women poets. The editors of *The Cambridge Companion to Irish Poets*, published in 2017, came under sharp censure for the collection's gender imbalance: of the thirty poets surveyed, only four were women, and just four of the scholarly contributors were women. In response, a group of Irish poets penned a pledge called "Fired! Irish Women Poets and the Canon," which calls for an interrogation of gender imbalance in anthologies, conferences, and other projects on Irish poetry. For more, see: Mary O'Donnell, "A Prosaic Lack of Women in *The Cambridge Companion to Irish Poets*," *The Irish Times*, January 8, 2018, https://www.irishtimes.com/culture/books/a-prosaic-lack-of-women-in-the-cambridge-companion-to-irish-poets-1.3336413; Deirdre Falvey, "Two-Thirds of Published Poets Are Male, So Does Poetry Have a Gender Issue?" *The Irish Times*, August 17, 2019, https://www.irishtimes.com/culture/books/two-thirds-of-published-poets-are-male-so-does-poetry-have-a-gender-issue-1.3984922.

57. In fact, the recent controversies over the work of conceptual poets Kenneth Goldsmith and Vanessa Place have highlighted how avant-garde poetic communities have historically excluded poets of color. As Cathy Park Hong succinctly puts it, "to encounter the history of avant-garde poetry is to encounter a racist tradition. . . . The avant-garde's 'delusion of whiteness' is the specious belief that renouncing subject and voice is anti-authoritarian, when in fact such wholesale pronouncements are clueless that the disenfranchised need such bourgeois niceties like voice to alter conditions forged in history." See: Hong, "Delusions of Whiteness in the Avant-Garde," *Lana Turner* 7 (November 3, 2014): https://arcade.stanford.edu/content/delusions-whiteness-avant-garde.

58. Ronda, *Remainders*, 15.

Chapter 1

1. Natasha Onwuemezi, "Poetry Sales Are Booming, LBF Hears," *The Bookseller*, April 13, 2018, https://www.thebookseller.com/news/poetry-summit-766826.

2. According to the Survey of Public Participation in the Arts (SPPA), 11.8 percent of US adults read a volume of poetry in 2018; the figure is even

more remarkable considering that 24 percent of adults surveyed did not read any books in that same year. Notably, the SPPA also revealed the largest increases in poetry readership occurred among young adults (ages 18–24), women, and people of color. See: "Taking Note: Poetry Reading Is Up—Federal Survey Results," *Art Works Blog*, National Endowment of the Arts, June 7, 2018, https://www.arts.gov/art-works/2018/taking-note-poetry-reading-—federal-survey-results.

3. Rebecca Watts ignited the critical firestorm around Instapoetry when she refused to review Hollie McNish's collection *Plum* and instead penned a withering essay in which she derided Instapoets for creating nothing more than "consumer driven content" and "instant gratification." The review sparked responses from McNish and other critics in the *Guardian*, the *New Statesman*, and the Poetry Foundation, among other outlets. See: Watts, "The Cult of the Noble Amateur," *PN Review* 239 44, no. 3 (2018), https://www.pnreview.co.uk/cgi-bin/scribe?item_id=10090.

4. See: Donna Ferguson, "Poetry Sales Soar as Political Millennials Search for Clarity," *The Guardian*, January 21, 2019, https://www.theguardian.com/books/2019/jan/21/poetry-sales-soar-as-political-millennials-search-for-clarity.

5. Jesse Lichtenstein, "How Poetry Came to Matter Again," *The Atlantic*, September 2018, https://www.theatlantic.com/magazine/archive/2018/09/chen-chen-aziza-barnes-layli-long-soldier/565781.

6. In the months after 9/11, Auden's poem was frequently reprinted in major newspapers and recited on public radio. See: Peter Steinfels, "Beliefs; After Sept. 11, a 62-Year-Old Poem by Auden Drew New Attention. Not All of It Was Favorable," *The New York Times*, December 1, 2001, https://www.nytimes.com/2001/12/01/us/beliefs-after-sept-11-62-year-old-poem-auden-drew-new-attention-not-all-it-was.html.

7. But Walsh more than simply recycles an old poem for a new occasion; his performance of the poem was crucial to its overnight popularity. At the climax of his reading, Walsh comes to a dramatic pause, points down to the steps of Manchester's town hall, and recites (to great applause following): "Manchester gives us such strength from the fact / That this is the place." With his conjoining of deixis and physical pointing, Walsh seems to literally cement his poem into the very ground of Manchester. See: 5 News, "This Is the Place: Poet Tony Walsh Reads Out His Tribute to Manchester," May 23, 2017, video, https://youtu.be/josaDi9ZBvE.

8. Stephen Wilson, "Poetry and Its Occasions: Undoing the Folded Line," in *A Companion to Poetic Genre*, ed. Erik Martiny (New York: Blackwell, 2011), 494.

9. W. H. Auden, "Yeats as an Example," *The Kenyon Review* 10, no. 2 (1948): 193.

10. That said, there have been valuable works of scholarship exploring the impact of the Celtic Tiger and its crash on contemporary Irish culture. Sarah

Brouillette has written several essays on the cultural industries of post-conflict Northern Ireland, particularly the phenomenon of "struggle tourism" that markets the violence of the Troubles to a voyeuristic foreign audience, such as with black cab tours and "Troubles trash" crime thrillers set during the sectarian conflict. For more, see: Brouillette, "Struggle Tourism and Northern Ireland's Culture Industries: The Case of Robert McLiam Wilson," *Textual Practice* 20, no. 2 (2006): 333–53; Brouillette, "On *Not* Safeguarding the Cultural Heritage: Glenn Patterson's *Black Night at Big Thunder Mountain*," *Irish Studies Review* 15, no. 3 (2007): 317–31. Breda Gray analyzes how the commodification of certain forms of Irish culture helped facilitate the sense of a global diasporic Irish identity during the late 1990s and early 2000s. (She borrows from Fintan O'Toole the term "Enyanomics" to describe this phenomenon.) See: Gray, "The Irish Diaspora: Globalised Belonging(s)," *Irish Journal of Sociology* 11, no. 2 (2002): 123–44. For work that concentrates on Irish theater after the crash of the Celtic Tiger, see: Laura Farrell-Wortman, "The Crisis and What Comes After," in *Routledge Handbook of Irish Studies*, ed. Renée Fox, Mike Cronin, and Brian Ó Conchubhair (Abingdon: Routledge, 2021), 300–10. There has been considerably more scholarship on this topic in the disciplines of geography and urban studies. For one illustrative example, see: Cian O'Callaghan, Sinéad Kelly, Mark Boyle, and Rob Kitchin, "Topologies and Topographies of Ireland's Neoliberal Crisis," *Space and Polity* 19, no. 1 (2015): 31–46.

    11. Joe Cleary, "'Horseman, Pass By!': The Neoliberal World System and the Crisis in Irish Literature," *boundary 2* 45, no. 1 (2018): 146.

    12. James English, *The Economy of Prestige: Prizes, Awards, and the Circulation of Cultural Value* (Cambridge: Harvard University Press, 2005), 12. Nathan Suhr-Sytsma makes a similar argument when he astutely reasons that any study of the politics of Northern Irish poetry (particularly the work of Seamus Heaney, Michael Longley, and other leading figures of the era) must also consider this body of work's publication and circulation in periodicals such as *The Believer* and *The Honest Ulsterman*: "[Critics must] account for how the language of poetry is actually embodied and mediated between poets and their publics, whether through performance, broadcasting, recording, or print. Any deconstruction or defense of poetry's autonomy from the political realm needs to be tempered by an awareness of how poetry is inflected by its publication in print venues along a spectrum of periodicity and perceived literariness." See: Suhr-Sytsma, *Poetry, Print, and the Making of Postcolonial Literature* (Cambridge: Cambridge University Press, 2017), 166.

    13. It is easiest to slide together the occasional poem and the ode, particularly as the latter has enjoyed being the subject of copious scholarship. The ode is also often defined by its ceremonial and public nature. For instance, Norman Maclean distinguishes the ode from other forms of lyric because it is "massive, public in its proclamations." However, as I will explain, for the purposes of this

chapter I remain with the category of occasional poetry because of its closer links with patronage. While there are numerous essays and monographs on the ode, Maclean remains the authoritative voice on the genre. See: Maclean, "From Action to Image: Theories of the Lyric in the Eighteenth Century," in *Critics and Criticism: Ancient and Modern*, ed. R. S. Crane (Chicago: University of Chicago Press, 1952), 408–60.

14. Marian Zwerling Sugano offers a nuanced and thorough history of the occasional poem's evolution. She explains that occasional poetry's waning in literary status went hand in hand with the decline of courtly patronage of the arts. During the Renaissance, occasional poetry was the poet's means of securing favor, stability, and protection with her courtly patrons. But the gradual dissolution of the monarchy and court over the seventeenth and eighteenth centuries completely transformed previous systems of patronage and with it the status and function of occasional poetry: "By the end of the eighteenth century the genre of occasional poetry had fallen into disrepute for many reasons: the sheer proliferation of undistinguished verse celebrating persons and occasions of dubious importance, the growing sense that the occasional poet was little more than a literate schemer in pursuit of social advancement or financial remuneration, an increasing conviction that the writing prompted by objective rather than subjective stimuli was no more than literary prostitution." See: Sugano, *The Poetics of the Occasion: Mallarmé and the Poetry of Circumstance* (Palo Alto: Stanford University Press, 1992), 8.

15. BBC, "Laureate Bemoans 'Thankless Job,'" September 10, 2008, http://news.bbc.co.uk/2/hi/entertainment/7607897.stm.

16. Adam Kirsch, "On Elizabeth Alexander's Bureaucratic Verse," *The New Republic*, January 20, 2009, https://newrepublic.com/article/47178/adam-kirsch-elizabeth-alexanders-bureaucratic-verse. The ungenerous reception of Alexander's poem seems even stranger considering the near-universal acclaim for Amanda Gorman's "The Hill We Climb," delivered at the 2021 presidential inauguration of Joseph Biden. But Virginia Jackson and Meredith Martin nonetheless argue for reading Gorman's work specifically as an occasional poem. Jackson and Martin explain that Black poets have long troubled the presumption of a racially unmarked and therefore presumed white speaker in lyric poetry. For these reasons, as well as Gorman's celebrity status as the inaugural Youth Poet Laureate, it becomes impossible to detach her poem from the occasion of its delivery at the 2021 presidential inauguration: "You cannot read her poem and say 'the speaker' this or that. It is virtually impossible to detach 'The Hill We Climb' from the person of Amanda Gorman . . . Gorman was already a recognizable person and personality when she took the stage, and her public delivery of her poetry burned through the expectation that a listener would detach the poem from its occasion of its performance." See: Jackson and Martin, "The

Poetry of the Future," *Avidly*, January 29, 2021, http://avidly.lareviewofbooks.org/2021/01/29/the-poetry-of-the-future/.

17. Paul Bond, "Poet Ben Okri on London's Grenfell Tower Fire," World Socialist Web Site, September 11, 2017, https://www.wsws.org/en/articles/2017/09/11/okri-s11.html.

18. While this chapter focuses on the evolution of occasional poetry from the Romantic period onward, the genre's roots can be drawn back to the Classical period, notably with Pindar's victory odes. Again, for the most thorough history of the occasional poem, see: Sugano, *Poetics of the Occasion*.

19. M. H. Abrams, *The Correspondent Breeze: Essays on English Romanticism* (New York: Norton, 1984), 77.

20. In her analysis of "Tintern Abbey," Marjorie Levinson notes that occasional poetry operates around a central tension between its seeming "complete spontaneity and . . . most diffuse and ineffable motivations" and its "occasional, topical character": "Consider the title of 'Tintern Abbey,' which, with its prolix explicitness, underlines the multiple anniversaries, national and personal, marked by the date of composition, and the very public meanings lodged in the landscape that the poem registers by negation." See: Levinson, *Wordsworth's Great Period Poems: Four Essays* (Cambridge: Cambridge University Press, 1986), 5.

21. Marjorie Perloff, "Yeats and the Occasional Poem: Easter 1916," *Papers on Language & Literature* 50, nos. 3 and 4 (2014): 330, 334. Edward Whitley makes a similar argument in the context of nineteenth-century American poetry, arguing that "'cultural situations' of occasional poetry are 'concrete' in ways that other literary productions are not." The reason for this, Whitley argues, is because occasional poets address their work to two differing audiences: that of the "immediate events of the occasion" and the "larger audience that will later participate in the occasion through print." See: Whitley, "Whitman's Occasional National: 'A Broadway Pageant' and the Space of Public Poetry," *Nineteenth-Century Literature* 60, no. 4 (2006): 452–3.

22. G. W. F. Hegel, *Aesthetics: Lectures on Fine Art*, trans. T. M. Knox, vol. 2 (Oxford: Clarendon Press, 1975), 995–6.

23. Robert Pinsky, "Occasional Poetry and Poetry on Occasions," *The Paris Review* 42, no. 154 (2000): 82.

24. Sometimes there is a distinction drawn between "cultural industry" (which includes museums, libraries, arts councils, heritage centers) and "creative industry" (which includes instead a broader range of media, including film, television, and advertising). However, because these distinctions are often unclear and blurred, I use the term "creative economy" to encapsulate these many industries.

25. Sarah Brouillette, *Literature and the Creative Economy* (Palo Alto: Stanford University Press, 2014), 17, emphasis in original.

26. Brouillette, *Literature and the Creative Economy*, 8.

27. Fintan O'Toole, "Island of Saints and Silicon: Literature and Social Change in Contemporary Ireland," in *Cultural Contexts and Literary Idioms in Contemporary Irish Literature*, ed. Michael Kenneally (Totowa: Barnes and Noble Books, 1988), 13.

28. In various interviews, Kinsella praises Whitaker as a generous colleague and his time in the Civil Service as ultimately a positive influence on his poetry. In *A Dublin Documentary*, Kinsella describes the Department of Finance as the "site of my first off-key career; and of certain finding matter and method, that I have appreciated more and more for writing, as the years have passed." See: Dennis O'Driscoll, "Interview with Thomas Kinsella," *The Poetry Ireland Review* 25 (1989): 60; Adrienne Leavy, "An Interview with Thomas Kinsella," *New Hibernia Review* 15, no. 2 (2011): 146; Kinsella, *A Dublin Documentary* (Dublin: O'Brien Press, 2012), 90.

29. Thomas Kinsella, *Collected Poems* (Winston-Salem: Wake Forest University Press, 2006), 77–78.

30. Kinsella, *Collected Poems*, 78.

31. Lionel Pilkington explains that in addition to promoting export-oriented manufacturing, the Lemass–T. K. program for economic expansion jump-started the cultivation of cultural tourism as an industry in Ireland. Irish drama was an especially valuable cultural commodity, as plays could be either staged abroad or produced domestically and draw tourism into the country, and so several public arts festivals were founded in Ireland in the midcentury, such as the Dublin Theater Festival in 1957. See: Pilkington, "Reading History in the Plays of Brian Friel," in *A Companion to Modern British and Irish Drama, 1880–2005*, ed. Mary Luckhurst (Malden: Blackwell, 2006), 500.

32. Kinsella, *Collected Poems*, 46.

33. Helen Vendler, *Our Secret Discipline: Yeats and Lyric Form* (Oxford: Oxford University Press, 2007), 24.

34. Stephen Spender, Patrick Kavanagh, Thomas Kinsella, and W. D. Snodgrass, "Poetry Since Yeats: An Exchange of Views," *Tri-Quarterly* 4 (1965): 106–7.

35. The main origin of foreign direct investment in Ireland has always been and remains the US. US foreign direct investment in Ireland exploded after 1973 when Ireland joined the EEC and therefore was able to offer US companies access to the European market. Recently, there has been speculation that a new "special relationship" between Ireland and the US will develop after Brexit when the Republic replaces the UK as the main bridge between the US and the EU Common Market. For more on the history on the Ireland-US economic relationship, see: Vanessa Broullet, "The Irish-U.S. Economic Relations: End of an Era or a Promising Future?," in *Revisiting the UK and Ireland's Transatlantic Relationship with the United States in the 21st Century*, ed. Anne Groutel,

Marie-Christine Pauwels, and Valérie Peyronel (London: Palgrave Macmillan, 2017), 57–74.

36. Kinsella was a close friend of and collaborator with Liam Miller, who with his wife Josephine Browne founded the famed Dolmen Press in 1951 and provided an outlet for Irish poetry at a time when there were nearly no professional publishers in Ireland. Kinsella's most famous publication with the Dolmen Press (and perhaps the Press's best-known publication) is his translation of *The Táin*, published in 1969. In numerous interviews, Kinsella explains that he partly modeled Peppercanister Press after the success of the Dolmen Press and describes what he considers the pathetic state of Irish publishing after Miller's death and Dolmen's closure. For more, see: Kinsella, *The Dual Tradition: An Essay on Poetry and Politics in Ireland* (Manchester: Carcanet Press, 1995).

37. The three Peppercanister poems following *Butcher's Dozen* were also occasional poems, including two elegies for the composer Seán Ó Riada (*A Selected Life* and *Vertical Man*) and *The Good Fight*, which commemorated the tenth anniversary of the assassination of John F. Kennedy. For more on the history of the Peppercanister poems, see: Derval Turbidy, *Thomas Kinsella: The Peppercanister Poems* (Dublin: University College Dublin Press, 2001).

38. Sean O'Reilly, "Butcher's Dozen by Thomas Kinsella," *The Stinging Fly*, January 25, 2022, https://stingingfly.org/review/butchers-dozen/.

39. Trevor Joyce, "Irish Terrain: Alternate Planes of Cleavage," in *Assembling Alternatives: Reading Postmodern Poetries Transnationally*, ed. Romana Huk (Middletown: Wesleyan University Press, 2003), 158; Denis Donoghue, *We Irish: Essays on Literature and Society* (Berkeley: University of California Press, 1986), 187.

40. Leavy, "An Interview with Thomas Kinsella," 141–2. Kinsella goes on to describe how he approached the publication of *Butcher's Dozen* as an ephemeral "pamphlet": "I had published it instantly—it was written and published in a week, operating like a tenpenny pamphlet, or a news sheet. Others didn't think that poetry was the medium for discussion; or that I was qualified to discuss. Some thought I had written it for money, or for public attention."

41. Julia Obert, "Space and the Trace: Thomas Kinsella's Postcolonial Placelore," *New Hibernia Review* 13, no. 4 (2009): 84.

42. Thomas Kinsella, *Peppercanister Poems 1972–1978* (Winston-Salem: Wake Forest University Press, 1979), 13.

43. Kinsella, *Peppercanister Poems*, 13.

44. Kinsella, *Peppercanister Poems*, 19.

45. Patrick Crotty, "Stunning Places: Thomas Kinsella's Locations," *The Poetry Ireland Review* 87 (2006): 37.

46. For more on the history of the Wood Quay protests, see: John Bradley, *Viking Dublin Exposed: The Wood Quay Saga* (Dublin: O'Brien Press, 1984).

47. Kinsella, *Collected Poems*, 291.
48. Kinsella, *Collected Poems*, 274.
49. Obert, "Space and the Trace," 78.
50. *Wood Quay Occupation News* no. 2, June 12, 1979. For the reprinted poem, see: Kinsella, *Collected Poems*, 291.

51. Many economists have deemed Ireland the largest tax haven in the world with an estimated $106 billion of corporate profits in 2015 (the bulk of which came from US multinationals), outpacing other better-known tax shelters like Switzerland and the Caribbean. While the Organization for Economic Cooperation and Development (OECD) has not officially designated Ireland a tax haven, it has never in its history given the label to any EU country, only ever awarding the title to Trinidad and Tobago in 2015. See: Mark Paul, "Ireland Is the World's Biggest Corporate 'Tax Haven,' Say Academics," *The Irish Times*, June 13, 2018, https://www.irishtimes.com/business/economy/ireland-is-the-world-s-biggest-corporate-tax-haven-say-academics-1.3528401.

52. Alexandra Slaby, "Whither Cultural Policy in Post-Celtic Ireland?" *The Canadian Journal of Irish Studies* 37, nos. 1 and 2 (2011): 76–97. Slaby argues that the recession accelerated the transformation of the Arts Council from an entity supporting cultural organizations to one that invests in cultural corporations: "The Arts Council sees itself . . . no longer as assisting artists but as mentoring managers, while discussions of quality or diversity of artistic contributions have been replaced by discussions of value for money" (90).

53. World Cities Culture Forum, "Global Cities Sharing a Belief in the Importance of Culture," accessed December 3, 2020, http://www.worldcitiescultureforum.com/about.

54. UNESCO Creative Cities Network, "Mission Statement," accessed December 3, 2020, https://en.unesco.org/creative-cities/sites/creative-cities/files/uccn_mission_statement_rev_nov_2017.pdf.

55. Although no additional funding is offered to cities awarded the designation of City of Literature, the program is often seen to provide a major economic boost to the local economy. Brouillette observes that cities often justify their applications to the City of Literature program with the hope that it will increase cultural tourism, which would stimulate private-sector (especially service-sector) growth. Therefore, she argues, the UNESCO City of Literature program specifically targets developed economies. See: Brouillette, *UNESCO and the Fate of the Literary* (Palo Alto: Stanford University Press, 2019), 102.

56. Charlie Taylor, "UNESCO City of Literature Status Sought for Dublin," *The Irish Times*, March 6, 2009, https://www.irishtimes.com/news/unesco-city-of-literature-status-sought-for-dublin-1.837102.

57. "Site-specific art" usually refers to large-scale sculptures and installations that are designed to exist in a particular location and includes the work of artists such as Robert Smithson and Richard Serra. However, in the context

of this chapter, I use the term more generally to refer to art and literature that are either located in or explicitly reference a specific place.

58. Again, Brouillette's scholarship proves an exception. Brouillette studies the odd phenomenon of writer-consultants, who are hired by property developers to communicate with local communities so that they feel included in and therefore less resistant to urban renewal projects that often gentrify neighborhoods and push out longtime residents. But her perceptive study does not note how these writer-consultants predominantly turn to poetry in these urban renewal projects. A quick glance at the writer-consultant groups that she cites (such as UrbanWords and A Place for Words) reveals that much of public arts literature is specifically poetry. For instance, one of the projects that Brouillette cites is the Poetry Society's Poetry Places 1998–2000, a scheme funded by the Arts Council of England that commissioned site-specific poetry and established residencies for poets at specific locales. See: Brouillette, "The Strange Case of the Writer-Consultant," in *Literature and the Creative Economy* (Palo Alto, Stanford University Press, 2014), 154–74.

59. Dublin: One City One Book Festival is a Dublin City Council initiative that selects one book about Dublin and encourages people to read it during the month of April. The festival puts on numerous events, including many geared toward tourists, such as Dublin City Bike Tours and Liffey Cruises. See: One Dublin One Book, *If Ever You Go: A Map of Dublin in Poetry and Song*, accessed December 3, 2020, http://www.dublinonecityonebook.ie/books/if-ever-you-go/.

60. Jessica Traynor, "Hungering: A Poetry Jukebox for Dublin's Docklands," *The Irish Times*, July 4, 2019, https://www.irishtimes.com/culture/books/hungering-a-poetry-jukebox-for-dublin-s-docklands-1.3946528.

61. The Poetry Project, "Oliver Comerford—Distance / Eavan Boland, In Our Own Country," accessed December 3, 2020, http://thepoetryproject.ie/poems/distance-oliver-comerford-in-our-own-country-eavan-boland/.

62. Eavan Boland, *Domestic Violence* (New York: Norton, 2007), 27.

63. Boland makes a similar critique in her poem "Making Money," in which she describes the mill workers who literally make the paper that is exported and used as banknote paper for Euro bills: "they do not and they never will see . . . / the crimson and indigo features / of the prince who will stare out from / the surfaces they have made / the ruin of a Europe / he cannot see from the surface / of a wealth he cannot keep." See: Boland, *New Collected Poems* (New York: Norton, 2008), 292–3.

64. "Programme for the Irish Presidency of the Council of the European Union," accessed December 3, 2020, http://www.eu2013.ie/media/eupresidency/content/documents/EU-Pres_Prog_A4.pdf.

65. Slaby points out that after the financial crisis, Irish culture was explicitly named a key part of the revitalization of the Irish economy: "It was only in 2009 . . . that Irish cultural policy became explicitly economized, in that it

was not just encouraged to contribute to economic growth but was to acquire an active role in leading the economy to a new stage." See: Slaby, "Whither Cultural Policy," 84.

66. Cleary, "'Horseman, Pass By!,'" 171.

67. Jody Allen Randolph, "The Body Politic: A Conversation with Paula Meehan," *An Sionnach: A Journal of Literature, Culture, and the Arts* 5, nos. 1 and 2 (2009): 262.

68. In its reprinting in the collection *Painting Rain*, Meehan includes an endnote for "Six Sycamores" that gives the context of its commissioning and the history it draws on: "Poems commissioned under the Per Cent for Art Scheme by the Office of Public Works on the occasion of the opening of the Link Building between number 51, (at one stage the Museum of Industry), and number 52, (built in 1771 by the banker David La Touche) on the east side of St Stephen's Green, Dublin, in 2001." See: Meehan, *Painting Rain* (Winston-Salem: Wake Forest University Press, 2009), 100.

69. Eileen O'Halloran and Kelli Maloy, "An Interview with Paula Meehan," *Contemporary Literature* 43, no. 1 (2002): 5.

70. Meehan, *Painting Rain*, 30.

71. Randolph, "The Body Politic," 265.

72. The Per Cent for Art Scheme is not unique to Ireland, and similar programs are found across the world, including the US, Australia, and other countries in Europe.

73. Although many new arts programs were established during the boom period, the Per Cent for Art Scheme is unique for commissioning works of literature in addition to visual and plastic arts, which are the more usual genres represented in the public arts. The Scheme's latest guidelines specifically call to expand the kinds of art they wish to sponsor: "While public art has traditionally been conceived primarily in terms of the plastic arts—most particularly permanent outdoor sculpture—a broader range of possibilities has been fruitfully explored in recent years. The scope of public art has widened to include not just sculpture's close relations, architecture and painting, but also music, literature, film, video, multimedia and sound art, as well as the various performing arts including theatre, dance, opera, performance and live art" (9). This is partly for budgetary reasons: because the Per Cent for Art Scheme aims to house artwork in all of its public buildings, it must commission a large amount of original art and therefore often gravitates toward smaller scaled and more affordable pieces. See: "Public Art: Per Cent for Art Scheme: General National Guidelines—2004," accessed December 3, 2020, https://publicart.ie/fileadmin/user_upload/PDF_Folder/Public_Art_Per_Cent_for_Art.pdf.

74. *General National Guidelines: Per Cent for Art Scheme*, official government ed. (2004), 5, 29, 46. In the guidelines, the former minister for arts, sports, and tourism stresses the importance of public art that "can contribute to the dis-

tinctiveness of the local area and can offer a different reading or interpretation of history or the environment. In Ireland, we look to artists' work and their interpretation of place to gauge our own development as a community. This interpretation gains more significance when it is placed in a particular site or area."

75. Yvonne Scott, *Art in State Buildings, 1995–2005*, official government ed. (Dublin: Stationery Office, 2006), vii–viii.

76. Randolph, "Body Politic," 261.

77. Meehan, *Painting Rain*, 32.

78. Meehan's allusion to Hopkins is not incidental; from 1884 to 1889, the English poet briefly worked as a professor of classics at University College Dublin, which at the time was located on Stephen's Green.

79. Meehan, *Painting Rain*, 31.

80. Meehan, *Painting Rain*, 28.

81. Randolph, "Body Politic," 268.

82. Sarah Jaffe, *Work Won't Love You Back: How Devotion to Our Jobs Keeps Us Exploited, Exhausted, and Alone* (New York: Bold Type Books, 2021), 181, 191.

Chapter 2

1. Eavan Boland, "Rereading Oliver Goldsmith's 'Deserted Village' in a Changed Ireland," *The American Scholar* 80, no. 1 (2011): 54–56. While Boland's work was first published in 2011, she wrote the poem in the years prior to the crash of the Celtic Tiger.

2. For other scholarship that examines the pastoral mode in contemporary Irish literature, see: Sidney Burris, *The Poetry of Resistance: Seamus Heaney and the Pastoral Tradition* (Athens: Ohio University Press, 1990); Oona Frawley, *Irish Pastoral: Nostalgia and Twentieth-Century Irish Literature* (Dublin: Irish Academic Press, 2005); Donna L. Potts, *Contemporary Irish Poetry and the Pastoral Tradition* (Columbia: University of Missouri Press, 2011); Iain Twiddy, *Pastoral Elegy in Contemporary British and Irish Poetry* (New York: Continuum, 2012).

3. While the pastoral has been sometimes classified as a genre, in this chapter I follow Paul Alpers's designation of it as a mode that operates across literature, music, and drama. For Alpers, the pastoral mode is defined by its "feelings and attitudes as such, as distinguished from their realization or manifestation in specific devices, conventions, structures." Leo Marx similarly defines pastoral as a mode rather than a genre, arguing that the pastoral "derives its identity not from any formal convention but from a particular perspective on human experience." See: Alpers, *What Is Pastoral?* (Chicago: University of Chicago Press, 1996), 46–47; Marx, "Pastoralism in America," in *Ideology and Classic American Literature*, ed. Sarcran Bercovitch and Myra Jehlan (Cambridge: Cambridge University Press, 1986), 46.

4. William Empson, *Some Versions of Pastoral* (New York: New Directions, 1974), 11; Samuel Johnson, *Samuel Johnson: Selected Writings*, ed. Martin Peter (Cambridge: Harvard University Press, 2011), 422.

5. Raymond Williams, *The Country and the City* (Oxford: Oxford University Press, 1973), 12. David Harvey employs a near identical allegory to explain Marx's complex understanding of capitalism: "Marx sees each relation as a separate 'window' from which we can look at the inner structure of capitalism. The view from any one window is flat and lacks perspective. When we move to another window we can see things that were formerly hidden from view. Armed with that knowledge, we can reinterpret and reconstitute our understanding of what we saw through the first window, giving it greater depth and perspective. By moving from window to window and carefully recording what we see, we come closer and closer to understanding capitalist society and all of its inherent contradictions." See: David Harvey, *Limits to Capital* (New York: Verso, 1982), 2.

6. One notable exception is John Goodby's excellent study *Irish Poetry Since 1950: From Stillness into History*. Goodby incisively situates postwar Irish poetry within a circuit of transatlantic crosscurrents, particularly in his examination of the institutional relationships between Irish poets and US universities. However, such a study requires a fresh lens, given the seismic upheavals in Ireland's recent history and the new wave of global poetics scholarship that has emerged over the past decade. See: Goodby, *Irish Poetry since 1950: From Stillness into History* (Manchester: Manchester University Press, 2000).

7. Patrick Fessenbecker and Bryan Yazell, "Literature, Economics, and a Turn to Content," *minnesota review* 96 (2021): 79. For more interdisciplinary scholarship that examines the intersections between economics and literature, see: Michelle Chihara and Matt Seybold, eds., *The Routledge Companion to Literature and Economics* (New York: Routledge, 2019).

8. Laura Finch, "It's the Economy, Stupid: On the Costs of Marginalizing the Aesthetic," *American Literary History* 31, no. 4 (2019): 820.

9. In his study of Heaney, Sidney Burris includes his correspondence with an IRA political prisoner, who condemned the poet's move to the Republic as an act of betrayal. Burris explains that such strident sentiments were common and profoundly shaped Heaney's career: "To many American readers, it will seem extraordinary that my correspondent had heard of the arguments marshaled against Heaney's decision to leave the North . . . But these firm alignments are typical of many readers and critics in Northern Ireland, and with a sophistication and urbanity rarely encountered by the American reader who faces 'political' verse, these alignments appear throughout Heaney's work as one of its major structural elements." See: Burris, *The Poetry of Resistance*, viii.

10. Heaney himself describes the landscape of Wicklow as distinctively pastoral: "The countryside where we live in Wicklow [is] pastoral rather than rural, trying to impose notions of a beautified landscape on the word, in order to

keep 'rural' for the unself-conscious face of raggle-taggle farmland." See: Heaney, "In the Country of Convention: English Pastoral Verse," in *Preoccupations: Selected Prose, 1968–1978* (New York: Farrar, Straus and Giroux, 1981), 173.

11. Quoted in: Henry Hart, *Seamus Heaney: Poet of Contrary Progressions*. Syracuse: Syracuse University Press (1992), 22.

12. Heaney, *Preoccupations*, 65.

13. Al Alvarez, "A Fine Way with Language," *New York Review of Books*, March 6, 1980, 16.

14. Rosanna Warren, *Fables of the Self: Studies in Lyric Poetry* (New York: Norton, 2008), 53–55.

15. Seamus Heaney, "Eclogues *In Extremis*: On the Staying Power of Pastoral," *Proceedings of the Royal Irish Academy* 103C, no. 1 (2003): 6.

16. Empson, *Some Versions of Pastoral*, 14. The specter of Soviet culture loomed large at this time in Empson's life; while writing *Some Versions*, Empson was working in Lianda (later National Southwestern Associated University) in Kunming after being forced to flee his post at Beijing University when the Japanese invaded China.

17. Empson, *Some Versions of Pastoral*, 18.

18. Paul de Man claims that Empson's study of the pastoral is in fact a meditation on the metaphysical dilemma of lyric poetry (what he calls the "cleavage of Being") disguised as a work of conventional literary criticism. See: de Man, "The Dead-End of Formalist Criticism," in *Blindness and Insight* (Minneapolis: University of Minnesota Press, 1971), 229–45.

19. Seamus Heaney, *Field Work* (New York: Farrar, Straus and Giroux, 1979), 15.

20. Éamon De Valera, *Speeches and Statements by Eamon de Valera, 1917–73*, ed. Maurice Moynihan (New York: St. Martin's Press, 1980), 466. The utopian image of the "cosy homestead" stands in stark contrast to the sober language of the Taoiseach's earlier speech for the Report on the Banking Commission in July 1939, in which he was forced to confront the realities of economically depleted rural areas that had been hit hard by the mass exodus of farmers (especially those of younger generations). De Valera claims that the government should be responsible for marketing a more idealized version of "country life" to a population fleeing the deprivations of rural life: "One of the things the Government has to examine is as to what method could be employed by which country life would be made more attractive for our own people. We want to make it attractive." In other words, for de Valera, the romanticized representation of the Irish countryside was a vital task of the nationalist agenda. See: Moynihan, *Speeches and Statements*, 402.

21. While the UK suffered little fallout from the Anglo-Irish Trade War, the Irish economy bore the brunt of the trade war and was essentially reduced to a state of barter for cattle farmers (who relied on importing their goods to

Britain), which led to mass emigration of young men and women from the 1940s onward. For more on the Economic War, see: Niamh Puirséil, "Political and Party Competition in Post-war Ireland," in *The Lemass Era*, ed. Brian Girvin and Gary Murphy (Dublin: University College Dublin Press, 2005), 12–27; Kevin O'Rourke, "Burn Everything British but Their Coal: The Anglo-Irish Economic War of the 1930s," *The Journal of Economic History* 51, no. 2 (1991): 357–66.

22. Clair Wills explains that Ireland's declaration of neutrality had a profound and long-lasting impact on the newly independent Republic's national identity, especially when the censorship ban was lifted in 1945 and reports of the Holocaust began to flood the Irish press: "But Ireland's wartime isolation had made it vulnerable to the charge of turning its back on humanity . . . [T]here was disturbing evidence, in letters to newspapers and in reviews of films of the camps, that 'neutral-mindedness' made it difficult to accept the facts of the Holocaust." See: Wills, *That Neutral Island: A Cultural History of Ireland during the Second World War* (Cambridge: Belknap Press, 2007), 268.

23. Frank Barry and John Bradley, "FDI and Trade: The Irish Host-Country Experience," *The Economic Journal* 107, no. 445 (1997): 1798.

24. For historical accounts that complicate the narrative of Irish economic modernization, see: Enda Delaney, "Modernity: The Past and Politics in Post-war Ireland," in *Turning Points in Twentieth-Century Irish History*, ed. T. E. Hachey (Dublin: Irish Academic Press, 2011), 103–18; Mervyn O'Driscoll, *Ireland, West Germany and the New Europe, 1949–73: Best Friend and Ally?* (Manchester: Manchester University Press, 2018); Mark S. Quigley, "Modernization's Lost Pasts: Sean O'Faolain, the "Bell," and Irish Modernization before Lemass," *New Hibernia Review* 18, no. 4 (2014): 44–67.

25. While the Common Agricultural Policy (CAP) was not able to completely stymie the flood of agricultural workers fleeing rural Ireland, it did allow for many Irish farms to survive the economic depression. D. S. Johnson and Liam Kennedy write that the CAP provided for 59 percent of the income for Irish farms by 1980, as compared to a mere 12 percent from the Irish state. See: Johnson and Kennedy, "The Two Economies in Ireland in the Twentieth Century," in *A New History of Ireland*, vol. 7, *Ireland 1921–1984*, ed. J. R. Hill (Oxford: Oxford University Press, 2003), 472.

26. For a detailed history of the Fianna Fáil and Fine Gael parties' involvement in the EEC petition, see: Dan Robinson, "The Bonded Republic: Ireland and the Visions of Europe," in *Natural and Necessary Unions: Britain, Europe, and the Scottish Question* (Oxford: Oxford University Press, 2020), 178–202.

27. Quoted in: Dermot Keogh, "Ireland, 1972–84," in *A New History of Ireland*, vol. 7, *Ireland 1921–1984*, ed. J. R. Hill (Oxford: Oxford University Press, 2003), 361.

28. Quoted in: Andrew Devenney, "Joining Europe: Ireland, Scotland, and the Celtic Response to European Integration, 1961–1975," *Journal of British Studies* 49, no. 1 (January 2010): 110.

29. See: John Lancester, "Once Greece Goes . . ." *London Review of Books*, July 14, 2011, http://www.lrb.co.uk/v33/n14/john-lanchester/once-greece-goes; Suzy Khimm and Henry Farrell, "The Fundamental Problem Here Is a Profoundly Political Problem," *The Washington Post*, September 29, 2011, https://www.washingtonpost.com/blogs/ezra-klein/post/farrell-the-fundamental-problem-here-is-a-profoundly-political-problem-euromess/2011/09/29/gIQAvIzD7K_blog.html.

30. Joe Cleary, *Outrageous Fortune: Capital and Culture in Modern Ireland* (Dublin: Field Day, 2006), 97.

31. Seamus Deane, "Unhappy and at Home: Interview with Seamus Heaney," *The Crane Bag* 1, no. 1 (1977): 66.

32. Williams, *The Country and the City*; Leo Marx, *The Machine in the Garden: Technology and the Pastoral Ideal in America* (Oxford: Oxford University Press, 1964).

33. Frawley, *Irish Pastoral*.

34. John Montague, *The Rough Field* (Winston-Salem: Wake Forest University Press, 2005), 3.

35. Empson, *Some Versions of Pastoral*, 11.

36. Montague, *The Rough Field*, vii.

37. For a comparative analysis of the economic histories of the Republic and Northern Ireland, see: Johnson and Kennedy, "The Two Economies," 474–77.

38. Montague even excerpts in its entirety a flyer (which he had actually received in the mail) from a Unionist organization that threatens to seek legal action to block the UK from joining the EEC on the grounds that integration would cede too much control to foreign (and, more to the point, Catholic) powers: "We fail to see how Her Majesty could be advised to sign away Her powers to an assembly, the membership of which is composed of people not of the Reformed Faith. What happens to the Coronation Oath?" See: Montague, *The Rough Field*, 24.

39. Montague, *The Rough Field*, 68.

40. Montague, *The Rough Field*, 58–9.

41. Montague, *The Rough Field*, 61.

42. Montague, *The Rough Field*, 67.

43. Montague, *The Rough Field*, 34–35.

44. Montague, *The Rough Field*, 69.

45. Andrew Devenney, "'A Unique and Unparalleled Surrender of Sovereignty': Early Opposition to European Integration in Ireland, 1961–72," *New Hibernia Review* 12, no. 4 (2008): 29.

46. Montague, *The Rough Field*, 82–83.

47. Graham Huggan and Helen Tiffin, *Postcolonial Ecocriticism: Literature, Animals, Environment* (Oxford: Routledge, 2010), 85.

48. Edward Said, *Culture and Imperialism* (New York: Vintage, 1993), 51.

49. Said, *Culture and Imperialism*, 96, emphasis mine.

50. In "Narrative and Social Space," Said similarly describes the task of contrapuntal reading as "reading a text with an understanding of what is involved when an author shows, for instance, that a colonial sugar plantation is seen as important to the process of maintaining a particular style of life in England." See: Said, *Culture and Imperialism*, 66.

51. This is a very abbreviated summary of Williams's much more thorough analysis of the evolution of pastoral literature in the twentieth century. Williams argues that while the landed aristocracy had lost much of its particular identity and political power over the course of industrial and imperialist development, the imagery of its country estates thrived in Victorian and Edwardian fiction—as he puts it, the fetishized images of "field sports, fishing, and above all horses." The "rural mode of display" in British literature is countered by "true rural literature," which feature the more traditional pastoral themes of struggles with landlords, failures of crops and debts, and the penetration of capital into peasant lands. Williams locates the latter in the work of postcolonial writers like Chinua Achebe, George Lamming, and Ngugi wa Thiong'o. See: Williams, *The Country and the City*, 282.

52. Williams, *The Country and the City*, 284–87.

53. Williams's analysis dovetails with the arguments of world-systems analysis by theorists like Immanuel Wallerstein, whose groundbreaking *The Modern World-System* was published in 1980, one year after *The Country and the City*.

54. Montague, *The Rough Field*, 32. In his extensive writings on "Ireland and the Irish Question," Karl Marx frequently draws attention to cattle farming in Ireland, noting how the country acts as an "agricultural district" that supports the industrialization of England and its imperial expansion: "England, a pre-eminently industrial country with fully developed capitalist production, would have bled to death under such a drain of population as Ireland has suffered. But Ireland is at present merely an agricultural district of England which happens to be divided by a wide stretch of water from the country for which it provides corn, wool, cattle and industrial and military recruits." See: Marx, *Capital*, vol. 1, *A Critique of Political Economy*, trans. Ben Fowkes (New York: Penguin, 1967), 860.

55. Montague, *The Rough Field*, 60–61.

56. Goodby, *Irish Poetry since 1950*, 105.

57. Richard Kirkland, "Ballygawley, Ballylynn, Belfast: Writing about Modernity and Settlement in Northern Ireland," *The Irish Review* 40/41 (2009): 20.

58. Montague, *The Rough Field*, 50.

59. Montague, "Oliver Goldsmith: A Sentimental Prophecy," in *The Figure in the Cave and Other Essays* (Syracuse: Syracuse University Press, 1989), 73–74.
60. Montague, *Figure in the Cave*, 3, emphasis in original.

Chapter 3

1. Hugh Kenner, *The Pound Era* (Berkeley: University of California Press, 1973), 45–46.
2. Patrick Duffy, "*Genius Loci*: The Geographical Imagination of Tim Robinson," in *Unfolding Irish Landscapes: Tim Robinson, Culture, and Environment*, ed. Derek Gladwin and Christine Cusick (Manchester: Manchester University Press, 2016), 22, 24–25.
3. Samuel Johnson, *The Lives of the Most Eminent English Poets; With Critical Observations on Their Works (1779–81)*, ed. Roger Lonsdale, vol. 1 (Oxford: Clarendon Press, 2006), 238, emphasis in original. Robert Aubin recommends "topographical poetry" as a more accurate term to use than Johnson's "local poetry," arguing that poems such as John Denham's "Cooper's Hill" are distinguished by their focus on "specifically named actual localities." See: Aubin, *Topographical Poetry in 18th-Century England* (New York: Modern Language Association of America, 1936), vii. M. H. Abrams and Geoffrey Galt Harpham use the terms "topographical poetry" and "local poetry" as synonyms, defining the genre as the "description of a specific natural scene with historical, political, or moral reflections that are associated with the scene or suggested by its details." See: M. H. Abrams and Geoffrey Galt Harpham, *A Glossary of Literary Terms* (Independence: Cengage Learning, 2011), 403.
4. John Barrell, *The Idea of Landscape and the Sense of Place, 1730–1840: An Approach to the Poetry of John Clare* (Cambridge: Cambridge University Press, 1972).
5. For examples of scholarship that situate Carson's poetry within the traditions of regionalism and *dinnseanchas*, see: Fran Brearton, "Mapping the Trenches: Gyres, Switchbacks and Zig-zag Circles in W. B. Yeats and Ciaran Carson," *Irish Studies Review* 9, no. 3 (2001): 373–86; Alex Houen, "Re-placing Terror: Poetic Mappings of Northern Ireland's 'Troubles,'" in *Terrorism and Modern Literature: From Joseph Conrad to Ciaran Carson* (Oxford: Oxford University Press, 2002), 235–78; Elmer Kennedy-Andrews, "Ciaran Carson: The New Urban Poetics," in *Writing Home: Poetry and Place in Northern Ireland, 1968–2008* (Cambridge: D. S. Brewer, 2008), 203–24.
6. Jim Cocola, *Places in the Making: A Cultural Geography of American Poetry* (Iowa City: University of Iowa Press, 2016), 3.
7. Johnson, *Lives of the Poets*, 238.

8. Georg Lukács, "Narrate or Describe?," in *Writer and Critic*, ed. and trans. Arthur Kahn (London: Merlin, 1970), 110–48.

9. Naomi Schor, *Reading in Detail: Aesthetics and the Feminine* (New York: Routledge, 2007), 3, emphasis mine.

10. Sharon Marcus, Heather Love, and Stephen Best, "Building a Better Description," *Representations* 135, no. 1 (2016): 4–5.

11. There already exist many razor-sharp rebuttals of surface reading and postcritique. For some of the finer examples, see: Sheila Leming, "Fighting Words," *Los Angeles Review of Books*, December 14, 2020, https://lareviewofbooks.org/article/fighting-words; Anna Kornbluh, "Extinct Critique," *The South Atlantic Quarterly* 119, no. 4 (2020): 767–77.

12. Marcus, Love, and Best, "Building a Better Description," 10.

13. Sarah Manguso, *500 Arguments* (New York: Graywolf Press, 2017), 51.

14. Patricia Craig, "Ciaran Carson Obituary," *The Guardian*, October 6, 2019, https://www.theguardian.com/books/2019/oct/06/ciaran-carson-obituary; "Award Winning Belfast Poet Ciaran Carson Passes Away Aged 70," *Belfast Telegraph*, October 6, 2019, https://www.belfasttelegraph.co.uk/news/northern-ireland/award-winning-belfast-poet-ciaran-carson-passes-away-aged-70-38567100.html.

15. Ciaran Carson, *Belfast Confetti* (Winston-Salem: Wake Forest University Press, 1989), 67.

16. Ciaran Carson, "Introduction," in *The Inferno of Dante Alighieri*, trans. Ciaran Carson (New York: New York Review of Books, 2002), xii–xiii.

17. Carson, *Belfast Confetti*, 52.

18. Ciaran Carson, *The Star Factory* (New York: Arcade, 1997), 153.

19. Rand Brandes, "Ciaran Carson," *The Irish Review* 8 (1990): 88.

20. William J. V. Neill, *Urban Planning and Cultural Identity* (New York: Routledge, 2004), 188–91.

21. Carson, *Belfast Confetti*, 67–68, emphasis in original.

22. Between 1969 and 1999, sectarian violence was the cause of 1,597 deaths in Belfast, the majority occurring between 1970 and 1977 and nearly 20 percent of them in a single year, 1972. At the same time, Northern Ireland had the highest unemployment rates in the UK. (Belfast had especially high unemployment rates, which reached as high as 17 percent in 1987.) For more on this period of Belfast's history, see: Alan F. Parkinson, *Belfast's Unholy War* (Dublin: Four Courts Press, 2004).

23. By comparison, such subsidies accounted for only 3.7 percent of Scotland's GDP. For more, see: John McGarry and Brendan O'Leary, "Mammon and Utility: Liberal Economic Reasoning," in *Broken Images: Explaining Northern Ireland* (Oxford: Blackwell, 1995), 265–310.

24. Bob Rowthorn, "Northern Ireland: An Economy in Crisis," *Cambridge Journal of Economics* 5, no. 1 (1981): 11.

25. In part, this wave of urban development in 1980s Belfast was poised as a remedy to the previous decade's botched city planning, which had been focused on containing sectarian violence and installing infrastructure for British military occupation. For more, see: Neill, *Urban Planning and Cultural Identity*.

26. The emphasis on economic development came partly as a result of a change in the IRA's bombing campaigns, which had shifted from political targets, such as government buildings and military bases, to specifically financial attacks, like the bombing of the Baltic Exchange in London, which cost a staggering 800 million pounds in damages. (The IRA presumed that the increasing costs of governing Northern Ireland would sap Britain's will to stay.) For more on the economic tactics of the IRA, see: McGarry and O'Leary, "Green Political Economy: British Imperialism as the Prime Mover," in *Broken Images*, 62–91.

27. F. W. Boal, *Shaping a City: Belfast in the Late Twentieth Century* (Belfast: Institute of Irish Studies, Queen's University, 1995), 10.

28. Initial funding for the construction of Castlecourt was earmarked earlier in 1978 as part of a larger package to rehabilitate Belfast's city center. For more on this history, see: William J. V. Neill, "Physical Planning and Image Enhancement: Recent Developments in Belfast," *International Journal of Urban and Regional Research* 17, no. 4 (1993): 595–609.

29. The concept of "ethnically neutral" zones or "neutralized territory" is not specific to Belfast but a common term in urban-planning strategies that attempt to manage urban-based ethnic conflicts and diffuse intergroup tensions. Similar strategies have been implemented in other cities such as Jerusalem and Johannesburg. For an overview, see: Scott A. Bollens, "Urban Policy in Ethnically Polarized Societies," *International Political Science Review* 19, no. 2 (1998): 187–215.

30. Richard Needham, *Battling for Peace* (Belfast: Blackstaff Press, 1998), 171.

31. Neill, *Urban Planning and Cultural Identity*, 193.

32. Gerald Dawe, "The Revenges of the Heart: Belfast and the Poetics of Space," in *The Cities of Belfast*, ed. Nicholas Allen and Aaron Kelly (Dublin: Four Courts Press, 2003), 199, 202.

33. For the representative works of these two prolific scholars, see: Anthony D. King, *Spaces of Global Cultures: Architecture, Urbanism, Identity* (New York: Routledge, 2004); David Harvey, *Spaces of Capital: Towards a Critical Geography* (New York: Routledge, 2001).

34. Ciaran Carson, *The Irish for No* (Loughcrew: Gallery Press, 1987), 42.

35. Carson, *Belfast Confetti*, 107.

36. Aida Edemariam, "A Life in Poetry: Ciaran Carson," *The Guardian*, January 16, 2009, https://www.theguardian.com/books/2009/jan/17/poetry-ciaran-carson-belfast-ireland.

37. Carson, *Belfast Confetti*, 58. Julia Obert goes so far as to argue that Carson's suspicion of maps causes him to instead create an alternative "soundscape" of Belfast that is more reliable than any visual representation of the city. See: Obert, *Postcolonial Overtures: The Politics of Sound in Contemporary Northern Irish Poetry* (Syracuse: Syracuse University Press, 2015), 22–76.

38. Carson, *Opera et Cetera* (Oldcastle: Gallery Press, 1996), 46, emphasis in original.

39. John Goodby, "'Walking in the City': Space, Narrative and Surveillance in *The Irish for No* and *Belfast Confetti*," in *Ciaran Carson: Critical Essays*, ed. Elmer Kennedy-Andrews (Dublin: Four Courts Press, 2009), 66–85.

40. Neal Alexander, *Ciaran Carson: Space, Place, Writing* (Liverpool: Liverpool University Press, 2010), 90, 86–87.

41. Eric Falci, *Continuity and Change in Irish Poetry, 1966–2010* (Cambridge: Cambridge University Press, 2012), 123.

42. Barrell, *Idea of Landscape and Sense of Place*, 22.

43. Adam Potkay, "Ear and Eye: Counteracting Senses in Loco-descriptive Poetry," in *A Companion to Romantic Poetry*, ed. Charles Mahoney (Oxford: Blackwell, 2012), 176–94.

44. Bonnie Costello, "Landscape Poem," in *Princeton Encyclopedia of Poetry and Poetics*, 4th ed., ed. Roland Greene, Stephen Cushman, Clare Cavanagh, Jahan Ramazani, and Paul Rouzer (Princeton: Princeton University Press, 2012), 784.

45. Contra Potkay and Costello, John Wilson Foster defines loco-descriptive poetry as relying on "exhaustive description, the catalogue as a descriptive device," which grounds the poems in specifically named localities like Cooper's Hill. However, much of the criticism on loco-descriptive poetry instead emphasizes its selectiveness rather than its all-inclusiveness. See: John Wilson Foster, "A Redefinition of Topographical Poetry," *The Journal of English and Germanic Philology* 69, no. 3 (1970): 395.

46. The peripatetic poem has remained relatively understudied in comparison to its generic sibling, which has received the bulk of critical attention since Barrell's influential study. For a cultural history of pedestrian travel in nineteenth-century England and its representations in British literature at the time, see: Anne D. Wallace, *Walking, Literature, and Culture: The Origins and Uses of Peripatetic in the Nineteenth Century* (Oxford: Oxford University Press, 1994).

47. Robin Jarvis, *Romantic Writing and Pedestrian Travel* (London: Palgrave Macmillan, 1997), 69.

48. Harryette Mullen, *Urban Tumbleweed: Notes from a Tanka Diary* (Minneapolis: Graywolf Press, 2013), viii.

49. In fact, Walt Hunter has persuasively shown how contemporary Anglophone poets such as J. H. Prynne, Kofi Awoonor, and Natasha Trethewey have recaptured the prospect poem as a literary device that can register the experience of precarity in life under neoliberal globalization. See: Hunter, "The No-Prospect Poem," *minnesota review* 85 (2015): 144–52.

50. For instance, Neal Alexander argues that the activity of walking is a "utopian spatial politics through which resistance to various forms of sociospatial regulation might be both imagined and effected." See: Alexander, *Ciaran Carson*, 86.

51. Carson, *Belfast Confetti*, 34.

52. Carson, *Irish For No*, 100.

53. Jarvis, *Romantic Writing and Pedestrian Travel*, 68–69.

54. Carson, *Belfast Confetti*, 60.

55. Carson, *Belfast Confetti*, 62, italics in original.

56. Allen Feldman, *Formations of Violence: The Narrative of the Body and Political Terror in Northern Ireland* (Chicago: University of Chicago Press, 1991), 49.

57. Daniel Weston, "'I Know This Labyrinth So Well': Narrative Mappings in the Poetry of Ciaran Carson," in *Poetry and Geography: Space and Place in Post-war Poetry*, ed. Neal Alexander and David Cooper (Liverpool: Liverpool University Press, 2013), 115.

58. Ciaran Carson, *Collected Poems* (Winston-Salem: Wake Forest University Press, 2009), 107, emphasis mine.

59. Leontia Flynn, *Drives* (London: Cape Books, 2008), 8.

60. Flynn, *Drives*, 2.

61. The Ulster Renaissance refers to the flourishing of poetry in Northern Ireland in the 1960s and 1970s, particularly the work of the coterie known as the "Belfast Group," whose members included Seamus Heaney, Michael Longley, Derek Mahon, and Paul Muldoon. For a thorough overview of the Belfast Group's activities, as well as their friendships and rivalries, see: Heather Clark, *The Ulster Renaissance: Poetry in Belfast, 1962–1972* (Oxford: Oxford University Press, 2006).

62. Catherine Switzer and Sara McDowell, "Redrawing Cognitive Maps of Conflict: Lost Spaces and Forgetting in the Centre of Belfast," *Memory Studies* 2, no. 3 (2009): 343.

63. For more, see: John A. McCord, Michael J. McCord, Peadar T. Davis, Martin E. Haran, and Sean MacIntyre, "The Political Cost? Religious Segregation, Peace Walls, and House Prices," *Peace and Conflict Studies* 24, no. 1 (2017): 1–37.

64. See: Paul Nolan, *The Northern Ireland Peace Monitoring Report, No. 2* (Belfast: Community Relations Council, 2013), 87–88.

65. Brendan Murtagh, "Desegregation and Place Restructuring in the New Belfast," *Urban Studies* 48, no. 6 (2011): 1119–35.

66. Aaron Kelly, "The Troubles with the Peace Process," *The Irish Review* 40/41 (2009): 2.

67. Alan Gillis, *Hawks and Doves* (Oldcastle, Ireland: Gallery Press, 2007), 35.

68. Gillis, *Hawks and Doves*, 14.

69. Leontia Flynn, *The Radio* (Winston-Salem: Wake Forest University Press, 2017), 30.

70. Sinéad Morrissey, *Parallax* (Manchester: Carcanet Press, 2013), 145, 147.

71. Northern Ireland certainly does not follow the same trajectory and breakneck speed of globalization that has characterized the Republic's economic development over the past decades. (In the year before the 2008 financial crisis, Northern Ireland received $1 billion in foreign direct investments, whereas the Republic received $27 billion.) But nor has Northern Ireland been sequestered altogether, particularly with the US's deep involvement in the brokering of the Peace Agreement and the EU's hefty contribution of Peace and Reconciliation funds (estimated at over €240 million) that helped finance the development of Belfast's cultural quarters. The unique circumstances of Northern Ireland—its dependency on public subsidies as well as its persistent cultures of atavism and ethnonationalism—make it sit awkwardly within the processes of globalization and neoliberalism, if not render it altogether incongruous with them. But as Liam O'Dowd and Milena Komarova argue, it is more useful to understand neoliberalism as existing in a hybridized form in Northern Ireland, where public funding is used as leverage for private real estate developments: "Somewhat paradoxically, high levels of public expenditure subsidized a neo-liberal economic strategy as means of promoting and consolidating a political settlement." See: O'Dowd and Komarova, "Contesting Territorial Fixity? A Case Study of Regeneration in Belfast," *Urban Studies* 48, no. 10 (2011): 2015.

72. Philip Boland, John Bronte, and Jenny Muir, "On the Waterfront: Neoliberal Urbanism and the Politics of Public Benefit," *Cities* 61 (2017): 122. The irony, of course, is that the shipyards represented one of the most segregated spaces in the city, as the shipbuilding industries excluded Catholics from their workforce in the nineteenth and twentieth centuries.

73. John Nagle, "Potemkin Village: Neo-liberalism and Peace-Building in Northern Ireland?" *Ethnopolitics* 8, no. 2 (1990): 173–4.

74. Carson, *Belfast Confetti*, 27.

75. Carson, *Collected Poems*, 311.

76. Carson, *The Star Factory*, 166–7, emphasis mine.

77. David Laskowski, "Inventing Carson: An Interview," *Chicago Review* 45, nos. 3 and 4 (1999): 94.

78. Foster, "Redefinition of Topographical Poetry," 396.

79. Carson, *The Star Factory*, 37.

80. Carson, *Belfast Confetti*, 79.

81. Miriam Gamble, "'A Potted Peace/Lily?' Northern Irish Poetry since the Ceasefires," in *The Oxford Handbook of Modern Irish Poetry*, ed. Fran Brearton and Alan Gillis (Oxford: Oxford University Press, 2018), 673.

82. Naomi Marklew, "The Future of Northern Irish Poetry: Fragility, Contingency, Value and Beauty," *English Academy Review* 31, no. 2 (2014): 75.

83. Gillis, *Hawks and Doves*, 73.

84. Alan Gillis, *Somebody, Somewhere* (Oldcastle: Gallery Press, 2005), 17.

85. Miriam Gamble, "'The Gentle Art of Re-perceiving': Post-ceasefire Identity in the Poetry of Alan Gillis," *Irish Studies* 17, no. 3 (2009): 368.
86. Gillis, *Somebody, Somewhere*, 17.
87. Carson, *Belfast Confetti*, 81–82, ellipsis in original.
88. Gillis, *Somebody, Somewhere*, 9.
89. Carson, *The New Estate* (Winston-Salem: Wake Forest University Press, 1976), 41.
90. Gillis, *Somebody, Somewhere*, 46–47, emphasis mine.
91. Walt Hunter, *Forms of a World: Contemporary Poetry and the Making of Globalization* (New York: Fordham University Press, 2019). 112.
92. Hunter, *Forms of a World*, 97.
93. Gillis, *Hawks and Doves*, 11.
94. Gillis, *Hawks and Doves*, 12.
95. Gillis, *Hawks and Doves*, 15, 14.
96. Gamble, "Gentle Art of Re-perceiving," 369.

Chapter 4

1. Lachlan Mackinnon, "A Dream Diffused in Words," *Times Literary Supplement*, October 12–18, 1990, 1105.
2. Rajeev S. Patke, "'Responsibility' and 'Difficulty' in the Poetry of Paul Muldoon," *Criticism* 50, no. 2 (2008): 279–99.
3. Charles McGrath, "Word Freak," *The New York Times*, November 19, 2006, https://www.nytimes.com/2006/11/19/magazine/word-freak.html.
4. T. S. Eliot, "Review of *Metaphysical Lyrics and Poems of the Seventeenth Century: Donne to Butler*, ed. Herbert J. C. Grierson," *Times Literary Supplement*, October 20, 1921, 669, emphasis in original.
5. Robert Archambeau, "Postnational Ireland," *Contemporary Literature* 50, no. 3 (2009): 610.
6. Dwight Garner, "Shared Homeland, Different Worldview," *New York Times*, September 16, 2010, https://www.nytimes.com/2010/09/17/books/17book.html. Garner also suggests that the emphasis on Muldoon's Irish identity is not only the result of the nation-bound myopia of literary critics but also a commercial strategy: publishers seek to market Muldoon toward a wider audience by associating him with other more popular and accessible Irish writers like Heaney.
7. Trinh Minh-ha, *Woman Native Other: Writing Postcolonialism and Feminism* (Bloomington: Indiana University Press, 1989), 15.
8. Fran Brearton, "Muldoon 'Goes Native' across the Pond? Review of *Horse Latitudes* by Paul Muldoon," *Tower Poetry*, no. 3 (2007): 7. Other scholars have made similar points about the associative structure of Muldoon's poetry. See: Guinn Batten, "'He Could Barely Tell One from the Other': The Border-

line Discourses of Paul Muldoon's Poetry," *South Atlantic Quarterly* 95, no. 1 (1996): 171–204; Eric Falci, *Continuity and Change in Irish Poetry, 1966–2010* (Cambridge: Cambridge University Press, 2012); Ruben Moi, *Paul Muldoon and the Language of Poetry* (Leiden: Brill, 2020).

9. Paul Muldoon, *Poems 1968–1998* (New York: Farrar, Straus and Giroux, 2001), 371.

10. Michel Foucault, *Archaeology of Knowledge* (New York: Routledge, 1972), 10.

11. Jahan Ramazani, *A Transnational Poetics* (Chicago: University of Chicago Press, 2010), 54, emphasis mine.

12. For more on the history of lyric reading, see: Virginia Jackson, *Dickinson's Misery: A Theory of Lyric Reading* (Princeton: Princeton University Press, 2005).

13. Virginia Jackson and Yopie Prins, eds., *The Lyric Theory Reader: A Critical Anthology* (Baltimore: Johns Hopkins University Press, 2014), 569, 575.

14. Eric Hayot, "Against Historical Fundamentalism," *PMLA* 131, no. 5 (2016): 1419. Hayot goes on: "Ask the question one way—did the Chinese have the lyric?—and the self-evidence of the answer (no, they did not have the word *lyric* in their language) allows us to ignore them. Ask it another way—does the history of Chinese poetry have something to teach us about the lyric?—and the willful self-impoverishment of the first way of asking becomes clear" (1420).

15. For a selection of the most prominent discussions of this topic, see: Susan Gubar, "Prosopopoeia and Holocaust Poetry in English: Sylvia Plath and Her Contemporaries," *Yale Journal of Criticism* 14, no. 1 (2001): 191–215; Matthew Hart, *Nations of Nothing but Poetry: Modernism, Transnationalism, and Synthetic Vernacular Writing* (Oxford: Oxford University Press, 2011); Ramazani, "Traveling Poetry," in *A Transnational Poetics* (Chicago: University of Chicago Press, 2010), 51–70.

16. Jacob Edmond, *A Common Strangeness: Contemporary Poetry, Cross-Cultural Encounter, Comparative Literature* (New York: Fordham University Press, 2012), 3–4.

17. Chris Chen and Tim Kreiner, "Free Speech, Minstrelsy, and the Avant-Garde," *Los Angeles Review of Books*, December 10, 2015, https://lareviewofbooks.org/article/free-speech-minstrelsy-and-the-avant-garde/.

18. This is not to elide the foundational work of labor historians like Noel Ignatiev, Matthew Frye Jacobsen, and David Roediger or the more recent generation of scholars like Ronit Lentin, Steve Garner, Diane Negra, and Sinéad Moynihan, who work at the nexus of Irish studies and critical race theory. But there remains a near-complete void of scholarship on race and Irish poetry.

19. Rayna Green, "The Tribe Called Wannabee: Playing Indian in American and Europe," *Folklore* 99, no. 1 (1988): 30–55.

20. Adrienne Rich, "Notes towards a Politics of Location," in *Blood, Bread, and Poetry: Selected Prose, 1979–1985* (New York: Norton, 1994), 224.

21. Muldoon, *Poems*, 395.
22. Muldoon, *Poems*, 398–9.
23. Lawrence Norfolk, "The Abundant Braes of Yarrow," *Times Literary Supplement*, August 21, 1994, 32–33.
24. Maureen McLane, "Paul Muldoon's Poems and Essays Pulse with Emotional and Intellectual Vigor," *Chicago Tribune*, October 8, 2006, https://www.chicagotribune.com/news/ct-xpm-2006-10-08-0610080230-story.html.
25. Clair Wills, *Reading Paul Muldoon* (Northumberland: Bloodaxe Books, 1998), 166.
26. Robert MacFarlane, "High and Dry in the Flood," *Times Literary Supplement*, October 11, 2002, 24.
27. Peter Davison, "Darkness at Muldoon," *The New York Times*, October 13, 2002, https://www.nytimes.com/2002/10/13/books/darkness-at-muldoon.html.
28. Cynthia Huntington, Heather McHugh, Paul Muldoon, and Charles Simic, "How to Peel a Poem: Five Poets Dine Out on Verse," *Harper's*, September 1, 1999, https://harpers.org/archive/1999/09/how-to-peel-a-poem/.
29. Natalie Melas, *All the Difference in the World: Postcolonialism and the Ends of Comparison* (Palo Alto: Stanford University Press, 2006), 93.
30. J. H. Prynne, "Difficulties in the Translation of 'Difficult' Poems," *Cambridge Literary Review* 1, no. 3 (2010): 154–55.
31. Muldoon, *Poems*, 24.
32. Muldoon, *Poems*, 134.
33. Charles L. O'Neill, "Paul Muldoon's *Madoc: A Mystery* and the Romantic Poets," *The Wordsworth Circle* 24, no. 1 (1993): 54–56.
34. For representative examples, see: John Kerrigan, "Paul Muldoon's Transits: Muddling after *Madoc*," in *Paul Muldoon: Critical Essays*, ed. Tim Kendall and Peter McDonald (Liverpool: Liverpool University Press, 2004), 125–49; Jacqueline McCurry, "A Land 'Not "Borrowed" but "Purloined"': Paul Muldoon's Indians," *New Hibernia Review* 1, no. 3 (1997): 40–51.
35. Omaar Hena, "Playing Indian/Disintegrating Irishness: Globalization and Cross-Cultural Identity in Paul Muldoon's 'Madoc: A Mystery,'" *Contemporary Literature* 49, no. 2 (2008): 258. In his monograph, Hena reconsiders his assessment of Muldoon's poetry in his original article, arguing that the poet's work can be read as guilty of cultural appropriation. See: Hena, *Global Anglophone Poetry: Literary Form and Social Critique in Walcott, Muldoon, de Kok, and Nagra* (New York: Palgrave Macmillan, 2015), 55–86.
36. Elizabeth Butler Cullingford, *Ireland's Others: Gender and Ethnicity in Irish Literature and Popular Culture* (Notre Dame: University of Notre Dame Press, 2001), 99. That said, Cullingford also cites bell hooks's critical reading of Neil Jordan's film *The Crying Game*, which features a relationship between a white IRA man and a Black British soldier during the Troubles: "While Neil Jordan . . . saw Fergus as a portrait of the IRA man as disenfranchised subject,

alienated by the presence of the British in the North, the black American feminist bell hooks sees the power differentials between white and black, masculine and feminine, as more important than the power differential between Brits and Paddies . . . Analogies, then, are slippery things: one man's sympathetic identification is another woman's 'cannibalistic' appropriation, and the construction of aesthetic parallels that elide historical differences or asymmetries of power may appear racist or falsely totalizing" (133). But later, Cullingford praises Muldoon's subtle connections between the "viral holocaust" of Native Americans at the hands of British colonists during the French Indian War and the Irish experience of the Famine (172).

37. Luke Gibbons, *Edmund Burke and Ireland: Aesthetics, Politics and the Colonial Sublime* (Cambridge: Cambridge University Press, 2003), 13.

38. Eóin Flannery, *Ireland and Postcolonial Studies: Theory, Discourse, Utopia* (London: Palgrave Macmillan, 2010), 69.

39. Lynn Keller, "Interview with Paul Muldoon," *Contemporary Literature* 35, no. 1 (1994): 19.

40. Franz Fanon, *Black Skin, White Masks*, trans. Charles Lam Markman (London: Pluto Press, 2008), 163.

41. For more work on the limits of comparative methodology, see: Rey Chow, "The Old/New Question of Comparison in Literary Studies: A Post-European Perspective," *ELH* 71, no. 2 (2004): 289–311.

42. Paul Muldoon, *Horse Latitudes* (New York: Farrar, Straus and Giroux, 2006), 85.

43. Kenneth Keating, *Contemporary Irish Poetry and the Canon: Critical Limitation and Textual Liberations* (Cham: Springer International, 2017), 80–81.

44. Moi, *Muldoon and the Language of Poetry*, 323.

45. Quoted in: Ian Duhig, "Sinéad Morrissey: A Maker of Intricate Poem Machines," *The Irish Times*, October 21, 2017, https://www.irishtimes.com/culture/books/sinéad-morrissey-a-maker-of-intricate-poem-machines-1.3260694.

46. James S. F. Wilson, "The Art of Poetry No. 87, Paul Muldoon," *The Paris Review* 169 (2004): 83.

47. Chen and Kreiner, "Free Speech, Minstrelsy, and the Avant-Garde."

48. Sarah Dowling, "Property, Priority, Place: Rethinking the Poetics of Appropriation," *Contemporary Literature* 60, no. 1 (2019): 119.

49. Ramazani, *Transnational Poetics*, 59–60.

50. Eve Tuck and K. Wayne Yang, "Decolonization Is Not a Metaphor," *Decolonization: Indigeneity, Education & Society* 1, no. 1 (2012): 3, emphasis mine.

51. This is not to reduce metaphor to what Max Black calls the "comparison view" of metaphor, in which one thing is merely substituted for another ("A is B"). For New Critics, most notably I. A. Richards and Monroe C. Beardsley, metaphor is not based on substitution but instead an "interaction" between words and things, which create new meanings. Roman Jakobson defines metaphor in

opposition to metonymy, arguing that metaphor is based on substitution (and associated more with poetry, especially that of the Romantics) while metonymy is based on contiguity (and aligned instead with prose and realism). See: Black, "How Metaphors Work: A Reply to Donald Davidson," *Critical Inquiry* 6, no. 1 (1979): 131–43; Jakobson, "Two Aspects of Language and Two Types of Aphasic Disturbances," in *On Language*, ed. Linda R. Waugh and Monique Monville-Burston (Cambridge: Harvard University Press, 1995), 115–33; George Lakoff and Mark Johnson, *Metaphors We Live By* (Chicago: University of Chicago Press, 1980).

52. The terms "tenor" and "vehicle" were coined by I. A. Richards in his seminal work *Philosophy of Rhetoric*. Richards does argue that it would be wrong to dismiss vehicle as a "mere embellishment of a tenor which is otherwise unchanged by it" and instead insists that "vehicle and tenor in co-operation give a meaning of more varied powers than can be ascribed to either." But while the interaction between these two components is vital to how metaphor makes meaning, the tenor is nonetheless the principal subject illuminated by the vehicle. See: Richards, *The Philosophy of Rhetoric* (Oxford: Oxford University Press, 1936), 100.

53. Similarly, Rayna Green pinpoints metaphor as central to the performances of "playing Indian" in the US. Green explains how the late nineteenth century saw both the end of Indian removal and the emergence of Wild West vaudeville shows that prominently featured "white Indian" frontiersmen like Sam Houston and Buffalo Bill: "In the West, the Indian has become the primary metaphor of the Americanization process, and the metaphor signs the real Indian's death warrant." See: Green, "The Tribe Called Wannabee," 31, 37.

54. While this chapter concentrates on the work of Irish studies scholars, this strain of cross-cultural comparative thinking is certainly not limited to this body of scholarship. Matthew Eatough traces what he calls the "analogic imaginary" in early-twentieth-century Irish nationalist discourse, Irish missionary work, and international humanitarianism in the 1990s, particularly the 1985 Live Aid concert, cofounded by Irish musician Bob Geldof. See: Matthew Eatough, "The Global Contemporary: The Humanitarian Legacy in Irish Fiction," in *The New Irish Studies*, ed. Paige Reynolds (Cambridge: Cambridge University Press, 2020), 113–28.

55. Cullingford, *Ireland's Others*, 99.

56. Mary Mullen, "How the Irish Became Settlers: Metaphors of Indigeneity and the Erasure of Indigenous Peoples," *New Hibernia Review* 20, no. 3 (2016): 96. In a footnote, Mullen makes a direct criticism of Muldoon's poetry, which she sees as asserting cross-cultural solidarity between Irish and Native anticolonial histories at the expense of acknowledging Irish involvement in settler colonialism in the Americas (87–88).

57. Andrew Fox, "Transnational Displacement: 'Native American Material' in Paul Muldoon's *New Weather*," *New Hibernia Review* 17, no. 4 (2013): 65.

58. David Lloyd, *Anomalous States: Irish Writing and the Post-colonial Moment* (Durham: Duke University Press, 1993), 9. Lloyd does not dismiss all forms of comparative analysis, and indeed he acknowledges how the Northern Irish civil rights movement in the 1960s productively looked to the US civil rights movement for inspiration. But Lloyd argues that it is vital to begin with a "differential analysis of cultural forms" in order to produce the most cogent forms of comparative analysis: "I have been constantly aware of the points of contact between historically very different cultural situations and have at moments attempted to address these explicitly. A paradoxical thesis that derives from this exploration is that by and large the more specific the cultural analysis, the more useful is the articulation of different histories with one another." Later, Lloyd rearticulates his critique of metaphor and upholds conceit as the superior poetic figure: "Unlike metaphor, which Étienne Bonnot de Condillac more succinctly and classically describes as 'thinking of the properties in which things agree,' wit and conceit derive their effects from the salience of difference . . . [M]etaphor is not merely the oscillation between sameness and difference but the process of subordinating difference to identity." See: Lloyd, *Under Representation: The Racial Regime of Aesthetics* (New York: Fordham University Press, 2018), 8, 78.

59. Samuel Johnson, *The Lives of the Most Eminent English Poets; With Critical Observations on Their Works (1779–81)*, ed. Roger Lonsdale, vol. 1 (Oxford: Oxford University Press, 2006), 200.

60. Helen Gardner, "Introduction," in *The Metaphysical Poets* (New York: Penguin, 1967), 20.

61. Paul Muldoon, "Getting Round: Notes towards an Ars Poetica," *Essays in Criticism* 48, no. 2 (1998): 108–9.

62. Wilson, "Art of Poetry No. 87," 75.

63. Christopher Johnson also argues that the contrivance of conceit distinguishes it from metaphor and other literary figures: "Unlike a simile or strong metaphor, [conceit's] terms are frequently allusive or qualified by argument, thus its perceived artificiality." See Roland Greene, Stephen Cushman, Clare Cavanagh, Jahan Ramazani, and Paul Rouzer, eds., *Princeton Encyclopedia of Poetry and Poetics*, 4th ed. (Princeton: Princeton University Press, 2012), 289.

64. Wilson, "Art of Poetry No. 87," 75.

65. Muldoon makes a similar distinction of meaning in *To Ireland, I* when he writes that Irish writers often feel compelled to conflate poetic subjectivity with political and national identity: "One way or another, it does seem that Irish writers again and again find themselves challenged by the violent juxtaposition of the concepts of 'Ireland' and 'I.' Irish writers have a tendency to interpose themselves between the two . . . either to bring them closer together, or to force them further apart. It's as if they feel obliged to extend the notion of being a 'medium' to becoming a 'mediator.'" See: Muldoon, *To Ireland, I* (Oxford: Oxford University Press, 2001), 35.

66. Wilson, "Art of Poetry No. 87," 75.

67. Muldoon, *Madoc: A Mystery* (New York: Farrar, Straus and Giroux, 1991), 10–11, emphases mine.

68. Prynne, "Difficulties in the Translation," 154.

69. Wilson, "Art of Poetry No. 87," 73.

70. Falci, *Continuity and Change in Irish Poetry*, 50. In an interview, Muldoon uses similar language to explain how his poetry resembles the "associative accretion" of Elizabeth Bishop's work: "John Donne is interested in the continuation of a comparison, to make it last for as long as he can, and there is another tradition—though they are most certainly connected—of an associative accretion, the piling of one thing on top of another. A great modern example would be Elizabeth Bishop, who's perfectly happy to leave one system and go to the next, to follow the poem wherever it wants to bring her . . ." See: Wilson, "Art of Poetry No. 87," 70.

71. Muldoon, *Poems*, 343.

72. Muldoon, *Poems*, 336–7.

73. Muldoon, *Poems*, 335.

74. Sianne Ngai, *Ugly Feelings* (Cambridge: Harvard University Press, 2005), 68, emphasis in original.

75. Ramazani, *Transnational Poetics*, 54–55.

76. Muldoon, *Poems*, 340.

77. Wilson, "Art of Poetry No. 87," 83.

78. John Brannigan, "'Ireland, and Black!': The Cultural Politics of Racial Figuration," in *Race in Modern Irish Literature and Culture* (Edinburgh: Edinburgh University Press, 2009), 214; Joe Cleary, "Irish Studies, Colonial Questions: Locating Ireland in the Colonial World," in *Outrageous Fortune: Capital and Culture in Modern Ireland* (Dublin: Field Day, 2006), 21, 16–17.

79. Renée Fox, Mike Cronin, and Brian Ó Conchubhair, "Introduction," in *The Routledge International Handbook of Irish Studies*, ed. Fox, Cronin, and Ó Conchubhair (Abingdon: Routledge, 2021), 8.

80. For another example of a call for new reformulations of Irish studies, see: Paige Reynolds, "Coda: A New Irish Studies," in *The New Irish Studies*, ed. Reynolds (Cambridge: Cambridge University Press, 2020), 275–82.

Coda

1. Caelainn Hogan, "Trump's Other Wall: Is His Irish Resort a Sign He Believes in Climate Change?" *The Guardian*, November 17, 2016, https://www.theguardian.com/us-news/2016/nov/17/donald-trump-ireland-golf-resort-wall-climate-change.

2. Griff Witte, "A Wall Denied May Have Made Trump Dislike E.U.," *The Washington Post*, February 7, 2017, https://www.washingtonpost.com/opinions/

as-europe-well-knows-big-walls-dont-make-good-neighbors/2017/02/10/07c54dc6-ee3e-11e6-a100-fdaaf400369a_story.html.

3. Similar language was echoed in the controversy over Trump's resort in Balmedie, Scotland, where he built a fifteen-foot wall along the golf course's perimeter, to the consternation of his neighbors. See: Katrin Bennhold, "In Scotland, Trump Built a Wall. Then He Sent Residents the Bill," *The New York Times*, November 25, 2016, https://www.nytimes.com/2016/11/25/world/europe/donald-trump-scotland-wall.html.

4. Liam Hogan penned an open letter condemning several websites for disseminating and legitimizing false articles about Irish slavery; the letter was cosigned by dozens of historians. See: "Open Letter to *Irish Central, Irish Examiner*, and *Scientific American* about Their 'Irish Slaves' Misinformation," Medium, last modified March 8, 2016, https://limerick1914.medium.com/open-letter-to-irish-central-irish-examiner-and-scientific-american-about-their-irish-slaves-3f6cf23b8d7f. While the myth of Irish slavery is hardly new, its reappearance in the form of internet memes (circulating everywhere from Irish American Facebook pages to mainstream history websites to neo-Nazi message boards) has been reported by journalists from the *New York Times* and the *Washington Post* as well as by advocacy groups like the Southern Poverty Law Center.

5. Since the ascent of *Hillbilly Elegy*, many writers have taken to task Vance's inaccurate portrayal of white Appalachians as a homogenous population sharing a common "pure" Scots-Irish heritage and ethnicity. What's more disturbing, as Bob Hutton notes, is how Vance's fetishization of Scots-Irish identity eerily echoes the "Celtic thesis," or the theory that US southerners are racially and culturally distinct because they descended from Celtic tribes in Ireland, Scotland, and Wales. Notably, two historians who tout the Celtic thesis are Forrest McDonald and Grady McWhiney, who also founded the white supremacist group the League of the South. See: Hutton, "Hillbilly Elitism," *Jacobin*, October 1, 2016, https://www.jacobinmag.com/2016/10/hillbilly-elegy-review-jd-vance-national-review-white-working-class-appalachia/; Elizabeth Catte, "The Mythical Whiteness of Trump Country," *Boston Review*, November 7, 2017, http://bostonreview.net/race-politics/elizabeth-catte-mythical-whiteness-trump-country; John Thomason, "Hillbilly Ethnography," *The New Inquiry*, November 29, 2016, https://thenewinquiry.com/hillbilly-ethnography/.

6. Diane Negra, *The Irish in Us: Irishness, Performativity, and Popular Culture* (Durham: Duke University Press, 2006), 2.

7. In particular, Irish studies has benefited from the recent work of scholars such as John Brannigan, Amy Clukey, Catherine Eagan, Catherine McIvor, Gerardine Meaney, Sinéad Moynihan, and Sarah Townsend. However, these scholars have primarily concentrated on the genres of fiction and drama, as opposed to poetry, and this coda hopes to spark more analyses of race in Irish poetry. See: Brannigan, *Race in Modern Irish Literature and Culture* (Edinburgh:

Edinburgh University Press, 2009); Amy Clukey, "White Troubles: The Southern Imaginary in Northern Ireland 2008–2016," *Arizona Quarterly* 73, no. 4 (2017): 61–92; Gerardine Meaney, *Gender, Ireland, and Cultural Change: Race, Sex, and Nation* (New York: Routledge, 2010); Sinéad Moynihan, *Other People's Diasporas: Negotiating Race in Contemporary Irish and Irish-American Culture* (Syracuse: Syracuse University Press, 2013); Sarah Townsend, "Undocumented Irish Need Apply: Ethnic Whiteness, Immigrant Rights, and the Campaign for US Diversity Visas in the 1980s," *Radical History Review* 143 (2022): 125–40.

8. Alison Garden and David Rankin Russell have examined race in Heaney's poetry, but their analyses emphasize the cross-racial affinities in Heaney's work, highlighting the poet's comparisons between the experience of Northern Irish Catholics and those of other oppressed peoples. While it is worthwhile to situate Heaney's poetry in broader comparative frameworks, such approaches necessarily situate the Irish as the racialized other, obscuring how these poems also participate in the construction of whiteness as fundamental to Irish identity. See: Garden, "'We Listen for What the Waves Intone': Intertextuality and the Circum-Atlantic Poetics of Seamus Heaney, Natasha Trethewey and Kwame Dawes," *Comparative American Studies: An International Journal* 14, no. 2 (2016): 1–18; Russell, "The Black and Green Atlantic: Violence, History, and Memory in Natasha Trethewey's 'South' and Seamus Heaney's 'North,'" *Southern Literary Journal* 46 (2014): 155–72.

9. Dorothy Wang, *Thinking Its Presence: Form, Race, and Subjectivity in Contemporary Asian American Poetry* (Palo Alto: Stanford University Press, 2013), 19.

10. Brannigan, *Race in Modern Irish Literature and Culture*, 21.

11. Garner's use of the term "soil" here is borrowed from Edmund Spenser's *View of the Present State of Ireland*: "And to say though Ireland is by nature counted a great soil of pasture, yet had I rather few cows kept and men better mannered than to have such huge increase of cattle and no increase of good conditions." See: Steve Garner, "Reflections on Race in Contemporary Ireland," in *Race and Immigration in the New Ireland*, eds. Julieann Veronica Ulin and Heather Edwards (Notre Dame: Notre Dame University Press, 2013), 178.

12. David Lloyd, "Black Irish, Irish Witness and Atlantic State Formation," in *The Black and Green Atlantic: Cross-Currents of the African and Irish Diasporas*, ed. Peter D. O'Neill and David Lloyd (London: Palgrave Macmillan, 2009), 10–11.

13. Sara Maurer, *The Dispossessed State: Narratives of Ownership in Nineteenth-Century Britain and Ireland* (Baltimore: Johns Hopkins University Press, 2012), 118, 120. As Mary Mullen points out, this rhetoric of fusing together property and identity took on dangerous forms when it crossed the Atlantic. The Young Irelanders' arguments that the Irish were naturally predisposed to "love of land and love of arms" helped legitimize the Irish as settler colonialists and therefore

justified the dispossession of Indigenous peoples' land in the US. See: Mullen, "How the Irish Became Settlers: Metaphors of Indigeneity and the Erasure of Indigenous Peoples," *New Hibernia Review* 20, no. 3 (2016): 81–96. 86–87.

14. For more on the Young Irelanders' use of racial rhetoric, see: Julie M. Duggers, "Black Ireland's Race: Thomas Carlyle and the Young Ireland Movement," *Victorian Studies* 48, no. 3 (Spring 2006): 461–85.

15. David Lloyd, *Under Representation: The Racial Regime of Aesthetics* (New York: Fordham University Press, 2018), 15, 77.

16. James Fintan Lalor, *The Writing of James Fintan Lalor: With an Introduction Embodying Personal Recollections* (Dublin: T. G. O'Donoghue, 1895), 64, 68.

17. Seamus Deane, *Strange Country: Modernity and Nationhood Since 1790* (Oxford: Oxford University Press, 1999), 76.

18. Eamon de Valera, "Aims of Fianna Fáil in Office, 17 March 1932," in *Speeches and Statements by Eamon de Valera, 1917–73*, ed. Maurice Moynihan (New York: St. Martin's Press, 1980), 194.

19. Brannigan, *Race in Modern Irish Literature and Culture*, 150.

20. Bernard Ryan, "The Celtic Cubs: The Controversy over Birthright Citizenship in Ireland," *European Journal of Migration and Law* 6 (2004): 176.

21. Ireland's policy of *jus soli* was in keeping with that of many other former British colonies, including the US, Canada, India, Pakistan, Australia, and New Zealand, which had based their original nationality laws on those of the UK. (The UK had unqualified *jus soli* until the British Nationality Act of 1981.)

22. Children's Rights Alliance, "Immigration and Citizenship in Ireland," accessed December 1, 2022, https://www.childrensrights.ie/sites/default/files/submissions_reports/files/Immigration%26Citizenship_0.pdf.

23. Houses of the Oireachtas, Tithe an Oireachtais, "Twenty-Seventh Amendment of the Constitution Bill 2004: Second Stage," *Dáil Éireann Debate* 583, no. 6 (April 21, 2004), https://www.oireachtas.ie/en/debates/debate/dail/2004-04-21/3.

24. While outside the scope of this essay, another important component to this conversation is the history of discrimination against Irish Travellers in Ireland. The racialization of Travellers often revolves around their nomadism, and their nomadic cultural practices became increasingly criminalized (usually in the form of trespassing laws) during the Celtic Tiger, when large tracts of land were rapidly developed as real estate. For more, see: Sindy Joyce, "Divided Spaces: An Examination of Everyday Racism and Its Impact on Young Travellers' Spatial Mobility," *Irish Journal of Anthropology* 18, no. 1 (2015): 15–23.

25. Mary Robinson, "Cherishing the Irish Diaspora: President Mary Robinson on a Matter of Public Importance," transcript of address delivered at the House of the Oireachtas, Dublin, Ireland, February 2, 1995, https://president.ie/en/media-library/speeches/cherishing-the-irish-diaspora.

26. Ronit Lentin, "Illegal in Ireland, Irish Illegals: Diaspora Nation as Racial State." *Irish Political Studies* 22, no. 4 (2007): 433–53.

27. What is also unique about the Citizenship Referendum is that the growing xenophobia and racism occurred during not an era of economic decline but instead the boom times of the Celtic Tiger, arguably the most "prosperous" moment of Ireland's economic history.

28. No other works of Irish poetry have generated as much simultaneous praise and ire. Depending on the critic, Heaney's poetry is either the defining work of the Troubles or a sacrilegious aestheticization of the sectarian conflict. For the major voices in the critical reception of Heaney's bog poems, see: David Lloyd, *Anomalous States: Irish Writing and the Post-colonial Moment* (Durham: Duke University Press, 1993); Helen Vendler, *Seamus Heaney* (Cambridge: Harvard University Press, 2000); Ciaran Carson, "Escaped from the Massacre?," in *Honest Ulsterman* 50 (1975): 183–86.

29. Such misunderstandings of Vikings as homogeneously white belie the multicultural and multiracial realities of this period of history. More disturbingly, the fantasia of Viking history—and the medieval period more largely—as a "preracial" white space has been a large part of white supremacist culture. For more, see Dorothy Kim, "White Supremacists Have Weaponized an Imaginary Viking past," *Time*, April 15, 2019, https://time.com/5569399/viking-history-white-nationalists/.

30. Seamus Heaney, *North* (London: Faber and Faber, 1975), 3.

31. Heaney, *North*, 46.

32. Catherine Nash, "Irish Origins, Celtic Origins: Population Genetics, Cultural Politics," *Irish Studies Review* 14, no. 1 (2006): 25.

33. See: Seamus Heaney, *Preoccupations: Selected Prose, 1968–1978* (New York: Farrar, Straus and Giroux, 1981), 54; Denis O'Driscoll, *Stepping Stones: Interviews with Seamus Heaney* (New York: Farrar, Straus and Giroux, 2008), 163.

34. Heaney, *North*, 33.

35. Heather O'Donoghue, "Heaney, *Beowulf* and the Medieval Literature of the North," in *The Cambridge Companion to Seamus Heaney*, ed. Bernard O'Donoghue (Cambridge: Cambridge University Press, 2009), 196.

36. Heaney, *North*, 4–5.

37. See: O'Donoghue, "Heaney, *Beowulf* and Medieval Literature," 193.

38. Henry Hart, *Seamus Heaney: Poet of Contrary Progressions* (Syracuse: Syracuse University Press, 1992), 82. However, this pluralistic rendering of the Yggdrasil tree is deeply ironic considering how it, along with other Nordic symbols, has become popular insignia for white supremacist groups. In the 2021 insurrection at the US Capitol, one of the prominent insurrectionists donned a quasi-Nordic costume and had a large and visible tattoo of the Yggdrasil tree. See: Kim Kelly, "Is the 'QAnon Shaman' from the MAGA Capitol Riot Covered in Neo-Nazi Imagery?" *Rolling*

Stone, January 8, 2021, https://www.rollingstone.com/culture/culture-features/qanon-shaman-maga-capitol-riot-rune-pagan-imagery-tattoo-1111344/.

39. Heaney, *North*, 34.

40. Toni Morrison, *Playing in the Dark: Whiteness and the Literary Imagination* (Cambridge: Harvard University Press, 1992), xii.

41. Quoted in: Breda Gray, "Irish State Diaspora Engagement: 'The Network State' and 'Netizens,'" *Éire-Ireland* 47, nos. 1–2 (2012): 252.

42. Paul Cullen, "We Need to Build on Arts and Culture, Says Desmond," *The Irish Times*, September 21, 2009, https://www.irishtimes.com/news/we-need-to-build-on-arts-and-culture-says-desmond-1.741928.

43. Carmel Crimmins, "Singing and Dancing Seen Helping Ireland out of Crisis," *Reuters*, September 19, 2009, https://www.reuters.com/article/uk-ireland-forum/singing-dancing-seen-helping-ireland-out-of-crisis-idUKTRE58I1BQ20090919.

44. Crimmins, "Singing and Dancing."

45. Moreover, Jordan's inflated comments about the status of culture in Ireland had a mercenary agenda. Joe Cleary points out that Colm Tóibín used Jordan's same exculpatory argument as justification for why public arts funding should not be cut as a part of austerity measures: "Like every other profession, artists had sectoral state funding and other interests to protect . . . The reflex impulse, in short, was not to launch a campaign to consider how writers might find the means to address the acute crisis that had befallen Irish society . . . [but] to safeguard its funding and to shore up its position as best it could to combat the resource onslaught ahead." See: Joe Cleary, "'Horseman, Pass By!': The Neoliberal World System and the Crisis in Irish Literature," *Ireland: From Boom to Bust and Beyond*, special issue of *boundary 2*, vol. 45, no. 2 (2018): 143.

46. Gray, "Irish State Diaspora Engagement," 269, 252.

47. Ciaran Carson, *Still Life* (Winston-Salem: Wake Forest University Press, 2020), 70, 78–79.

48. Carson, *Still Life*, 12.

49. Carson, *Still Life*, 81.

50. Carson, *Still Life*, 83–84.

51. Carson, *Still Life*, 84.

Bibliography

5 News. "This Is the Place: Poet Tony Walsh Reads Out His Tribute to Manchester." May 23, 2017. Video. https://youtu.be/josaDi9ZBvE.

Abrams, M. H. *The Correspondent Breeze: Essays on English Romanticism*. New York: Norton, 1984.

Abrams, M. H., and Geoffrey Galt Harpham. *A Glossary of Literary Terms*. Independence: Cengage Learning, 2011.

Alexander, Neal. *Ciaran Carson: Space, Place, Writing*. Liverpool: Liverpool University Press, 2010.

———. "Remembering the Future: Poetry, Peace, and the Politics of Memory in Northern Ireland." *Textual Practice* 32, no. 1 (2018): 59–79.

Alpers, Paul. *What Is Pastoral?* Chicago: University of Chicago Press, 1996.

Alvarez, Al. "A Fine Way with Language." *New York Review of Books*, March 6, 1980, 16.

Archambeau, Robert. "Postnational Ireland." *Contemporary Literature* 50, no. 3 (2009): 610–18.

Aubin, Robert. *Topographical Poetry in 18th-Century England*. New York: Modern Language Association of America, 1936.

Auden, W. H. "Yeats as an Example." *The Kenyon Review* 10, no. 2 (1948): 187–95.

"Award Winning Belfast Poet Ciaran Carson Passes Away Aged 70." *Belfast Telegraph*, October 6, 2019. https://www.belfasttelegraph.co.uk/news/northern-ireland/award-winning-belfast-poet-ciaran-carson-passes-away-aged-70-38567100.html.

Barrell, John. *The Idea of Landscape and the Sense of Place, 1730–1840: An Approach to the Poetry of John Clare*. Cambridge: Cambridge University Press, 1972.

Barry, Frank, and John Bradley. "FDI and Trade: The Irish Host-Country Experience." *The Economic Journal* 107, no. 445 (1997): 1798–1811.

Batten, Guinn. "'He Could Barely Tell One from the Other': The Borderline Discourses of Paul Muldoon's Poetry." *South Atlantic Quarterly* 95, no. 1 (1996): 171–204.

BBC. "Laureate Bemoans 'Thankless Job.'" September 10, 2008. http://news.bbc.co.uk/2/hi/entertainment/7607897.stm.

Bennhold, Katrin. "In Scotland, Trump Built a Wall. Then He Sent Residents the Bill." *The New York Times*, November 25, 2016. https://www.nytimes.com/2016/11/25/world/europe/donald-trump-scotland-wall.html.

Black, Max. "How Metaphors Work: A Reply to Donald Davidson." *Critical Inquiry* 6, no. 1 (1979): 131–43.

Boal, F. W. *Shaping a City: Belfast in the Late Twentieth Century*. Belfast: Institute of Irish Studies, Queen's University, 1995.

Boland, Eavan. *Domestic Violence*. New York: Norton, 2007.

———. *New Collected Poems*. New York: Norton, 2008.

———. "Rereading Oliver Goldsmith's 'Deserted Village' in a Changed Ireland." *The American Scholar* 80, no. 1 (2011): 54–56.

Boland, Philip, John Bronte, and Jenny Muir. "On the Waterfront: Neoliberal Urbanism and the Politics of Public Benefit." *Cities* 61 (2017): 117–27.

Bollens, Scott A. "Urban Policy in Ethnically Polarized Societies." *International Political Science Review* 19, no. 2 (1998): 187–215.

Bond, Paul. "Poet Ben Okri on London's Grenfell Tower Fire." World Socialist Web Site, September 11, 2017. https://www.wsws.org/en/articles/2017/09/11/okri-s11.html.

Bradley, John. *Viking Dublin Exposed: The Wood Quay Saga*. Dublin: O'Brien Press, 1984.

Brandes, Rand. "Ciaran Carson." *The Irish Review* 8 (1990): 77–90.

Brannigan, John. *Race in Modern Irish Literature and Culture*. Edinburgh: Edinburgh University Press, 2009.

Brearton, Fran. "Mapping the Trenches: Gyres, Switchbacks and Zig-zag Circles in W. B. Yeats and Ciaran Carson." *Irish Studies Review* 9, no. 3 (2001): 373–86.

———. "Muldoon 'Goes Native' across the Pond? Review of *Horse Latitudes* by Paul Muldoon." *Tower Poetry*, no. 3 (2007): 7–8.

———. "'The Nothing-Could-Be-Simpler Line': Form in Contemporary Irish Poetry." In *The Oxford Handbook of Modern Irish Poetry*, edited by Fran Brearton and Alan Gillis, 629–47. Oxford: Oxford University Press, 2012.

Brouillette, Sarah. *Literature and the Creative Economy*. Palo Alto: Stanford University Press, 2014.

———. "On *Not* Safeguarding the Cultural Heritage: Glenn Patterson's *Black Night at Big Thunder Mountain*." *Irish Studies Review* 15, no. 3 (2007): 317–31.

———. "Struggle Tourism and Northern Ireland's Culture Industries: The Case of Robert McLiam Wilson." *Textual Practice* 20, no. 2 (2006): 333–53.

———. *UNESCO and the Fate of the Literary*. Palo Alto: Stanford University Press, 2019.

Broullet, Vanessa. "The Irish-U.S. Economic Relations: End of an Era or a Promising Future?" In *Revisiting the UK and Ireland's Transatlantic Relationship with the United States in the 21ˢᵗ Century*, edited by Anne Groutel, Marie-Christine Pauwels, and Valérie Peyronel, 57–74. London: Palgrave Macmillan, 2017.
Burris, Sidney. *The Poetry of Resistance: Seamus Heaney and the Pastoral Tradition*. Athens: Ohio University Press, 1990.
Carson, Ciaran. *Belfast Confetti*. Winston-Salem: Wake Forest University Press, 1989.
———. *Collected Poems*. Winston-Salem: Wake Forest University Press, 2009.
———. "Escaped from the Massacre?" *Honest Ulsterman* 50 (1975): 183–6.
———. "Introduction." In *The Inferno of Dante Alighieri*, translated by Ciaran Carson, xi–xv. New York: New York Review of Books, 2002.
———. *The Irish for No*. Loughcrew: Gallery Press, 1987.
———. *The New Estate*. Winston-Salem: Wake Forest University Press, 1976.
———. *Opera et Cetera*. Oldcastle: Gallery Press, 1996.
———. *The Star Factory*. New York: Arcade, 1997.
———. *Still Life*. Winston-Salem: Wake Forest University Press, 2020.
Casanova, Pascale. *The World Republic of Letters*. Translated by Malcolm DeBevoise. Cambridge: Harvard University Press, 2007.
Catte, Elizabeth. "The Mythical Whiteness of Trump Country." *Boston Review*, November 7, 2017. http://bostonreview.net/race-politics/elizabeth-catte-mythical-whiteness-trump-country.
Chen, Chris, and Tim Kreiner. "Free Speech, Minstrelsy, and the Avant-Garde." *Los Angeles Review of Books*, December 10, 2015. https://lareviewofbooks.org/article/free-speech-minstrelsy-and-the-avant-garde/.
Chihara, Michelle, and Matt Seybold, eds. *The Routledge Companion to Literature and Economics*. New York: Routledge, 2019.
Children's Rights Alliance. "Immigration and Citizenship in Ireland." Accessed December 1, 2022. https://www.childrensrights.ie/sites/default/files/submissions_reports/files/Immigration%26Citizenship_0.pdf.
Chow, Rey. "The Old/New Question of Comparison in Literary Studies: A Post-European Perspective." *ELH* 71, no. 2 (2004): 289–311.
Clark, Heather. *The Ulster Renaissance: Poetry in Belfast, 1962–1972*. Oxford: Oxford University Press, 2006.
Cleary, Joe. "'Horseman, Pass By!': The Neoliberal World System and the Crisis in Irish Literature." *Ireland: From Boom to Bust and Beyond*, special issue of *boundary 2* 45, no. 2 (2018): 135–79.
———. "Introduction." In *The Cambridge Companion to Irish Modernism*, edited by Joe Cleary, 1–18. Cambridge: Cambridge University Press, 2014.
———. *The Irish Expatriate Novel in Late Capitalist Globalization*. Cambridge: Cambridge University Press, 2021.

———. *Outrageous Fortune: Capital and Culture in Modern Ireland*. Dublin: Field Day Publications, 2006.
Cocola, Jim. *Places in the Making: A Cultural Geography of American Poetry*. Iowa City, University of Iowa Press, 2016.
Craig, Patricia. "Ciaran Carson Obituary." *The Guardian*, October 6, 2019. https://www.theguardian.com/books/2019/oct/06/ciaran-carson-obituary.
Crimmins, Carmel. "Singing and Dancing Seen Helping Ireland out of Crisis." *Reuters*, September 19, 2009. https://www.reuters.com/article/uk-ireland-forum/singing-dancing-seen-helping-ireland-out-of-crisis-idUKTRE58I1BQ20090919.
Crotty, Patrick. "Stunning Places: Thomas Kinsella's Locations." *The Poetry Ireland Review* 87 (2006): 35–48.
Cullen, Paul. "We Need to Build on Arts and Culture, Says Desmond." *The Irish Times*, September 21, 2009. https://www.irishtimes.com/news/we-need-to-build-on-arts-and-culture-says-desmond-1.741928.
Cullingford, Elizabeth Butler. "American Dreams: Emigration or Exile in Contemporary Irish Fiction?" *Éire-Ireland* 49, nos. 3 and 4 (2014): 60–94.
———. *Ireland's Others: Gender and Ethnicity in Irish Literature and Popular Culture*. Notre Dame: University of Notre Dame Press, 2001.
———. "'Thinking of Her . . . as . . . Ireland': Yeats, Pearse, and Heaney." *Textual Practice* 4, no. 1 (1990): 1–21.
Davis, Thomas S., and Nathan Hensley. "Scale and Form; or, What Was Global Modernism?" *Modernism/modernity* Print Plus 2, no. 4 (2018). https://doi.org/10.26597/mod.0033.
Davison, Peter. "Darkness at Muldoon." *The New York Times*, October 13, 2002. https://www.nytimes.com/2002/10/13/books/darkness-at-muldoon.html.
Dawe, Gerald. "The Revenges of the Heart: Belfast and the Poetics of Space." In *The Cities of Belfast*, edited by Nicholas Allen and Aaron Kelly, 199–210. Dublin: Four Courts Press, 2003.
Deane, Seamus. *Strange Country: Modernity and Nationhood Since 1790*. Oxford: Oxford University Press, 1999.
———. "Unhappy and at Home: Interview with Seamus Heaney." *The Crane Bag* 1, no. 1 (1977), 66–72.
Deckard, Sharae. "World-Ecology and Ireland: The Neoliberal Ecological Regime." *Journal of World-Systems Research* 22, no. 1 (2016): 145–76.
Delaney, Enda. "Modernity, the Past and Politics in Post-war Ireland." In *Turning Points in Twentieth-Century Irish History*, edited by T. E. Hachey, 103–18. Dublin: Irish Academic Press, 2011.
De Man, Paul. "The Dead-End of Formalist Criticism." In *Blindness and Insight*, 229–45. Minneapolis: University of Minnesota Press, 1971.
De Valera, Éamon. *Speeches and Statements by Eamon de Valera, 1917–73*. Edited by Maurice Moynihan. New York: St. Martin's Press, 1980.

Devenney, Andrew. "Joining Europe: Ireland, Scotland, and the Celtic Response to European Integration, 1961–1975." *Journal of British Studies* 49, no. 1 (2010): 97–116.

———. "'A Unique and Unparalleled Surrender of Sovereignty': Early Opposition to European Integration in Ireland, 1961–72." *New Hibernia Review* 12, no. 4 (2008), 15–32.

Donoghue, Denis. *We Irish: Essays on Literature and Society*. Berkeley: University of California Press, 1986.Dowling, Sarah. "Property, Priority, Place: Rethinking the Poetics of Appropriation," *Contemporary Literature* 60, no. 1 (2019): 98–125.

Dreher, Alex, Noel Gaston, Pim Martens, and Willem Jozef Meine Martens, eds. *Measuring Globalisation: Gauging Its Consequences*. New York: Springer, 2008.

Duffy, Patrick. "*Genius Loci*: The Geographical Imagination of Tim Robinson." In *Unfolding Irish Landscapes: Tim Robinson, Culture, and Environment*, edited by Derek Gladwin and Christine Cusick, 21–40. Manchester: Manchester University Press, 2016.

Duggers, Julie M. "Black Ireland's Race: Thomas Carlyle and the Young Ireland Movement." *Victorian Studies* 48, no. 3 (Spring 2006): 461–85.

Duhig, Ian. "Sinéad Morrissey: A Maker of Intricate Poem Machines." *The Irish Times*, October 21, 2017. https://www.irishtimes.com/culture/books/sinéad-morrissey-a-maker-of-intricate-poem-machines-1.3260694.

Eatough, Matthew. "The Global Contemporary: The Humanitarian Legacy in Irish Fiction," in *The New Irish Studies*, edited by Paige Reynolds, 113–28. Cambridge: Cambridge University Press, 2020.

Edemariam, Aida. "A Life in Poetry: Ciaran Carson." *The Guardian*, January 16, 2009. https://www.theguardian.com/books/2009/jan/17/poetry-ciaran-carson-belfast-ireland.

Edmond, Jacob. *A Common Strangeness: Contemporary Poetry, Cross-Cultural Encounter, Comparative Literature*. New York: Fordham University Press, 2012.

Eliot, T. S. "Review of *Metaphysical Lyrics and Poems of the Seventeenth Century: Donne to Butler*, ed. Herbert J. C. Grierson." *Times Literary Supplement*, October 20, 1921, 669–70.

Empson, William. *Some Versions of Pastoral*. New York: New Directions, 1974.

English, James. *The Economy of Prestige: Prizes, Awards, and the Circulation of Cultural Value*. Cambridge: Harvard University Press, 2005.

Falci, Eric. *Continuity and Change in Irish Poetry, 1966–2010*. Cambridge: Cambridge University Press, 2012.

———. "Rethinking Form (Yet Again) in Contemporary Irish Poetry." *Irish University Review* 50, no. 1 (2020): 164–74.

Falvey, Deirdre. "Two-Thirds of Published Poets Are Male, So Does Poetry Have a Gender Issue?" *The Irish Times*, August 17, 2019. https://www.irishtimes.

com/culture/books/two-thirds-of-published-poets-are-male-so-does-poetry-have-a-gender-issue-1.3984922.

Fanon, Franz. *Black Skin, White Masks*. Translated by Charles Lam Markman. London: Pluto Press, 2008.

Feinsod, Harris. *The Poetry of the Americas: From Good Neighbors to Countercultures*. Oxford: Oxford University Press, 2017.

Feldman, Allen. *Formations of Violence: The Narrative of the Body and Political Terror in Northern Ireland*. Chicago: University of Chicago Press, 1991.

Ferguson, Donna. "Poetry Sales Soar as Political Millennials Search for Clarity." *The Guardian*, January 21, 2019. https://www.theguardian.com/books/2019/jan/21/poetry-sales-soar-as-political-millennials-search-for-clarity.

Fessenbecker, Patrick, and Bryan Yazell, "Literature, Economics, and a Turn to Content." *minnesota review* 96 (2021).

Finch, Laura. "It's the Economy, Stupid: On the Costs of Marginalizing the Aesthetic." *American Literary History* 31, no. 4 (2019): 818–28.

Flannery, Eóin. *Ireland and Postcolonial Studies: Theory, Discourse, Utopia*. Basingstoke: Palgrave Macmillan, 2009.

Flynn, Leontia. *Drives*. London: Cape Books, 2008.

———. *The Radio*. Winston-Salem: Wake Forest University Press, 2017.

Foster, John Wilson. "A Redefinition of Topographical Poetry." *The Journal of English and Germanic Philology* 69, no. 3 (1970): 394–406.

Foucault, Michel. *Archaeology of Knowledge*. New York: Routledge, 1972.

Fox, Andrew. "Transnational Displacement: 'Native American Material' in Paul Muldoon's *New Weather*." *New Hibernia Review* 17, no. 4 (2013): 55–73.

Fox, Renée, Mike Cronin, and Brian Ó Conchubhair, eds. *The Routledge International Handbook of Irish Studies*. Abingdon: Routledge, 2021.

Frawley, Oona. *Irish Pastoral: Nostalgia and Twentieth-Century Irish Literature*. Dublin: Irish Academic Press, 2005.

Friedman, Susan Stanford. *Planetary Modernisms: Provocations of Modernity across Time*. New York: Columbia University Press, 2015.

Gamble, Miriam. "'The Gentle Art of Re-perceiving': Post-ceasefire Identity in the Poetry of Alan Gillis," *Irish Studies* 17, no. 3 (2009): 361–76.

———. "'A Potted Peace/Lily?' Northern Irish Poetry since the Ceasefires." In *The Oxford Handbook of Modern Irish Poetry*, edited by Fran Brearton and Alan Gillis, 668–83. Oxford: Oxford University Press, 2018.

Garden, Alison. "'We Listen for What the Waves Intone': Intertextuality and the Circum-Atlantic Poetics of Seamus Heaney, Natasha Trethewey and Kwame Dawes." *Comparative American Studies: An International Journal* 14, no. 2 (2016): 1–18.

Gardner, Helen, ed. *The Metaphysical Poets*. New York: Penguin, 1967.

Garner, Dwight. "Shared Homeland, Different Worldview." *The New York Times*, September 16, 2010. https://www.nytimes.com/2010/09/17/books/17book.html.

Garner, Steve. "Reflections on Race in Contemporary Ireland." In *Race and Immigration in the New Ireland*, edited by Julieann Veronica Ulin, 175–204. Notre Dame: Notre Dame University Press, 2013.

Gibbons, Luke. *Edmund Burke and Ireland: Aesthetics, Politics and the Colonial Sublime*. Cambridge: Cambridge University Press, 2003.

Giddens, Anthony. *The Consequences of Modernity*. Palo Alto: Stanford University Press, 1990.

Gilligan, Chris. *Northern Ireland and the Crisis of Anti-racism*. Manchester: Manchester University Press, 2018.

Gillis, Alan. *Hawks and Doves*. Oldcastle, Ireland: Gallery Press, 2007.

———. *Somebody, Somewhere*. Oldcastle, Ireland: Gallery Press, 2005.

Goodby, John. *Irish Poetry since 1950: From Stillness into History* (Manchester: Manchester University Press, 2000).

———. "'Walking in the City': Space, Narrative and Surveillance in *The Irish for No* and *Belfast Confetti*." In *Ciaran Carson: Critical Essays*, edited by Elmer Kennedy-Andrews, 66–86. Dublin: Four Courts Press, 2009.

Gray, Breda. "The Irish Diaspora: Globalised Belonging(s)." *Irish Journal of Sociology* 11, no. 2 (2002), 123–44.

———. "Irish State Diaspora Engagement: 'The Network State' and 'Netizens.'" *Éire-Ireland* 47, nos. 1 and 2 (2012): 244–70.

Greaves, Margaret. "Punishing the Lyric: Seamus Heaney and the Poetics of a Communal Europe." *Éire-Ireland* 51, nos. 3 and 4 (2016): 216–43.

Green, Rayna. "The Tribe Called Wannabee: Playing Indian in America and Europe." *Folklore* 99, no. 1 (1988): 30–55.

Greene, Roland, Stephen Cushman, Clare Cavanagh, Jahan Ramazani, and Paul Rouzer, eds. *Princeton Encyclopedia of Poetry and Poetics*. 4th ed. Princeton: Princeton University Press, 2012.

Gubar, Susan. "Prosopopoeia and Holocaust Poetry in English: Sylvia Plath and Her Contemporaries." *Yale Journal of Criticism* 14, no. 1 (2001): 191–215.

Hart, Henry. *Seamus Heaney: Poet of Contrary Progressions*. Syracuse: Syracuse University Press, 1992.

Hart, Matthew. *Nations of Nothing but Poetry: Modernism, Transnationalism, and Synthetic Vernacular Writing*. Oxford: Oxford University Press, 2011.

Harvey, David. "Globalization and the 'Spatial Fix.'" *Geographische revue* 2 (2001): 23–30.

———. *Limits to Capital* (New York: Verso Books, 1982).

———. *Spaces of Capital: Towards a Critical Geography*. New York: Routledge, 2001.

Haughey, Anthony. "A Landscape of Crisis: Photographing Post–Celtic Tiger Ghost Estates." *The Canadian Journal of Irish Studies* 40 (2017): 53–71.

Hayot. "Against Historical Fundamentalism." *PMLA* 131, no. 5 (2016): 1414–22.

Heaney, Seamus. "Eclogues *In Extremis*: On the Staying Power of Pastoral." *Proceedings of the Royal Irish Academy* 103C, no. 1 (2003): 1–12.

———. *Field Work*. New York: Farrar, Straus and Giroux, 1979.
———. *North*. London: Faber and Faber, 1975.
———. *Preoccupations*. New York: Farrar, Straus and Giroux, 1980.
Hegel, G. W. F. *Aesthetics: Lectures on Fine Art*. Translated by T. M. Knox. Vol. 2. Oxford: Clarendon Press, 1975.
Heise, Ursula. *Sense of Place and Sense of Planet: The Environmental Imagination of the Global*. Oxford: Oxford University Press, 2008.
Hena, Omaar. "Playing Indian/Disintegrating Irishness: Globalization and Cross-Cultural Identity in Paul Muldoon's 'Madoc: A Mystery.'" *Contemporary Literature* 49, no. 2 (2008): 232–62.
———. *Global Anglophone Poetry: Literary Form and Social Critique in Walcott, Muldoon, de Kok, and Nagra*. New York: Palgrave Macmillan, 2015.
Hogan, Caelainn. "Trump's Other Wall: Is His Irish Resort a Sign He Believes in Climate Change?" *The Guardian*, November 17, 2016. https://www.theguardian.com/us-news/2016/nov/17/donald-trump-ireland-golf-resort-wall-climate-change.
Hogan, Liam. "Open Letter to *Irish Central, Irish Examiner*, and *Scientific American* about Their 'Irish Slaves' Misinformation." Medium, last modified March 8, 2016. http://medium.com/open-letter-to-irish-central-irish-examiner-and-scientific-american-about-their-irish-slaves-3f6cf23b8d7f.
Holdridge, Jefferson, and Brian Ó Conchubhair. *Post-Ireland? Essays on Contemporary Irish Poetry*. Winston-Salem: Wake Forest University Press, 2017.
Hong, Cathy Park. "Delusions of Whiteness in the Avant-Garde." *Lana Turner*, November 3, 2014. https://arcade.stanford.edu/content/delusions-whiteness-avant-garde.
Houen, Alex. *Terrorism and Modern Literature: From Joseph Conrad to Ciaran Carson*. Oxford: Oxford University Press, 2002.
Houses of the Oireachtas, Tithe an Oireachtais. "Twenty-Seventh Amendment of the Constitution Bill 2004: Second Stage." *Dáil Éireann Debate* 583, no. 6 (April 21, 2004). https://www.oireachtas.ie/en/debates/debate/dail/2004-04-21/3.
Huggan, Graham, and Helen Tiffin. *Postcolonial Ecocriticism: Literature, Animals, Environment*. Oxford: Routledge, 2010.
Hunter, Walt. *Forms of a World: Contemporary Poetry and the Making of Globalization*. New York: Fordham University Press, 2019.
———. "The No-Prospect Poem." *minnesota review* 85 (2015): 144–52.
Huntington, Cynthia, Heather McHugh, Paul Muldoon, and Charles Simic. "How to Peel a Poem: Five Poets Dine Out on Verse." *Harper's*, September 1, 1999. https://harpers.org/archive/1999/09/how-to-peel-a-poem/.
Hutton, Bob. "Hillbilly Elitism." *Jacobin*, October 1, 2016. https://www.jacobinmag.com/2016/10/hillbilly-elegy-review-jd-vance-national-review-white-working-class-appalachia/.

Jackson, Virginia. *Dickinson's Misery: A Theory of Lyric Reading*. Princeton: Princeton University Press, 2005.

Jackson, Virginia, and Meredith Martin. "The Poetry of the Future." *Avidly*, January 29, 2021. http://avidly.lareviewofbooks.org/2021/01/29/the-poetry-of-the-future/.

Jackson, Virginia, and Yopie Prins, eds. *The Lyric Theory Reader: A Critical Anthology*. Baltimore: Johns Hopkins University Press, 2014.

Jaffe, Sarah. *Work Won't Love You Back: How Devotion to Our Jobs Keeps Us Exploited, Exhausted, and Alone*. New York: Bold Type Books, 2021.

Jakobson, Roman. "Two Aspects of Language and Two Types of Aphasic Disturbances." In *On Language*, edited by Linda R. Waugh and Monique Monville-Burston, 115–33. Cambridge: Harvard University Press, 1995.

Jameson, Fredric. "Culture and Finance Capital." *Critical Inquiry* 24, no. 1 (1997): 246–65.

Jarvis, Robin. *Romantic Writing and Pedestrian Travel*. London: Palgrave Macmillan, 1997.

Jay, Paul. *Global Matters: The Transnational Turn in Literary Studies*. Ithaca: Cornell University Press, 2010.

Jennison, Ruth. "29 | 73 | 08: Poetry, Crisis, and a Hermeneutic of Limit." *Mediations* 28, no. 2 (2015): 37–46.

Johnson, Barbara. "Apostrophe, Animation, and Abortion." *Diacritics* 16, no. 1 (1986): 28–47.

Johnson, D. S., and Liam Kennedy. "The Two Economies in Ireland in the Twentieth Century." In *A New History of Ireland*. Vol. 7, *Ireland 1921–1984*, edited by J. R. Hill, 452–86. Oxford: Oxford University Press, 2003.

Johnson, Samuel. *The Lives of the Most Eminent English Poets; With Critical Observations on Their Works (1779–81)*, edited by Roger Lonsdale. Vol. 1. Oxford: Clarendon Press, 2006.

———. *Samuel Johnson: Selected Writings*. Edited by Martin Peter. Cambridge: Harvard University Press, 2011.

Joyce, Sindy. "Divided Spaces: An Examination of Everyday Racism and Its Impact on Young Travellers' Spatial Mobility." *Irish Journal of Anthropology* 18, no. 1 (2015): 15–23.

Joyce, Trevor. "Irish Terrain: Alternate Planes of Cleavage." In *Assembling Alternatives: Reading Postmodern Poetries Transnationally*, edited by Romana Huk, 156–68. Middletown: Wesleyan University Press, 2003.

Keating, Kenneth. *Contemporary Irish Poetry and the Canon: Critical Limitation and Textual Liberations*. Cham: Springer International, 2017.

Keaveney, Karen, Rob Kitchin, Cian O'Callaghan, and Justin Gleeson. "A Haunted Landscape: Housing and Ghost Estates in Post–Celtic Tiger Ireland." National Institute for Regional and Spatial Analysis, Working Paper 59 (2010): 1–68.

Keller, Lynn. "Interview with Paul Muldoon." *Contemporary Literature* 35, no. 1 (1994): 1–29.
Kelly, Aaron "Geopolitical Eclipse: Culture and the Peace Process in Northern Ireland." *Third Text* 19, no. 5 (2005): 545–53.
———. "The Troubles with the Peace Process." *The Irish Review* 40/41 (2009): 1–17.
Kelly, Kim. "Is the 'QAnon Shaman' from the MAGA Capitol Riot Covered in Neo-Nazi Imagery?" *Rolling Stone*, January 8, 2021. https://www.rollingstone.com/culture/culture-features/qanon-shaman-maga-capitol-riot-rune-pagan-imagery-tattoo-1111344/.
Kennedy-Andrews, Elmer. *Writing Home: Poetry and Place in Northern Ireland, 1968–2008*. Cambridge: D. S. Brewer, 2008.
Kenner, Hugh. *The Pound Era*. Berkeley: University of California Press, 1973.
Kenny, Kevin, ed. *Ireland and the British Empire*. Oxford: Oxford University Press, 2004.
Keogh, Dermot. "Ireland, 1972–84." In *A New History of Ireland*. Vol. 7, *Ireland 1921–1984*, edited by J. R. Hill, 356–94. Oxford: Oxford University Press, 2003.
Kerrigan, John. "Paul Muldoon's Transits: Muddling after *Madoc*." In *Paul Muldoon: Critical Essays*, edited by Tim Kendall and Peter McDonald, 125–49. Liverpool: Liverpool University Press, 2004.
Khimm, Suzy, and Henry Farrell. "The Fundamental Problem Here Is a Profoundly Political Problem." *The Washington Post*, September 29, 2011. https://www.washingtonpost.com/blogs/ezra-klein/post/farrell-the-fundamental-problem-here-is-a-profoundly-political-problem-euromess/2011/09/29/gIQAvIzD7K_blog.html.
Kiberd, Declan. "After Ireland?" *The Irish Times*, August 29, 2009. https://www.irishtimes.com/news/after-ireland-1.728344.
———. *After Ireland: Writing the Nation from Beckett to the Present*. Cambridge: Harvard University Press, 2017.
Kim, Dorothy. "White Supremacists Have Weaponized an Imaginary Viking past." *Time*, April 15, 2019. https://time.com/5569399/viking-history-white-nationalists/.
King, Anthony D. *Spaces of Global Cultures: Architecture, Urbanism, Identity*. New York: Routledge, 2004.
Kinsella, Thomas. *Collected Poems*. Winston-Salem: Wake Forest University Press, 2006.
———. *The Dual Tradition: An Essay on Poetry and Politics in Ireland*. Manchester: Carcanet Press, 1995.
———. *A Dublin Documentary*. Dublin: O'Brien Press, 2012.
———. *Peppercanister Poems 1972–1978*. Winston-Salem: Wake Forest University Press, 1979.

Kirkland, Richard. "Ballygawley, Ballylynn, Belfast: Writing about Modernity and Settlement in Northern Ireland." *The Irish Review* 40/41 (2009): 18–32.

———. "Towards a Disciplinary History of Irish Studies." *The Irish Review* 48 (2014): 65–80.

Kirsch, Adam. "On Elizabeth Alexander's Bureaucratic Verse." *The New Republic*, January 20, 2009. https://newrepublic.com/article/47178/adam-kirsch-elizabeth-alexanders-bureaucratic-verse.

Kitchin, Rob, Cian O'Callaghan, and Justin Gleeson. "Post-politics, Crisis, and Ireland's 'Ghost Estates.'" *Political Geography* 42 (2014): 121–33.

Kornbluh, Anna. "Extinct Critique." *The South Atlantic Quarterly* 119, no. 4 (2020): 767–77.

Lakoff, George, and Mark Johnson. *Metaphors We Live By*. Chicago: University of Chicago Press, 1980.

Lalor, James Fintan. *The Writing of James Fintan Lalor: With an Introduction Embodying Personal Recollections*. Dublin: T. G. O'Donoghue, 1895.

Lancester, John. "Once Greece Goes . . ." *London Review of Books*, July 14, 2011. http://www.lrb.co.uk/v33/n14/john-lanchester/once-greece-goes.

Laskowski, David. "Inventing Carson: An Interview." *Chicago Review* 45, nos. 3 and 4 (1999): 92–100.

Leavy, Adrienne. "An Interview with Thomas Kinsella." *New Hibernia Review* 15, no. 2 (2011): 136–48.

Leming, Sheila. "Fighting Words." *Los Angeles Review of Books*, December 14, 2020. https://lareviewofbooks.org/article/fighting-words/.

Lentin, Ronit. "Illegal in Ireland, Irish Illegals: Diaspora Nation as Racial State." *Irish Political Studies* 22, no. 4 (2007): 433–53.

Levinson, Marjorie. *Wordsworth's Great Period Poems: Four Essays*. Cambridge: Cambridge University Press, 1986.

Lichtenstein, Jesse. "How Poetry Came to Matter Again." *The Atlantic*, September 2018. https://www.theatlantic.com/magazine/archive/2018/09/chen-chen-aziza-barnes-layli-long-soldier/565781.

Lloyd, David. *Anomalous States: Irish Writing and the Post-colonial Moment*. Durham: Duke University Press, 1993.

———. "Black Irish, Irish Witness and Atlantic State Formation." In *The Black and Green Atlantic: Cross-Currents of the African and Irish Diasporas*, edited by Peter D. O'Neill and David Lloyd, 3–19. London: Palgrave Macmillan, 2009.

———. "The Cultures of Poetry in Contemporary Ireland." In *Irish Literature in Transition: 1980–2020*, edited by Eric Falci and Paige Reynolds, 44–64. Cambridge: Cambridge University Press, 2020.

———. *Under Representation: The Racial Regime of Aesthetics*. New York: Fordham University Press, 2018.

Lukács, Georg. *Writer and Critic*. Edited and translated by Arthur Kahn. London: Merlin, 1970.
Lyons, Alice. *The Breadbasket of Europe*. Surrey: Veer Books, 2015.
MacFarlane, Robert. "High and Dry in the Flood." *Times Literary Supplement*, October 11, 2002, 24.
Mackinnon, Lachlan. "A Dream Diffused in Words." *Times Literary Supplement*, October 12–18, 1990, 1105.
Maclean, Norman. "From Action to Image: Theories of the Lyric in the Eighteenth Century." In *Critics and Criticism: Ancient and Modern*, edited by R. S. Crane, 408–50. Chicago: University of Chicago Press, 1952.
Manguso, Sarah. *500 Arguments*. New York: Graywolf Press, 2017.
Mao, Douglas, and Rebecca Walkowitz. "The New Modernist Studies." *PMLA* 123, no. 3 (2008): 737–48.
Marcus, Sharon, Heather Love, and Stephen Best. "Building a Better Description." *Representations* 136 (2016): 1–21.
Marklew, Naomi. "The Future of Northern Irish Poetry: Fragility, Contingency, Value and Beauty." *English Academy Review* 31, no. 2 (2014): 64–80.
Marx, Karl. *Capital*. Vol. 1, *A Critique of Political Economy*. Translated by Ben Fowkes. New York: Penguin, 1967.
Marx, Leo. *The Machine in the Garden: Technology and the Pastoral Ideal in America*. Oxford: Oxford University Press, 1964.
———. "Pastoralism in America." In *Ideology and Classic American Literature*, edited by Sarcran Bercovitch and Myra Jehlan, 36–69. Cambridge: Cambridge University Press, 1986.
Massey, Doreen. *Space, Place and Gender*. Minneapolis: University of Minnesota Press, 1994.
Maurer, Sara. *The Dispossessed State: Narratives of Ownership in Nineteenth-Century Britain and Ireland*. Baltimore: Johns Hopkins University Press, 2012.
McClanahan, Annie. *Dead Pledges: Debt, Crisis, and Twenty-First-Century Culture*. Palo Alto: Stanford University Press, 2017.
———. "Financialization." In *American Literature in Transition, 2000–2010*, edited by Rachel Greenwald Smith, 239–54. Cambridge: Cambridge University Press, 2017.
McConnell, Gail. "No 'Replicas / Atone': Northern Irish Poetry after the Peace Process." *boundary 2* 45, no. 1 (2018): 201–29.
McCord, John A., Michael J. McCord, Peadar T. Davis, Martin E. Haran, and Sean MacIntyre. "The Political Cost? Religious Segregation, Peace Walls, and House Prices." *Peace and Conflict Studies* 24, no. 1 (2017), 1–37.
McCurry, Jacqueline. "A Land 'Not "Borrowed" but "Purloined"': Paul Muldoon's Indians." *New Hibernia Review* 1, no. 3 (1997): 40–51.
McDonough, Terrence. "Economic Causes and Consequences of the Celtic Tiger Crash." *boundary 2* 45, no. 1 (2018): 7–30.

McGarry, John, and Brendan O'Leary. *Broken Images: Explaining Northern Ireland.* Oxford: Blackwell, 1995.
McGlynn, Mary. "Things Unexploded: The Calculus and Aesthetics of Risk in Two Post-Boom Irish Novels." *boundary 2* 45, no. 1 (2018): 181–200.
McGrath, Charles. "Word Freak." *The New York Times*, November 19, 2006. https://www.nytimes.com/2006/11/19/magazine/word-freak.html.
McLane, Maureen. "Paul Muldoon's Poems and Essays Pulse with Emotional and Intellectual Vigor." *Chicago Tribune*, October 8, 2006. https://www.chicagotribune.com/news/ct-xpm-2006-10-08-0610080230-story.html.
Meaney, Gerardine. *Gender, Ireland, and Cultural Change: Race, Sex, and Nation.* New York: Routledge, 2010.
Meehan, Paula. *Painting Rain.* Winston-Salem, NC: Wake Forest University Press, 2009.
Melas, Natalie. *All the Difference in the World: Postcolonialism and the Ends of Comparison.* Palo Alto: Stanford University Press, 2006.
Minh-ha, Trinh. *Woman Native Other: Writing Postcolonialism and Feminism.* Bloomington: Indiana University Press, 1989.
Moi, Ruben. *Paul Muldoon and the Language of Poetry.* Leiden: Brill, 2020.
Montague, John. *The Figure in the Cave and Other Essays.* Syracuse: Syracuse University Press, 1989.
———. *The Rough Field.* Winston-Salem: Wake Forest University Press, 2005.
Moore, Jason. *Capitalism in the Web of Life: Ecology and the Accumulation of Capital.* New York: Verso, 2015.
Morrison, Toni. *Playing in the Dark: Whiteness and the Literary Imagination.* Cambridge: Harvard University Press, 1992.
Morrissey, Sinéad. *Between Here and There.* Manchester: Carcanet Press, 2002.
———. *Parallax.* Manchester: Carcanet Press, 2013.
Moynihan, Sinéad. *Other People's Diasporas: Negotiating Race in Contemporary Irish and Irish-American Culture.* Syracuse: Syracuse University Press, 2013.
Muldoon, Paul. "Getting Round: Notes towards an Ars Poetica." *Essays in Criticism* 48, no. 2 (1998): 107–28.
———. *Horse Latitudes.* New York: Farrar, Straus and Giroux, 2006.
———. *Madoc: A Mystery.* New York: Farrar, Straus and Giroux, 1991.
———. *Poems 1968–1998.* New York: Farrar, Straus and Giroux, 2001.
———. *To Ireland, I.* Oxford: Oxford University Press, 2001.
Mullen, Harryette. *Urban Tumbleweed: Notes from a Tanka Diary.* Minneapolis: Graywolf Press, 2013.
Mullen, Mary. "How the Irish Became Settlers: Metaphors of Indigeneity and the Erasure of Indigenous Peoples." *New Hibernia Review* 20, no. 3 (2016): 81–96.
Murtagh, Brendan. "Desegregation and Place Restructuring in the New Belfast." *Urban Studies* 48, no. 6 (2011): 1119–35.

Nagle, John. "Potemkin Village: Neo-liberalism and Peace-Building in Northern Ireland?" *Ethnopolitics* 8, no. 2 (1990): 173–90.
Nash, Catherine. "Irish Origins, Celtic Origins: Population Genetics, Cultural Politics." *Irish Studies Review* 14, no. 1 (2006): 11–37.
Needham, Richard. *Battling for Peace.* Belfast: Blackstaff Press, 1998.
Negra, Diane. *The Irish in Us: Irishness, Performativity, and Popular Culture.* Durham: Duke University Press, 2006.
Neill, William J. V. "Physical Planning and Image Enhancement: Recent Developments in Belfast." *International Journal of Urban and Regional Research* 17, no. 4 (1993): 595–609.
———. *Urban Planning and Cultural Identity.* New York: Routledge, 2004.
Ngai, Sianne. *Ugly Feelings.* Cambridge: Harvard University Press, 2005.
Nolan, Paul. *The Northern Ireland Peace Monitoring Report, No. 2.* Belfast: Community Relations Council, 2013.
Norfolk, Lawrence. "The Abundant Braes of Yarrow." *Times Literary Supplement*, August 21, 1994, 32–33.
Obert, Julia. *Postcolonial Overtures: The Politics of Sound in Contemporary Northern Irish Poetry.* Syracuse: Syracuse University Press, 2015.
———. "Space and the Trace: Thomas Kinsella's Postcolonial Placelore." *New Hibernia Review* 13, no. 4 (2009): 77–93.
O'Callaghan, Cian, Sinéad Kelly, Mark Boyle, and Rob Kitchin. "Topologies and Topographies of Ireland's Neoliberal Crisis." *Space and Polity* 19, no. 1 (2015): 31–46.
O'Donnell, Mary. "A Prosaic Lack of Women in *The Cambridge Companion to Irish Poets*." *The Irish Times*, January 8, 2018. https://www.irishtimes.com/culture/books/a-prosaic-lack-of-women-in-the-cambridge-companion-to-irish-poets-1.3336413.
O'Donoghue, Heather. "Heaney, *Beowulf* and the Medieval Literature of the North." In *The Cambridge Companion to Seamus Heaney*, edited by Bernard O'Donoghue, 192–205. Cambridge: Cambridge University Press, 2009.
O'Dowd, Liam, and Milena Komarova. "Contesting Territorial Fixity? A Case Study of Regeneration in Belfast." *Urban Studies* 48, no. 10 (2011): 2013–28.
———. "Interview with Thomas Kinsella." *The Poetry Ireland Review* 25 (1989): 57–65.
———. *Stepping Stones: Interviews with Seamus Heaney.* New York: Farrar, Straus and Giroux, 2008.
O'Driscoll, Mervyn. *Ireland, West Germany and the New Europe, 1949–73: Best Friend and Ally?* Manchester: Manchester University Press, 2018.
O'Halloran, Eileen, and Kelli Maloy. "An Interview with Paula Meehan." *Contemporary Literature* 43, no. 1 (2002): 1–27.
One Dublin One Book. *If Ever You Go: A Map of Dublin in Poetry and Song.* Accessed December 3, 2020. http://www.dublinonecityonebook.ie/books/if-ever-you-go/.

O'Neill, Charles L. "Paul Muldoon's *Madoc: A Mystery* and the Romantic Poets." *The Wordsworth Circle* 24, no. 1 (1993): 54–56.
Onwuemezi, Natasha. "Poetry Sales Are Booming, LBF Hears." *The Bookseller*. April 13, 2018. https://www.thebookseller.com/news/poetry-summit-766826.
O'Reilly, Sean. "Butcher's Dozen by Thomas Kinsella." *The Stinging Fly*, January 25, 2022. https://stingingfly.org/review/butchers-dozen/.
Ó Riain, Seán. *The Rise and Fall of Ireland's Celtic Tiger: Liberalism, Boom and Bust*. Cambridge: Cambridge University Press, 2014.
O'Rourke, Kevin. "Burn Everything British but Their Coal: The Anglo-Irish Economic War of the 1930s." *The Journal of Economic History* 51, no. 2 (1991): 357–66.
O'Toole, Fintan. "Island of Saints and Silicon: Literature and Social Change in Contemporary Ireland." In *Cultural Contexts and Literary Idioms in Contemporary Irish Literature*, edited by Michael Kenneally, 11–35. Totowa: Barnes and Noble Books, 1988.
Parker, Michael. *Seamus Heaney: The Making of a Poet*. London: Macmillan, 2003.
Parkinson, Alan F. *Belfast's Unholy War*. Dublin: Four Courts Press, 2004.
Parsons, Cóilín. *The Ordnance Survey and Modern Irish Literature*. Oxford: Oxford University Press, 2016.
Patke, Rajeev S. "'Responsibility' and 'Difficulty' in the Poetry of Paul Muldoon." *Criticism* 50, no. 2 (2008): 279–99.
Paul, Mark. "Ireland Is the World's Biggest Corporate 'Tax Haven,' Say Academics." *The Irish Times*, June 13, 2018. https://www.irishtimes.com/business/economy/ireland-is-the-world-s-biggest-corporate-tax-haven-say-academics-1.3528401.
Perloff, Marjorie. "Yeats and the Occasional Poem: Easter 1916." *Papers on Language & Literature* 50, nos. 3 and 4 (2014): 326–51.
Pilkington, Lionel. "Reading History in the Plays of Brian Friel." In *A Companion to Modern British and Irish Drama, 1880–2005*, edited by Mary Luckhurst, 499–508. Malden: Blackwell, 2006.
Pinsky, Robert. "Occasional Poetry and Poetry on Occasions." *The Paris Review* 42, no. 154 (2000): 76–82.
The Poetry Project. "Oliver Comerford—Distance / Eavan Boland, In Our Own Country." Accessed December 3, 2020. http://thepoetryproject.ie/poems/distance-oliver-comerford-in-our-own-country-eavan-boland/.
Posmentier, Sonya. *Cultivation and Catastrophe: The Lyric Ecology of Modern Black Literature*. Baltimore: Johns Hopkins University Press, 2017.
Potkay, Adam. "Ear and Eye: Counteracting Senses in Loco-descriptive Poetry." In *A Companion to Romantic Poetry*, edited by Charles Mahoney, 176–94. Oxford: Blackwell, 2012.
Potts, Donna L. *Contemporary Irish Poetry and the Pastoral Tradition*. Columbia: University of Missouri Press, 2011.

Pratt, Geraldine, and Victoria Rosner. "Introduction: The Global and the Intimate." *Women's Studies Quarterly* 34, no. 1 and 2 (2006): 13–24.
"Programme for the Irish Presidency of the Council of the European Union." Accessed December 3, 2020. http://www.eu2013.ie/media/eupresidency/content/documents/EU-Pres_Prog_A4.pdf.
Prynne, J. H. "Difficulties in the Translation of 'Difficult' Poems." *Cambridge Literary Review* 1, no. 3 (2010): 151–65.
"Public Art: Per Cent for Art Scheme: General National Guidelines—2004." Accessed December 3, 2020. https://publicart.ie/fileadmin/user_upload/PDF_Folder/Public_Art_Per_Cent_for_Art.pdf
Puirséil, Niamh. "Political and Party Competition in Post-war Ireland." In *The Lemass Era*, edited by Brian Girvin and Gary Murphy, 12–27. Dublin: University College Dublin Press, 2005.
Quigley, Mark S. "Modernization's Lost Pasts: Sean O'Faolain, the "Bell," and Irish Modernization before Lemass." *New Hibernia Review* 18, no. 4 (2014): 44–67.
Quinn, Justin. "The Disappearance of Ireland." In *The Cambridge Introduction to Modern Irish Poetry, 1800–2000*, 194–210. Cambridge: Cambridge University Press, 2008.
Ramazani, Jahan. "The Local Poem in a Global Age." *Critical Inquiry* 43 (2017): 670–96.
———. *Poetry in a Global Age*. Chicago: University of Chicago Press, 2020.
———. *A Transnational Poetics*. Chicago: University of Chicago Press, 2010.
Randolph, Jody Allen. "The Body Politic: A Conversation with Paula Meehan." *An Sionnach: A Journal of Literature, Culture, and the Arts* 5, nos. 1 and 2 (2009), 239–71.
Reed, Anthony. *Freedom Time: The Poetics and Politics of Black Experimental Writing*. Baltimore: Johns Hopkins University Press, 2016.
Reynolds, Paige, ed. *The New Irish Studies*. Cambridge: Cambridge University Press, 2020.
Rich, Adrienne. *Blood, Bread, and Poetry: Selected Prose, 1979–1985*. New York: Norton, 1994.
Richards, I. A. *The Philosophy of Rhetoric*. Oxford: Oxford University Press, 1936.
Robinson, Dan. *Natural and Necessary Unions: Britain, Europe, and the Scottish Question*. Oxford: Oxford University Press, 2020.
Robinson, Mary. "Cherishing the Irish Diaspora: On a Matter of Public Importance." Transcript of address delivered at the House of the Oireachtas, Dublin, Ireland, February 2, 1995. https://president.ie/en/media-library/speeches/cherishing-the-irish-diaspora.
Ronda, Margaret. *Remainders: American Poetry at Nature's End*. Stanford: Stanford University Press, 2018.
Rowthorn, Bob. "Northern Ireland: An Economy in Crisis." *Cambridge Journal of Economics* 5, no. 1 (1981): 1–31.

Russell, David Rankin. "The Black and Green Atlantic: Violence, History, and Memory in Natasha Trethewey's 'South' and Seamus Heaney's 'North.'" *Southern Literary Journal* 46 (2014): 155–72.

Ryan, Bernard. "The Celtic Cubs: The Controversy over Birthright Citizenship in Ireland." *European Journal of Migration and Law* 6 (2004): 173–93.

Said, Edward. *Culture and Imperialism*. New York: Vintage, 1993.

Sassen, Saskia. *Expulsions: Brutality and Complexity in the Global Economy*. Cambridge: Harvard University Press, 2014.

Savaric, Michel. "Racism and Sectarianism in Northern Ireland." In *The Politics of Ethnic Diversity in the British Isles*, edited by Romain Garbaye and Pauline Schnapper, 174–88. London: Palgrave Macmillan, 2014.

Schor, Naomi. *Reading in Detail: Aesthetics and the Feminine*. New York: Routledge, 2007.

Scott, Yvonne. *Art in State Buildings, 1995–2005*. Dublin: Stationery Office, 2006.

Slaby, Alexandra. "Whither Cultural Policy in Post-Celtic Ireland?" *The Canadian Journal of Irish Studies* 37, nos. 1 and 2 (2011): 76–97.

Spender, Stephen, Patrick Kavanagh, Thomas Kinsella, and W. D. Snodgrass. "Poetry since Yeats: An Exchange of Views." *Tri-Quarterly* 4 (1965): 100–11.

Steinfels, Peter. "Beliefs; After Sept. 11, a 62-Year-Old Poem by Auden Drew New Attention. Not All of It Was Favorable." *The New York Times*, December 1, 2001. https://www.nytimes.com/2001/12/01/us/beliefs-after-sept-11-62-year-old-poem-auden-drew-new-attention-not-all-it-was.html.

Sugano, Marian Zwerling. *The Poetics of the Occasion: Mallarmé and the Poetry of Circumstance*. Palo Alto: Stanford University Press, 1992.

Suhr-Sytsma, Nathan. *Poetry, Print, and the Making of Postcolonial Literature*. Cambridge: Cambridge University Press, 2017.

Switzer, Catherine, and Sara McDowell. "Redrawing Cognitive Maps of Conflict: Lost Spaces and Forgetting in the Centre of Belfast." *Memory Studies* 2, no. 3 (2009), 337–53.

"Taking Note: Poetry Reading Is Up—Federal Survey Results." *Art Works Blog*. National Endowment of the Arts. Accessed June 7, 2018. https://www.arts.gov/art-works/2018/taking-note-poetry-reading-—federal-survey-results.

Taylor, Charlie. "UNESCO City of Literature Status Sought for Dublin." *The Irish Times*, March 6, 2009. https://www.irishtimes.com/news/unesco-city-of-literature-status-sought-for-dublin-1.837102.

Thomason, John. "Hillbilly Ethnography." *The New Inquiry*, November 29, 2016. https://thenewinquiry.com/hillbilly-ethnography/.

Townsend, Sarah. "Undocumented Irish Need Apply: Ethnic Whiteness, Immigrant Rights, and the Campaign for US Diversity Visas in the 1980s." *Radical History Review* 143 (2022), 125–40.

Traynor, Jessica. "Hungering: A Poetry Jukebox for Dublin's Docklands." *The Irish Times*, July 4, 2019. https://www.irishtimes.com/culture/books/hungering-a-poetry-jukebox-for-dublin-s-docklands-1.3946528.

Tsing, Anna. *The Mushroom at the End of the World: On the Possibility of Life in Capitalist Ruins*. Princeton: Princeton University Press, 2015.
Tuck, Eve, and K. Wayne Yang. "Decolonization Is Not a Metaphor." *Decolonization: Indigeneity, Education & Society* 1, no. 1 (2012): 1–40.
Tucker, Amanda, and Moira E. Casey, eds. *Where Motley Is Worn: Transnational Irish Literatures*. Cork: Cork University Press, 2014.
Turbidy, Derval. *Thomas Kinsella: The Peppercanister Poems*. Dublin: University College Dublin Press, 2001.
Twiddy, Iain. *Pastoral Elegy in Contemporary British and Irish Poetry*. New York: Continuum, 2012.
UNESCO Creative Cities Network. "Mission Statement." Accessed December 3, 2020. https://en.unesco.org/creative-cities/sites/creative-cities/files/uccn_mission_statement_rev_nov_2017.pdf.
Vendler, Helen. *Our Secret Discipline: Yeats and Lyric Form* (Oxford: Oxford University Press, 2007).
———. *Seamus Heaney*. Cambridge: Harvard University Press, 2000.
Vogl, Joseph. *The Spectre of Capital*. Palo Alto: Stanford University Press, 2014.
Walkowitz, Rebecca. "After Close and Distant: Modernist Studies and the New Turn to Scale." *Modernism/modernity* Print Plus 3, no. 4 (2019). https://doi.org/10.26597/mod.0085.
Wallace, Anne D. *Walking, Literature, and Culture: The Origins and Uses of Peripatetic in the Nineteenth Century*. Oxford: Oxford University Press, 1994.
Wang, Dorothy. *Thinking Its Presence: Form, Race, and Subjectivity in Contemporary Asian American Poetry*. Palo Alto: Stanford University Press, 2014.
Warren, Rosanna. *Fables of the Self: Studies in Lyric Poetry*. New York: Norton, 2008.
Watts, Rebecca. "The Cult of the Noble Amateur." *PN Review* 239 44, no. 3 (2018). https://www.pnreview.co.uk/cgi-bin/scribe?item_id=10090.
Weaver, Andrew. "It Is I: Robert Creely's Deictic Subjectivity and the Sublime Self." *Journal of Modern Literature* 41, no. 3 (2018): 77–96.
Weston, Daniel. "'I Know This Labyrinth So Well': Narrative Mappings in the Poetry of Ciaran Carson." In *Poetry and Geography: Space and Place in Post-war Poetry*, edited by Neal Alexander and David Cooper, 105–19. Liverpool: Liverpool University Press, 2013.
Whitley, Edward. "Whitman's Occasional National: 'A Broadway Pageant' and the Space of Public Poetry." *Nineteenth-Century Literature* 60, no. 4 (2006): 451–80.
Williams, Raymond. *The Country and the City*. Oxford: Oxford University Press, 1975.
Wills, Clair. *Reading Paul Muldoon*. Northumberland: Bloodaxe Books, 1998.
———. *That Neutral Island: A Cultural History of Ireland during the Second World War*. Cambridge: Belknap Press, 2007.

Wilson, James S. F. "The Art of Poetry No. 87, Paul Muldoon." *The Paris Review* 169 (2004): 52–91.
Wilson, Stephen. "Poetry and Its Occasions: Undoing the Folded Line." In *A Companion to Poetic Genre*, edited by Erik Martiny, 490–504. New York: Blackwell, 2011.
Witte, Griff. "A Wall Denied May Have Made Trump Dislike E.U." *The Washington Post*, February 7, 2017. https://www.washingtonpost.com/opinions/as-europe-well-knows-big-walls-dont-make-good-neighbors/2017/02/10/07c54dc6-ee3e-11e6-a100-fdaaf400369a_story.html.
Wolosky, Shira. "The Claims of Rhetoric: Toward a Historical Poetics (1820–1900)." *American Literary History* 15, no. 1 (2003): 14–21.
World Cities Culture Forum. "Global Cities Sharing a Belief in the Importance of Culture." Accessed December 3, 2020. http://www.worldcitiesculture-forum.com/about.

Index

Page numbers in **bold** refer to figures.

"A Country Walk" (Kinsella), 35–36, 37
"A Severed Head" (Montague), 77, **78–81**, 82
Abrams, M. H., 31
aesthetic autonomy, 15–16 30, 33, 53–54
agriculture, role of, 64–65, 66
Alexander, Elizabeth, 30
Alexander, Neal, 97–98
Alpers, Paul, 183n3
Alvarez, Al, 61
"Ambition" (Carson), 106–07
Anglo-Irish Trade War, 65, 185–86n21
Annals of Chile (Muldoon), 140
apostrophe, 16–19
Archambeau, Robert, 116
"Army" (Carson), 100
Arrighi, Giovanni, 11
Arts Council, 42–43, 180n52
Auden, W. H.
　Another Time, 28
　"September 1, 1939," 27
"Auditque Vocatus Apollo" (Carson), 107
austerity, 11, 16, 20, 44–47, 50, 206n45

authenticity, 83, 120

"Balance Sheet" (Montague), 70, **70, 71**, 72–73
Bank of Ireland, 49–50
Barrell, John, 89
"Belderg" (Heaney), 159–61
Belfast
　Carson and, 92–102, 106–13, 164–65
　Castlecourt shopping center, 96–97, 191n28
　city planning, 93–94, 101–02, 103
　commodification, 9–10, 90
　deindustrialization, 89, 93, 94–95
　Flynn and, 103–06
　"In Belfast" (Morrissey), 7–9
　IRA paramilitaries, 101, 191n26
　the loco-descriptive poem, 87–113
　post-conflict, 90, 103–13
　segregation, 89, 93, 194n72
　surveillance state, 90, 101
　Titanic Quarter, 89, 105
　tourism, 90, 103
　"Tourism" (Morrissey), 9–10
　the Troubles, 8–9, 93–102, 190n22
　urban redevelopment, 3, 21–22, 88–89, 95–96, 103–13, 191n25

227

228 | Index

Belfast Agreement, 1998, 22, 23, 88, 148
Belfast Confetti (Carson), 89, 93
Best, Stephen, 91–92
"Birth" (Muldoon), 139–40
Bishop, Elizabeth, 201n70
Bloody Sunday, 37–38
Boland, Eavan, 57–59
  "In Our Own Country," 45–46
  "Making Money," 181n63
Brannigan, John, 151, 155
Brearton, Fran, 117
Brexit, 3, 23, 59, 144, 147–48
Brouillette, Sarah, 32–3, 181n58
Burris, Sidney, 184n9
Butcher's Dozen (Kinsella), 37–39, 179n36

capitalism, 50, 184n5
  and the arts, 32–33, 35–37
  and crisis, 29
Carson, Ciaran, 3, 21–22, 88, 89–90, 92–102, 106–13, 192n37
  "Ambition," 106–07
  "Army," 100
  "Auditque Vocatus Apollo," 107
  Belfast Confetti, 89, 93
  "The Exiles' Club," 102
  fixation on Belfast, 92–93, 107
  "Hamlet," 97
  "I," 98
  "Intelligence," 108, 110–11
  The Irish for No, 89
  "Queen's Gambit," 100
  "Question Time," 100–01
  "Revised Version," 93–94
  The Star Factory, 89
  Still Life, 99, 164–66
  The Táin, 87
  topographical lists, 108–09
  translation of Dante's *Inferno*, 93
  "Travellers," 97
"Cauliflowers" (Muldoon), 137–38

Celtic Tiger, 3, 11, 16, 17, 20–21, 42–47
  creative economy projects, 45–47
  see also Kinsella, Thomas; Meehan, Paula
Chen, Chris, 120
Chen, Man Levette, 150
citizenship, 3, 23, 150, 155–57
Citizenship Referendum, 2004, 150, 155–56, 162, 205n27
Cleary, Joe, 29, 47, 67, 170–71n37, 206n45
Cocola, Jim, 90–91
colonialism, 12, 49, 63–64, 129, 134, 136, 150
commodification, 9–10, 35–37, 41–42, 54–55, 175n10
Common Agricultural Policy, 66, 186n25
conceit, 23, 135–36, 138, 144–45, 200n63
cosmopolitanism, 14, 84–85
Crabbe, George, 58
Craig, Patricia, 97
creative economy, 33, 42–44, 54–55, 163, 177n24
critical race studies, 150, 196n18
Cronin, Mike, 144
cross-cultural comparison, 3, 22–23, 84–85, 118–20, 121–22, 128–34, 135–43, 143–45, 199n56
Crotty, Patrick, 39
Cullingford, Elizabeth Butler, 6, 129, 133–34, 197–98n36
cultural appropriation, 23, 119, 120–21, 197n35
cultural industries, 28, 33, 43–44, 47, 178n31

Dark Decade, the, 65–66
Davis, Thomas S., 6
Dawe, Gerald, 96
de Paor, Liam, 69

de Valera, Éamon, St. Patrick's Day speech, 1943, 65, 154–55, 156, 185n20
Deane, Seamus, 143, 154
Death of a Naturalist (Heaney), 61, 68
Deckard, Sharae, 12, 170n30
decolonization, 3, 15, 133–34
description, 22, 91–92
"Developers" (Lyons), 16–19
Devenney, Andrew, 74
dinnseanchas, 40–41, 89
Donoghue, Denis, 38
Dublin, 20, 26–27, 87, 156
  "A Country Walk" (Kinsella), 35–36
  creative economy, 43–44, 45–47
  "Night Conference, Wood Quay, 6 June 1979," (Kinsella) 39–41
  Nightwalker (Kinsella), 34–35
  OPW headquarters, St. Stephen's Green, 48–54
  "Six Sycamores" (Meehan), 48–54
  Wood Quay, 39–41

Eatough, Matthew, 199n54
ecocriticism, 4, 17–18
economics
  economic nationalism, 64–65, 67
  economic policy, 59–60, 72
  and literature, 59–60
  and poetics, 35
  protectionism, 34, 42, 65–66, 74
  see also creative economy; financialization
Edmond, Jacob, 120
ekphrasis, 164–66
Electric Light (Heaney), 61
Eliot, T. S., 116
Empson, William, 58, 62–63, 64, 69, 185n16, 185n18
The End of the Poem (Muldoon), 124
English, James, 29
ethnonationalism, 2, 10, 23, 150

European Economic Community (EEC), 3, 21, 59, 64, 66–67, 74
European Union (EU), 46, 68, 144, 148, 178–79n35
"The Exiles' Club" (Carson), 102

Falci, Eric, 98, 139
Feldman, Allen, 101
Fessenbecker, Patrick, 59–60
Field Work (Heaney), 61, 83
financial crisis, 2008, 17–19, 67, 181–82n65
financialization, 18, 19, 20–21, 27, 42–43, 50
Finch, Laura, 60
The First Programme for Economic Expansion (1958–63), 34, 66
Flannery, Eóin, 129
Flynn, Leontia, 3, 22, 88, 90, 103–06
  "Leaving Belfast," 103–05
foreign direct investment, 37, 66, 69, 178–79n35
Foster, John Wilson, 107–08
Foucault, Michel, 118
Fox, Andrew, 134
Fox, Renée, 144
Frawley, Oona, 68
Friedman, Susan Stanford, 6

Gamble, Miriam, 112
Gardner, Helen, 135
Garner, Dwight, 116
Garner, Steve, 152
geopolitics, 23, 59, 144, 147–49, 162–66
ghost estates, 3, 16–19, 172n44
Gibbons, Luke, 129
Giddens, Anthony, 5
Gillis, Alan, 3, 22, 88, 90, 104, 109–13
  "Laganside," 109
  Somewhere, Somebody, 111–12
  "The Mournes," 112–13
  "Traffic Flow," 109–10

"Glanmore Sonnets" (Heaney), 61
Global Irish Economic Forum
 (GIEF), 163–64
globalization, 14–15, 27, 37, 96, 105,
 118, 149, 162
 definitions, 2, 4–5, 10–12, 167–
  68n5
 Ireland and, 33–34, 162–66
 Northern Ireland and, 194n71
 and poetic production, 27, 29–30
globalization studies, 4, 11–12
Goldsmith, Kenneth, 120–21, 173n57
Goldsmith, Oliver, "The Deserted
 Village," 57–58, 83–84
Goodby, John, 82, 97, 184n6
Gorman, Amanda, 176–77n16
Gray, Breda, 163–64
Gray, Thomas, 58
Greaves, Margaret, 16
Green, Rayna, 121, 199n53
Guzmán, Roy G., 26, 27

Halappanavar, Savita, 150
"Hamlet" (Carson), 97
Hart, Henry, 160–61
Harvey, David, 4–5, 59, 96, 184n5
Hayot, Eric, 119
Heaney, Seamus, 3, 12–13, 21, 59,
 60, 60–68, 83–85, 184n9
 "Belderg" 159–61
 bog poems, 23, 151, 157–62
 Death of a Naturalist, 61, 68
 Electric Light, 61
 Field Work, 61, 83
 "Glanmore Sonnets," 61
 "Kinship," 159
 North, 61, 157–58
 race in poetry, 151, 157–62, 203n8
 "The Sense of Place," 1–2
 "The Toome Road," 63–64, 83
Hegel, G. W. F., 31–32, 41–42
Heise, Ursula, 5
Hena, Omaar, 197n35

Hensley, Nathan, 6
Higgins, Michael D., 42
Hogan, Liam, 202n4
Holdridge, Jefferson, 13
Hong, Cathy Park, 173n57
Hopkins, Gerard Manley, 53
Horse Latitudes (Muldoon), 130–31
Huggan, Graham, 75
Hunter, Walt, 15, 111–12, 118
"Hymn to the New Omagh Road"
 (Montague), 70, **70**, **71**, 72–73,
 77, 82

"I" (Carson), 98
Ignatiev, Noel, 161
"In Belfast" (Morrissey), 7–10
"In Our Own Country" (Boland),
 45–46
"Incantata" (Muldoon), 140–43
"The Indians on Alcatraz" (Muldoon),
 128
Innes, C. L., 143
"Intelligence" (Carson), 108, 110–11
Iraq War, 112, 131, 132
Irish diaspora, 154–55, 156–57
The Irish for No (Carson), 89
Irish studies, 13, 29, 134, 143–44,
 150, 161–62, 196n18, 202–03n7

Jackson, Virginia, 15, 119
Jaffe, Sarah, 54
Jameson, Fredric, 11, 18
Jarvis, Robin, 99, 100
Jennison, Ruth, 19
Johnson, Barbara, 17
Johnson, Christopher, 200n63
Johnson, Samuel, 88, 91, 135, 189n3
Jordan, Neil, 163, 206n45
Joyce, James, 87
Joyce, Trevor, 14, 38

Kauffman, Angelica, 49
Kelly, Aaron, 104, 169n21

Kennedy-Andrews, Elmer, 12
Kiberd, Declan, 13
King, Anthony D., 96
Kinsella, Thomas, 20, 27, 28, 33, 34–42, 54, 87, 178n28, 179n36
   "A Country Walk," 35–36, 37
   Butcher's Dozen, 37–39, 179n36
   "Night Conference, Wood Quay, 6 June 1979," 39–41
   Nightwalker, 34–35, 37
"Kinship" (Heaney), 159
Kirkland, Richard, 82
Kreiner, Tim, 120

"Laganside" (Gillis), 109
Lalor, James Fintan, 154
Land Enclosure Acts, 57–58, 89, 98
Leary, John Pat, 54
"Leaving Belfast" (Flynn), 103–05
Lefebvre, Henri, 11
Lemass, Seán, 42, 66, 95
Lentin, Ronit, 156
Levinson, Marjorie, 177n20
Lichtenstein, Jesse, 26
Lloyd, David, 12, 19, 134, 200n58
loco-descriptive poetry, 22, 87–92
   conventions, 107–08
   definition, 91, 99, 108–09, 192n45
   detail, 88, 91, 99–100
   peripatetic poetry, 97, 98–99, 192n46
   prospect poetry, 98–99, 106–08, 110–12, 192n49
   see also Carson, Ciaran; Gillis, Alan
Love, Heather, 91–92
Lukács, Georg, 91
Lyons, Alice, 3
   "Developers," 16–19
lyric poetry, 16, 72, 116, 119

McClanahan, Annie, 11
McDonough, Terrence, 17
McDowell, Michael, 156

MacFarlane, Robert, 124
Madoc: A Mystery (Muldoon), 121, 129, 132, 138
Major, John, 103
"Making Money" (Boland), 181n63
Manchester Arena bombing, 2017, 25–26, 27–28
Manguso, Sarah, 92
Mao, Douglas, 168n9
Marcus, Sharon, 91–92
Marx, Karl, 184n5, 188n54
Marx, Leo, 68
Massey, Doreen, 1
Maurer, Sara, 153
Meehan, Paula, 3, 20–21, 27, 28, 33, 47–54, 54–55
   "Number Fifty-One," 48
   "Number Fifty-Two," 48, 49–50, 51
   "Six Sycamores," 48–54, 182n68
   "Them Ducks Died for Ireland," 52
Meeting the British (Muldoon), 121, 129, 132
Melas, Natalie, 126–27
metaphor, 122, 133–34, 135, 198–99n51, 199n53
Mill, John Stuart, 15, 152
Miller, Liam, 179n36
Minh-ha, Trinh, 117
modernism, 5–6, 13–14, 91, 170–71n37
Moi, Ruben, 131
Montague, John, 3, 59, 67, 83–85
   "A Severed Head," 77, **78–81**, 82
   ambivalences, 21, 72, 73–74
   "Balance Sheet," 70, **70**, **71**, 72–73
   "Hymn to the New Omagh Road," 70, **70**, **71**, 72–73, 77, 82
   "Oliver Goldsmith: Sentimental Prophecy," 83–84
   The Rough Field, 60, 68–82, 83, 187n38
Moore, Jason, 11–12

"The More a Man Has the More a Man Wants" (Muldoon), 128–29
Morrison, Toni, 161
Morrissey, Sinéad, 3, 22, 88, 90
  "In Belfast," 7–9
  "Photographs of Belfast by Alexander Robert Hogg," 105–06
  "Tourism," 9–10, 169n23
Motion, Andrew, 30
"The Mournes" (Gillis), 112–13
"The Mudroom" (Muldoon), 122–25
Muldoon, Paul, 3, 22–23, 97, 115–45
  allusions, 116, 117, 123–25
  Annals of Chile, 140
  "Birth," 139–40
  "Cauliflowers," 137–38
  cross-cultural comparisons, 128–34, 135–43, 143–45
  cultural appropriation, 121, 197n35, 199n56
  difficulty, 115–17, 122–28, 142
  The End of the Poem, 124
  Horse Latitudes, 130–31
  "Incantata," 140–43
  "The Indians on Alcatraz," 128
  To Ireland, I, 138, 200n65
  list poems, 138–43
  Madoc: A Mystery, 121, 129, 132, 138
  Meeting the British, 121, 129, 132
  "The More a Man Has the More a Man Wants," 128–29
  Moy Sand and Gravel, 124
  "The Mudroom," 122–25
  "Perdu," 130–32
  The Prince of Quotidian, 124, 138
  references to Native American culture, 121, 129, 130–32
  "Yarrow," 117–18, 138
Mullen, Harryette, 99

Mullen, Mary, 134
Murphy, Tom, 67
Murtagh, Brendan, 104

Nagle, John, 105
Naipaul, V. S., 126–27
Nash, Catherine, 158–59
national identity, 67, 153–55, 156–57, 200n65
nationalism, 2, 6–7, 14, 65, 117, 161, 163
nativism, 2, 10, 157, 162
naturalism, 67, 69
Needham, Richard, 96
Negra, Diane, 149
Neill, William, 93, 96
neoliberalism, 4, 11, 19, 34, 47, 60, 89, 194n71
Ngai, Sianne, 141
"Night Conference, Wood Quay, 6 June 1979" (Kinsella), 39–41
Nightwalker (Kinsella), 34–35, 37
North (Heaney), 61, 157–58
nostalgia, 1, 10, 58, 60, 74, 82, 102
"Number Fifty-One" (Meehan), 48
"Number Fifty-Two" (Meehan), 48, 49–50, 51

Ó Conchubhair, Brian, 13, 144
Obert, Julia, 192n37
occasional poetry, 20, 25–34, 175–76n14
  autonomy, 28, 30–32, 42, 177n21
  history of the genre, 31–32, 176n14
  role of, 25–6, 29–30, 55
  see also Kinsella, Thomas; Meehan, Paula
O'Donoghue, Heather, 159
Okri, Ben, 26, 27, 31
Olson, Charles, 90–91
O'Neill, Terrence, 95

Parsons, Cóilín, 170n37
pastoral, 21, 57–60, 68–82, 83–85
  definition, 77, 183n3
  nostalgia, 58, 60, 82
  spectrality, 75–77, **78–81**, 82, 83
  history, 58, 63–64, 84
  see also Heaney, Seamus;
    Montague, John
Patke, Rajeev, 115
Peace Poets, 8–9, 88, 90
Peace Process, 8–9, 21–22, 169n21
Peppercanister Press, 37, 41, 179n36
Per Cent for Art Scheme, 50–51, 54, 182–83n74, 182n68, 182n72, 182n73
"Perdu" (Muldoon), 130–32
peripatetic poetry, 97, 98–99, 192n46
Perloff, Marjorie, 31
"Photographs of Belfast by Alexander Robert Hogg" (Morrissey), 105–06
Pilkington, Lionel, 178n31
Pinsky, Robert, 32
Place, Vanessa, 120–21, 173n57
plantation era, 152–53
Plath, Sylvia, 119–20
postcolonial theory, 15, 41, 75–76, 118, 121, 126–27, 129–30, 134, 143, 167n4
Potkay, Adam, 98
Prashad, Vijay, 59
Pratt, Geraldine, 6–7
Priestley, Joseph, 4
The Prince of the Quotidian (Muldoon), 124, 138
Prins, Yopie, 15, 119
prospect poetry, 98–99, 106–08, 110–12, 192n49
Prynne, J. H., 116, 127–28, 138

"Queen's Gambit" (Carson), 100
"Question Time" (Carson), 100–01

Quinn, Justin, 13

race and racism, 148–52, 169n24, 205n27
  Citizenship Referendum and, 155–56
  in Heaney's poetry, 157–62, 203n8
  and place, 152–62
  rhetoric of soil, 152–57
Ramazani, Jahan, 7, 10, 118, 132
"Revised Version" (Carson), 93–94
Rich, Adrienne, 122
Richards, I. A., 199n52
Robinson, Mary, 156
Robinson, Tim, 87–88
Ronda, Margaret, 17, 19–20
Rosner, Victoria, 6–7
The Rough Field (Montague), 60, 68–82, 83, 187n38
  "A Severed Head," 77, **78–81**, 82
  "Balance Sheet," 70, **70**, **71**, 72–73
  "Hymn to the New Omagh Road," 70, **70**, **71**, 72–73, 77, 82
Ryan, Bernard, 155

Said, Edward, 75–76, 188n50
Moy Sand and Gravel (Muldoon), 124
Sassen, Saskia, 11
scale, 5–7, 168n9
Schor, Naomi, 91
Second World War, 27, 186n22
"The Sense of Place," Heaney, 1–2
site-specific art, 51, 180–81n57
"Six Sycamores" (Meehan), 48–54, 182n68
Slaby, Alexander, 43, 180n52, 181–82n65
soil, rhetoric of, 152–57
Somewhere, Somebody (Gillis), 111–12

Spenser, Edmund, 73
The Star Factory (Carson), 89
Still Life (Carson), 99, 164–66
Sugano, Marian Zwerling, 176n14
Suhr-Sytsma, Nathan, 175n12

The Táin (Carson), 87
Thelwall, John, 99
"Them Ducks Died for Ireland" (Meehan), 52
Tiffin, Helen, 75
To Ireland, I (Muldoon), 138, 200n65
"The Toome Road" (Heaney), 63–64, 83
tourism, 35, 43, 103, 178n31
"Tourism" (Morrissey), 9–10, 169n23
"Traffic Flow" (Gillis), 109–10
"Travellers" (Carson), 97
Troubles, the, 3, 8–9, 11, 12–13, 22, 89–90, 92–103, 125, 164, 169n21, 190n22
Tsing, Anna, 5–6
Tuck, Eve, 133

UNESCO, 44, 47, 180n55
urban redevelopment, 3, 68, 76–77, 88–89, 191n25

Varadkar, Leo, 147, 148

Vendler, Helen, 36
Vogl, Joseph, 18

Walkowitz, Rebecca, 168n9
Walsh, Tony, 25–26, 27–28, 174n7
Wang, Dorothy, 15, 151
Warren, Rosanna, 62
Watts, Rebecca, 174n3
Weaver, Andrew, 8
Weston, Daniel, 102
Whitaker, T. K., 34, 42, 66, 178n28
whiteness, 149, 157, 161, 161–62, 173n57
Williams, Raymond, 54, 58, 68, 76–77, 83, 188n51
Wills, Clair, 124, 126
Wilson, Stephen, 28
Wolosky, Shira, 15
Wordsworth, William, 30, 99

xenophobia, 23, 151, 157, 162, 169n24, 205n27

Yang, K. Wayne, 133
"Yarrow" (Muldoon), 117–18, 138
Yazell, Bryan, 59–60
Yeats, W. B., 12, 14, 28, 35–36, 67, 73, 91
  "Easter 1916," 27, 48
Young Ireland movement, 152–54, 203–04n13